Folger Documents of Tudor and Stuart Civilization

SELECTED SERMONS
OF
HUGH LATIMER

FOLGER DOCUMENTS

OF TUDOR AND STUART CIVILIZATION

THIS volume is one of a series of publications of Tudor and Stuart documents that the Folger Library proposes to bring out. These documents will consist of hitherto unprinted manuscripts as well as reprints of rare books in the Folger Library. An effort will be made to choose significant items that will throw light on the social and intellectual background of the period from 1485 to 1715. In response to almost unanimous requests of interested historians, the spelling, punctuation, and capitalization will be modernized in printed texts. In some cases, where the original printing is clear and easily read, texts may be photographically reproduced. The Folger Library is prepared to supply microfilm of original texts to scholars who require a facsimile.

THE FOLGER SHAKESPEARE LIBRARY IS ADMINISTERED
BY THE TRUSTEES OF AMHERST COLLEGE.

SELECTED SERMONS OF HUGH LATIMER

Edited by
ALLAN G. CHESTER

PUBLISHED FOR
The Folger Shakespeare Library

THE UNIVERSITY PRESS OF VIRGINIA
Charlottesville

First published 1968

The University Press of Virginia

Library of Congress Catalog Card Number: 68–14091

PRINTED IN THE UNITED STATES OF AMERICA

PREFACE

"I HAVE an ear for other preachers," said Sir John Cheke, "but I have a heart for Latimer." For four centuries readers of the sermons of the most popular preacher of the English Reformation have in one way or another echoed Cheke's words. Latimer's religious fervor, his social conscience, his eloquence, his homely humor, to mention a few of his outstanding qualities, have established for him a place in the history of Tudor England which is shared by no other preacher. It is fitting, therefore, that a selection from his sermons should be included in the Folger Shakespeare Library's series of Tudor and Stuart documents, particularly so since no other edition of the sermons is now in print.

For all but one of the sermons reprinted in the present volume the basic text is that of the Folger copy of the earliest printed edition. The first note to each sermon or group of sermons gives the title page of the volume from which the text is taken. The collected editions of 1562 (STC 15277) and 1571–1572 (STC 15284) provide the earliest texts of the last three sermons in the volume. The other sermons had all been printed earlier. For these, on the assumption, demonstrable at a number of points, that the text of the collected editions had been bowdlerized or otherwise censored by the Elizabethan editors, we have preferred the first printed text, except for the first sermon preached before King Edward VI. In the latter case the fourth edition (STC 15271) provides more reliable readings than the first edition (STC 15270.8). STC 15271 has accordingly been made the basis of the text, with some correction of faulty passages by reference to STC 15270.8. Since most of Latimer's sermons were recorded in shorthand by stenographers who confessed their inability to keep up with him, we have ventured a few silent emendations of obvious inaccuracies and have supplied a few obvious omissions in square brackets.

In accordance with the practice established for this series, spelling and punctuation have been modernized. On the other hand, obsolete or archaic forms—e.g., *ensample* (example), *mo* (more), *sithens* (since)—have been retained for their flavor and linguistic interest, even when the more familiar forms also occur. In the matter of paragraphing, it would be more accurate to say that the text has been divided into units of manageable length, since it is impossible to paragraph Latimer's discursive prose according to any principle known to modern rhetoric.

In only one other respect does the present text vary from the originals. In some, but not all, of the early editions Latimer's scriptural quotations are identified in the margins by book and chapter, but never by verse, since the Geneva Bible of 1558 was the first in English to give verse numberings. In this edition full citations are incorporated into the text. Anyone interested in the practice of sixteenth-century preachers will be fascinated by a comparison of Latimer's free handling of scripture with the English or Latin versions current in his day.

I am grateful to Dr. Louis B. Wright, the Director of the Folger Shakespeare Library, and to Professor Roland M. Frye, formerly of the Folger staff, for the suggestion that Latimer's sermons should be published in this series and for their choice of me as editor. The task has been a pleasurable one. I am especially indebted to Miss Virginia LaMar, of the Folger Library, for the editorial vigilance and patience which have saved me from more errors than I like to recall. My wife, as usual, has served as nonpaid editorial assistant, proofreader, and general encourager of good works.

ALLAN G. CHESTER

University of Pennsylvania
March 7, 1967

CONTENTS

Preface v

A Chronological Table ix

Introduction xiii

Convocation Sermon 1

Sermon on the Plowers 28

First Sermon before Edward VI 50

Second Sermon before Edward VI 70

Sixth Sermon before Edward VI 90

Seventh Sermon before Edward VI 114

Last Sermon before Edward VI 138

First Sermon on the Lord's Prayer 158

Sermon for Christmas Day 175

Sermon for St. Stephen's Day 188

Index 205

A CHRONOLOGICAL TABLE OF THE PRINCIPAL EVENTS IN THE LIFE OF HUGH LATIMER

ca. 1492 Hugh Latimer born near Thurcaston, Leicestershire.

ca. 1506 Enters Cambridge, probably Clare Hall.

1510 Proceeds B.A. Fellow of Clare Hall.

1514 M.A.

1515 Ordained to priesthood (July 15).

1522 Appointed University preacher and cross keeper.

1524 Receives B.D. "Converted" to New Learning by Thomas Bilney.

1528 Preaches in advocacy of English Bible and is examined by Cardinal Wolsey. Removed from office of cross keeper.

1529 Preaches the "Sermons on the Card," the first to be preserved (December).

1530 Active in procuring the approval of Cambridge University for the annulment of Henry VIII's marriage to Catherine of Aragon (March). Preaches for the first time at Windsor (March 13). Member of the commission for the suppression of heretical books (May). Writes letter to the King advocating authorized English Bible (December).

1531 Appointed rector of West Kington, Wiltshire (January). Preaches at St. Mary Abchurch, London, without license of Bishop Stokesley (January).

1532 Examined by Convocation at instigation of Stokesley and confesses to having preached erroneous doctrines (April 22).

1533 Denounces saint worship and Mariolatry at Bristol and engages in bitter controversy with conservative clergy (March).

1534 Preaches at Court (Lent).

1535 Appointed Bishop of Worcester (August). Consecrated (September 26).

1536 Preaches the "Convocation Sermon" (June 9). Helps to formulate the "Ten Articles" (July).

1537 Member of the commission which formulates the "Bishops' Book" (June).

1538 Visitation of diocese. Active in the work of suppressing shrines and relics.

1539 Resigns his bishopric following passage of the "Six Articles" (July 1). Under house arrest until July, 1540. Granted annual pension of 100 marks but forbidden to preach.

1540–46 In retirement, probably in Warwickshire and Lincolnshire.

1546 Returns to London and is examined by Privy Council in connection with charges against Dr. Edward Crome (May 13). Imprisoned in Tower.

1547 Released from prison (February) after accession of Edward VI.

1548 Preaches eight sermons at Paul's Cross, including "Sermon on the Plowers" (January). Preaches at Court during Lent.

1549 Preaches the seven sermons before Edward VI (Lent).

1550 Preaches at Court for the last time (Lent).

1550–53 Lives in semiretirement, chiefly in Lincolnshire at Grimsthorpe in the household of the Duchess of Suffolk, preaching twice each Sunday at Grimsthorpe and elsewhere. The seven sermons on the Lord's Prayer and twenty-two other "Lincolnshire" sermons.

1553 Death of Edward VI and accession of Mary Tudor (January). Latimer confined in Tower with Cranmer and Ridley (September).

1554 Removed to Bocardo prison, Oxford (March). The Oxford Disputations (April 14–20). Remains in confinement at Oxford.

1555 The trial for heresy (September 30–October 1). The martyrdom (October 16).

INTRODUCTION

HUGH LATIMER was the most popular, as he was the most influential, preacher of the English Reformation. For more than a generation Latimer preached his gospel of religious reform and personal and civic righteousness throughout the length and breadth of England, in cathedrals, in remote parish churches, in the courts of kings, and even in the fields. When he preached, people of all ranks listened as they did not listen to more scholarly or more formal preachers. To his admirers he was the only prophet in England, the "apostle to the English." His opponents, those to whom his doctrines were repugnant, responded with equal fervor. They called him a knave bishop and said they hoped to see him burned. As indeed he was, in 1555, at Oxford, where the Martyrs' Memorial stands as a reminder of his work and that of Cranmer and Ridley, his fellow sufferers.

The date of Latimer's birth is uncertain, but the weight of evidence points to 1492 or thereabouts. His father, we are told in one of the sermons, was a yeoman,[1] the yearly tenant of a farm which was probably part of the manor of Thurcaston in Leicestershire. The father prospered for a time and the son was sent to Cambridge, where he became a member of Clare Hall. He received the B.A. in 1510 and at the same time was given a fellowship at Clare. He proceeded M.A. in 1514.[2] He was ordained to the diaconate at Lincoln on April 7, 1515, and to the priesthood the following July

[1] "First Sermon before Edward VI." See below, p. 67.

[2] The dates of his degrees are recorded in the Cambridge Grace Books.

15.[3] Meanwhile he remained at Cambridge, reading in theology in preparation for the B.D., becoming most apt in "the labyrinth of the school doctors."[4] The University statutes required a minimum period of five years of such study, but Latimer took ten.

It was precisely during this period when Latimer was steeping himself in traditional theology that the ferment of the "New Learning"[5]—the New Testament studies of Erasmus and the doctrinal notions of Martin Luther—began to work at Cambridge. Certain of the brightest young dons—Thomas Bilney, George Stafford, John Frith, Robert Barnes, Thomas Cranmer, to name just a few—were fascinated by the new doctrines. Erasmus' Greek New Testament, with the accompanying Latin text which dared to revise the Vulgate in places, opened up a new world of religious thought to them, while Luther's version of the Pauline doctrine of justification by faith shook their confidence in the adequacy of the ceremonies and teachings of the medieval church as a means of salvation.

Down to 1524 Latimer remained hostile to these new ideas. He was devoted to the traditional ways and ceremonies. Years later he declared that at this time he was "as obstinate a papist as any was in England."[6] He was dismayed and angered at the freedom with which some of his contemporaries were proclaiming the new doctrines from their lecture platforms, and he denounced them vigorously. It is reported that he would interrupt their lectures to urge the students not to listen to them and that he would often break in upon the formal disputations of the students to denounce the "newfangled" study of the Holy Scriptures and persuade the young men to return to the study of traditional theology.[7]

[3] These dates are recorded in the Lincoln diocesan registers.

[4] Harleian MS 422, Art. 12. This manuscript is said to be in the handwriting of Ralph Morice, Archbishop Cranmer's secretary. The text is printed in *Sermons and Remains of Hugh Latimer,* ed. George E. Corrie (Cambridge: The Parker Society, 1845), II, xxvii–xxxi. Cited hereafter as *Sermons and Remains.*

[5] It was only in the nineteenth century that this term came to be applied to the revival of classical learning.

[6] "First Sermon on the Lord's Prayer." See below, p. 167.

[7] Harleian MS 422, Art. 12.

So it was that in 1524 he used the occasion of his own disputation for the degree of Bachelor of Divinity to attack the doctrines of Philip Melanchthon, the great German theologian whose *Loci communes rerum theologicarum* had been published three years before. The performance satisfied his examiners and the degree was conferred. But it did not satisfy Thomas Bilney of Trinity, who was present as an observer. "Little Bilney," as his friends affectionately called him, had taken fire from the study of Erasmus' Greek Testament and was already preaching the new doctrines with the fervor which was to lead him finally to martyrdom in the Lollards' Pit at Norwich. Now, listening to the disputation, Bilney perceived that Latimer was "zealous without knowledge." Afterward, says Latimer, "he came to me . . . in my study and desired me, for God's sake, to hear his confession. I did so; and, to say the truth, by his confession I learned more than afore in many years. So from that time forward I began to smell the Word of God and forsook the school doctors and such fooleries." [8]

The flat succinctness of this account suggests that Latimer's "conversion" came as a sudden revelation. Other passages in the sermons support that view. Indeed, there can be no doubt of the emotional intensity of the experience. But the extant sermons considered as a whole, as well as other evidence drawn from his public career, suggest that his progress in the new ideas was gradual. It is certain that at this period, the latter part of the year 1524, he still regarded all seven of the sacraments as valid, and it would be many years before he rejected the doctrine of transubstantiation, the issue over which the final battle was to be fought. On the other hand, he had rejected the vast body of patristic and scholastic literature which had recently been his whole study, and he had accepted the Bible as the sole authority in matters of doctrine. He had also accepted the doctrine of justification by "faith only" and the corollary opinion that "will-works"—pilgrimages, veneration of images, and the like—would in themselves avail little toward salvation.

[8] "First Sermon on the Lord's Prayer," See below, p. 167.

In what follows we shall be concerned chiefly with the record of Latimer's preaching. John Foxe tells us that he began to preach his new opinions immediately after his conversion.[9] There is some evidence—but not very reliable—that for so doing he was in trouble as early as 1526 with the Bishop of Ely, within whose diocese Cambridge lay, and even with the great Cardinal Wolsey. It is certain that in 1528, as a consequence of his insistent demand for an authorized English Bible, he was examined by the Cardinal. There were no formal proceedings against him, however, and he was dismissed with a warning.[10]

The earliest sermons which have been substantially preserved are the so-called "Sermons on the Card," which belong to the Christmas season of 1529. Foxe gives us full but garbled summaries of these sermons, as well as a confused account of the circumstances under which they were preached.[11] Early in December, it would appear, Latimer, preaching *ad clerum,* advocated an authorized English Bible and denounced such practices as devotion to the saints, veneration of relics, and pilgrimages to shrines—the voluntary or "will" works which were to be the principal matters of his denunciation during the next few years. The sermon offended the conservatives at Cambridge and provoked a reply from Dr. John Venutus, a Benedictine, who in 1529 was deputy vice-chancellor of the University. According to Foxe, Venutus called Latimer a "mad and brainless man." On December 19 in St. Edward's church, which served as a chapel for the students of Clare Hall, Latimer replied with the first of the two "Sermons on the Card."

These sermons take their title from the fact that as he preached Latimer drew a pack of playing cards from the sleeve of his gown and announced his intention to illustrate his points by playing a game of "triumph." The device was an old trick of the preaching friars, but Latimer was probably the first to try it on a learned

9 *Acts and Monuments,* ed. R. R. Mendham and Josiah Pratt (4th ed., London [1875]), VII, 489. Cited hereafter as Foxe.

10 Harleian MS 422, Art. 12.

11 Foxe, VII, 438–451.

audience. In the first sermon the first card was the trump to take all the other cards. It was a card spoken by Christ himself—"Whosoever shall say, 'Thou fool,' shall be in danger of hellfire." It is not clear how Latimer worked out the rest of the card game. But it is perfectly clear that this portion of the sermon was a direct attack upon Venutus, who had called him mad and brainless.

At this point Foxe's summary of the first "Sermon on the Card" breaks off. From the sequel, however, it is evident that Latimer continued with a further advocacy of an authorized English Bible, for it was to this point that Dr. Robert Buckenham, prior of the Dominican House at Cambridge, replied with a "Sermon on the Dice." Preaching a few days after Latimer, Buckenham drew from the sleeve of his gown a pair of dice and threw "cinque and quater." The four represented the Four Doctors, by whom he would prove that it was not expedient to have the scriptures in English. The five stood for five places in scripture which proved the same point. All this was so silly, according to the not impartial testimony of John Foxe, that Latimer, in his sermon a day or so later, turned Buckenham into the laughingstock of the whole University.

The second "Sermon on the Card" is in a different vein. It was preached shortly after the exchange with Buckenham. As we have it in summary, it is free from personal invective. Its text—its "card"—was Matthew 5:23–24, which was rendered as follows: "When thou makest thine oblation at mine altar, and there dost remember that thy neighbor has anything against thee, lay down there thine oblation and go first and reconcile thy neighbor, and then come offer thine oblation." By and large the sermon is a temperate but cogent statement of the primary importance of repentance for sin and of works of mercy. The peroration is eloquent; we must hope that the words are Latimer's own, unimproved by John Foxe:

Again, if you list to gild and paint Christ in your churches and honor Him in vestments, see that before your eyes the poor people die not for lack of meat, drink, and clothing. Then do you deck the very true temple of God and honor Him in vestures that will never be worn. . . . And then finally set up your candles, and they will report what a glorious light remaineth in your hearts. . . . Then, I say, go your pilgrimages, build your material churches, do all your voluntary works, and they will represent you unto God and testify with you that you have provided Him with a glorious place in your hearts.

But there must have been more to the "Sermons on the Card" than Foxe has reported; otherwise it would be difficult to account for the bitter controversy which ensued. No fewer than five heads of houses preached against Latimer, as did numerous other conservatives of lesser rank. Latimer responded with equal vehemence, and the affair became a threat to the peace and good order of the University. In the end Dr. Edward Fox, the provost of King's and almoner to Henry VIII, intervened in the latter's name. Latimer was warned to be more discreet in his sermons, but his opponents were rebuked for their slanderous and malicious attacks upon him. Clearly Latimer had carried the day.

Evidently it was through the episode of the "Sermons on the Card" that Latimer first came to the notice of the King. In the following year, 1530, when the question of the validity of Henry VIII's marriage to Catherine of Aragon was referred to the universities of Europe, Latimer was active in the group which finally secured from Cambridge University a decision favorable to the King's wishes. Shortly thereafter he preached for the first time before the King at Windsor, and early in the following year, through the good offices of Henry, he was appointed rector of the parish of West Kington in Wiltshire.[12]

No sermon survives from the five-year period during which Latimer served as a parish priest. But there is abundant testimony to the continuing vigor of his advocacy of the New Learning and the excitement and controversy which his sermons provoked. Almost immediately after his appointment to West Kington, and possibly

[12] He was instituted on January 14, 1531 (Campeggio Register, Salisbury Diocese, f. 24).

before he had visited his new parish, he was in trouble as a consequence of a sermon, preached at St. Mary Abchurch, London, in which, along with much else, he criticized the bishops for their methods in proceeding against alleged heretics. Unfortunately he had preached without the license of the Bishop of London, John Stokesley, an arch conservative. Although it took the better part of a year, Stokesley finally managed to have Latimer brought before Convocation to answer to charges of heresy.[13] Only through the intervention of the King did he escape condemnation as a heretic, but even so he experienced the humiliation of being forced to confess that in some of his utterances he had erred not only in discretion but also in doctrine.[14]

Latimer's encounter with Convocation came in April of 1532. During the year which followed, the "submission of the clergy" whereby the church became completely subservient to the state was effected; Thomas Cranmer, Latimer's Cambridge friend, was nominated to the archbishopric of Canterbury; Thomas Cromwell began his meteoric rise to power; and Henry VIII was married to Anne Boleyn. These events served to create an atmosphere favorable to the reformers, with the result that early in 1533 Latimer resumed his preaching with even greater vigor, in spite of the submission he had made a year earlier. In March he preached three sermons at Bristol which provoked fierce and protracted controversy. In these sermons Latimer denounced excessive veneration of the saints, excessive adoration of Our Lady, and the abuses arising from the doctrine of purgatory—masses for the dead, the sale of indulgences, and the like.[15] The conservative clergy responded immediately; laymen formed themselves into factions. The unseemly brawling continued until July, when Cromwell intervened by appointing a commission to look into the matter. Once again Latimer's enemies were routed

[13] The details are given in the correspondence between Latimer and Sir Edward Baynton (Foxe, VII, 484–498; *Sermons and Remains,* II, 322–351).

[14] *Conciliae Magnae Britanniae et Hiberniae,* ed. David Wilkins (London, 1737), III, 747.

[15] Foxe, VII, 466–484.

through government influence, and Archbishop Cranmer issued a license permitting Latimer to preach anywhere in the province of Canterbury.

By the spring of 1534 Latimer was again rising rapidly in the royal favor. Through Cranmer's influence he was invited to preach in the Chapel Royal every Wednesday in Lent of that year. The Archbishop warned him to be judicious in speech and to limit his preaching to an hour or an hour and a half at the most.[16] Evidently he followed the Primate's advice, for the King was pleased. Shortly thereafter Latimer was appointed one of Henry's chaplains. In the summer of 1535 he was nominated by the King to the bishopric of Worcester, and he was consecrated at Winchester on September 26, 1535.[17]

Since we are here primarily concerned with the sermons, it will not be necessary to recount the details of Latimer's career as Bishop of Worcester. One point, however, should be made. His elevation to the episcopal bench was a political appointment. Throughout his episcopacy he was occupied less with diocesan affairs than with the concerns of the newly nationalized church. He was one of the leaders of the reforming party in Convocation and in the House of Lords. He was directly involved in the preparation of the "Ten Articles" and the "Bishops' Book," the first two doctrinal formularies of the English Church. He was active in the work of suppressing the monasteries and destroying the shrines. And he was, of course, one of the chief official spokesmen for the state religion in sermons preached at Paul's Cross and elsewhere.

Although there are many references to Latimer's preaching during his episcopacy, only two sermons from this period have been preserved. One of them was addressed to the leaders of the "Pilgrimage of Grace," as the northern rebellion of 1535 was known. The sermon as preserved is obviously a fragment and of no great inter-

[16] *Miscellaneous Writings and Letters of Thomas Cranmer,* ed. John E. Cox (Cambridge: The Parker Society, 1845), p. 308.

[17] William Stubbs, *Registrum Sacrum Anglicanum* (2d ed., Oxford, 1897), p. 99.

est.[18] In the following year came the "Convocation Sermon," which was the first of Latimer's sermons to be printed and therefore has pride of place in the present volume.

The "Convocation Sermon" was the keynote speech of the Convocation which assembled concurrently with a new Parliament in June, 1536. The predetermined business of this session of Convocation was to formulate for the Church of England articles of faith which, it was vainly hoped, might resolve some of the differences between conservatives and reformers. Latimer was chosen to preach the opening sermon by Archbishop Cranmer, with the approval of the King. Yet his presence in the pulpit was shocking to the conservative prelates who constituted the majority of his audience. Only four years earlier he had been accused of heresy before a commission of this same Convocation. Now, as all his hearers knew, he represented the official point of view.

Since the English version of this sermon—the original, being *ad clerum,* was in Latin—is here reprinted, it is unnecessary to review its contents in detail. The sermon is in two parts, the first preached in the morning of June 9, 1536, the second in the afternoon. The morning sermon was devoted chiefly to a condemnation of those abuses which Latimer had been attacking for almost a decade. The second part was directed more specifically against the higher clergy —that is, against the preacher's audience. They had become the children of this world, said Latimer, and their record was one of shameful corruption and incompetence. In conclusion he proposed a specific program of reform of those abuses which were generally acknowledged.

Latimer's career as a bishop ended abruptly in June, 1539. During the preceding year the King had been increasingly disenchanted with the opinions which the more advanced reformers such as the Archbishop of Canterbury and the Bishop of Worcester were expressing with considerable freedom—the opinions, for example, that

[18] It was first printed in the 1578 edition of *Frutefull Sermons* (STC 15279).

the clergy might be permitted to marry, that auricular confession was unnecessary, that both the Bread and the Wine should be administered to the laity at communion, and even that the doctrine of transubstantiation was of doubtful validity. Accordingly, on June 28, 1539, at the King's insistence, Parliament approved "An Act Abolishing Diversity of Opinions," commonly called the "Six Articles" or, by the reformers, the "Whip with the Six Strings." By this legislation the following six matters were written into the law of the land: that in the Sacrament of the Altar the natural body and blood of Christ are really present under the form of bread and wine; that communion in both kinds is not necessary; that priests may not marry; that vows of chastity must be kept; that private masses must be continued; that auricular confession is expedient and necessary. Penal clauses of the greatest severity were attached.

Thomas Cranmer managed to adjust his opinions to the new law and retained his archbishopric. Latimer, who in theological matters usually followed Cranmer's lead, would probably have conformed also. But he was led to resign his bishopric by Thomas Cromwell, who told him it was the King's will that he should do so. According to Latimer, the King later denied that he had ever suggested such a course.[19] Nevertheless, the country at large was led to believe that Latimer had resigned in protest against the "Six Articles." His treatment by the government was not calculated to dispel this opinion. He was placed under house arrest in the London establishment of the Bishop of Chichester and was not released until July, 1540.[20] Then he was prohibited from preaching and was forbidden to come within ten miles of London and of the universities or to go anywhere within his old diocese of Worcester.[21] As if in compensa-

[19] *Letters and Papers, Foreign and Domestic, of the Reign of Henry VIII,* XXI, Part 1 (London, 1908), No. 823.

[20] *Ibid.,* XIV, Part 2 (London, 1895), No. 255.

[21] There is no official record of this prohibition. It is mentioned in a letter from Richard Hilles to Heinrich Bullinger, the Swiss reformer.

tion for these severities, the Crown awarded him an annual pension of one hundred marks (£66 13*s*. 4*d*).[22]

There is almost no record of Latimer's activities during the next seven years. Much of the time, John Foxe tells us, was spent in the country, possibly at Baxterley in Warwickshire in the household of a beloved niece and her husband, Mary and Robert Glover. But in the spring of 1546 Latimer's name reappears in the public record. He had been seriously injured by the fall of a tree, and in defiance of the prohibition of 1539 he came up to London to seek medical attention.[23] Courageously but injudiciously he allowed himself to become involved in the affairs of an old Cambridge associate, Dr. Edward Crome, who was under examination by the Privy Council for proclaiming the nonexistence of purgatory. Latimer was also brought before the Council and was bold to express views concerning purgatory and transubstantiation which came dangerously close to contravening the "Six Articles."[24] As a result, he was imprisoned in the Tower, where he remained until the death of Henry VIII in January, 1547. In the meantime, however, the King, partly under the influence of Cranmer and partly for political reasons too complex to be entered into here, was preparing to permit the substitution of a communion service for the mass, with a corresponding modification of the official attitude toward the doctrine of transubstantiation. It was probably as a result of this latest vagary of the royal theologian that Latimer was saved from more extreme punishment at this time.

With the accession of Edward VI and the rise to power of the Protestant Seymours, Latimer was released from the Tower and shortly thereafter was licensed to preach once again. According to John Stow, he preached for the first time in eight years on January 1, 1548. Thereafter his services as a preacher on behalf of the officially reformed religion were in great demand. The extent to which his eloquence was used may be suggested by the fact that in January,

22 *Letters and Papers . . . of Henry VIII,* XIV, Part 2, No. 236.

23 Foxe, VII, 463.

24 *Letters and Papers . . . of Henry VIII,* XXI, Part 1, Nos. 810 and 823.

1548, he preached no fewer than eight sermons at Paul's Cross [25] in support of the liberalizing Royal Injunctions of 1547.[26] The only one of these sermons to survive is the famous "Sermon on the Plowers," the second selection in the present volume.

By many critics the "Sermon on the Plowers" is regarded as the finest of Latimer's extant sermons. It was the last of four Wednesday sermons of January, 1548, all of which were based upon the parable of the Sower. The people were God's plowland, the Word of God was the seed, and the clergy were the sowers, the plowers, whose responsibility it was to prepare the field so that the seed would fall upon good ground. Much of the sermon is an attack upon "unpreaching prelates" and a plea for a preaching clergy who would bring their people to the living faith which is the way of salvation. The central metaphor suggested to the preacher the designation "spiritual enclosers" for nonpreaching prelates, by analogy with the landlords who were enclosing and converting plowland to pasture for sheep, with consequent economic distress to the displaced farm workers. Thus Latimer was able to bring religious reform and economic reform into a meaningful relationship. If the clergy preached as they should, the living faith which ensued would result in a collective righteousness from which would emerge a truly Christian commonwealth, wherein greed and self-interest would give place to a concern for the welfare of all.

The Paul's Cross sermons of January, 1548, were followed by a series preached at Court during Lent of the same year. The fame of Latimer's eloquence was now so great that all who wished to hear him could not be crowded into the Chapel Royal, and a temporary pulpit was erected in the private gardens of Westminster Palace. Here—the scene is perpetuated in a crude woodcut in Foxe's *Acts and Monuments*—he preached before the boy King, the Lord Protector Somerset, other members of the Council, and a vast concourse of dignitaries of the Court and city.

[25] John Stow, *The Annales of England* (London, 1600), p. 1002.

[26] See the first note to the "Sermon on the Plowers" in the present volume, pp. 28–29.

The Lenten sermons of 1548 have not survived. In the following year, however, Latimer preached at Court on each of the seven Fridays in Lent, and all these sermons were taken down in shorthand and published shortly thereafter. It is chiefly upon them and the earlier "Sermon on the Plowers" that Latimer's later fame is based.

In the seven Court sermons of 1549, four of which are here reprinted, Latimer is not much concerned with matters of doctrine or correcting superstition or castigating the "Italian bishop yonder." These battles, he mistakenly believed, had already been won. Indeed, only one of the seven, the Good Friday sermon, which is an eloquent meditation on the Agony in the Garden, is primarily religious. In the others he directs his eloquence to the task of bringing the English nation, and especially its rulers, to the faith-righteousness which he saw as the means whereby the ills of England might be cured. He addresses himself to the gravest problems of the day: the difficulties arising from the fact that England had a boy king; the question of the succession to the throne; the economic ills arising from enclosures and rack-renting; the Tudor theory of the divine right and the evil of rebellion against the Crown. To students of the period it is clear that he is speaking on behalf of the Lord Protector's policies and that the sermons are in large measure propaganda. But Latimer believed fervently in the rightness of Seymour's policies. There is no reason to question the preacher's sincerity, nor is there any doubt of his confidence that he knew the remedy for the political, economic, and social ills of England. Again and again he insists upon the need for a preaching clergy. By preaching, men will be brought to a true and lively faith, by faith to individual and collective righteousness, and by righteousness a truly Christian commonwealth will be established.

During Lent of the following year Latimer preached but a single sermon at Court. He was old, according to sixteenth-century life expectancy, and ill, and he realized that this would be his last appearance, his *ultimum vale,* as he called it, in this pulpit. "When I was appointed to preach here," he said at the outset, "I was new come out of a sickness whereof I looked to have died; and weak I was. Yet . . . when I was appointed unto it I took it upon me. . . . I think I shall no more come here, for I think I have not long to live, so that I judge I take my leave now of the Court forever and shall no more come in this place."[27] It may indeed have been because of illness that he preached only once in 1550. But another reason suggests itself. In the year that had just passed the Protector Somerset, Edward Seymour, had been overthrown, and the government was now in the hands of the cynical and unscrupulous John Dudley, Earl of Warwick and Duke of Northumberland. It is not unlikely that Dudley, no friend to reform in either economics or government, wished to hear no more of Latimer's continuing attacks on enclosers, rack-renters, and corruption and incompetence in high places.

During the time when his services were in frequent demand as a preacher at Court or at Paul's Cross, Latimer had made his home with Archbishop Cranmer at Lambeth Palace. Now that he was no longer able to render such service—or perhaps because it was no longer called for—he retired once again to the country. During most of the next five years he was an honored guest at Grimsthorpe in Lincolnshire, in the household of Katherine Willoughby, the widowed Duchess of Suffolk, who had now in a real sense become his patroness. But he could scarcely be said to have been living in retirement. His Swiss friend and servant, Augustine Bernher, who prepared many of the sermons for the press, tells us that during this period, despite age and illness, Latimer preached two sermons on most Sundays, and "every morning ordinarily, winter and summer, about two of the clock in the morning he was at his book most diligently."[28]

It is chiefly with Grimsthorpe that the last and largest group (twenty-eight out of a total of forty-one) of Latimer's extant ser-

[27] See below, pp. 144, 147, 152–153.

[28] Dedication to the Duchess of Suffolk in Latimer's *27 Sermons* (1562), reprinted in *Sermons and Remains,* I, 320.

mons is associated. Of these, seven sermons on the Lord's Prayer were "lectures," as the preacher called them, addressed to the servants of the Duchess of Suffolk in the private chapel at Grimsthorpe. The remaining twenty-one sermons, described by Bernher as "preached in Lincolnshire," were also preached at Grimsthorpe or in neighboring parishes. The "First Sermon on the Lord's Prayer" and two of the other Lincolnshire sermons are reprinted in the present volume.

Like all good preachers, Latimer was always acutely aware of the composition and capacities of his audiences. It is not surprising, therefore, that these later sermons, addressed to the servants of the Duchess or the congregation of a country church, are quite different in substance and tone from the sermons at the Court of Edward VI, which were largely concerned with the responsibilities of kings and magistrates. The Lincolnshire sermons are concerned with the duties of servants and subjects—with the importance of obedience, of good manners, of faithful work, of virtuous living. Little points of doctrine are carefully explained for an unsophisticated audience; stories from the Bible are expanded and dramatized in order to emphasize their moral or typological significance. Such homilies are of less historical interest than the "Convocation Sermon" or the Court sermons. But they have their own charm—the charm of homely simplicity, of quaintness, and of heartfelt earnestness.

Such, in summary, is the record of Latimer's career as preacher. Out of hundreds of sermons, forty-one have survived. As we turn to a brief consideration of the literary or stylistic qualities of the extant sermons, we must bear in mind the circumstances of their preservation. The "Convocation Sermon" of 1535, originally in Latin, was printed almost immediately, possibly from Latimer's own manuscript. The English version, published shortly thereafter, is so much in Latimer's English vein that we may suppose the preacher himself had a large share in the translation. All the other extant sermons were preserved through the agency of friends and admirers. The Edward VI sermons, and probably the "Sermon on the Plowers," were taken down by one Thomas Some, perhaps at the direction of the Duchess of Suffolk. Some was expert in a kind of shorthand, but he ruefully confesses, in the dedication of the printed text to the Duchess, that his skill was inadequate to keep pace with the torrent of the preacher's eloquence. The sermons on the Lord's Prayer and the other Lincolnshire sermons were prepared for the press by Augustine Bernher, whose references to the provenance of his text are vague. At the end of the earliest printed text of the Lord's Prayer sermons occur the words *Excerptae per me Augustinum Bernerum, Helvetium*. The Lincolnshire sermons, first printed in 1571, are said to have been "Faithfully gathered . . . by Augustine Bernher, his servant." I doubt that any of these later sermons were preached from a manuscript and would guess that "Excerptae" and "gathered" must be taken to mean that the texts as we have them are based on Bernher's copious notes.

The probability that the sermons were so recorded would partly account for their principal weakness—a noticeable lack of careful organization and orderly progression of ideas. But the fault was largely Latimer's own, for he had a darting rather than a logical mind. As he preached, with his eye on his audience, not on a manuscript, something—one of his own words, perhaps, or a sudden awareness of a familiar face in the audience, or the recollection of something he had neglected to say in an earlier sermon to the same congregation—would send him haring off on a tangent.

But if the loose organization is in one respect a weakness, it also accounts for one of the most delightful qualities of the sermons, the touches of wit and humor, so rare in the sermons of other preachers of this period. Latimer can introduce the story of the bishop who visited a town in his diocese where the clapper of the church bell was missing, so that the reverend visitor could not be ceremoniously rung into the parish, only to be told by a local wag that the bell was no worse than the pulpit, which had lacked a voice for twenty years.[29] He can tell with wry amusement of his own remembered

[29] See below, pp. 104–105.

chagrin on the occasion when, having announced his intention to preach in one of the churches of his diocese, he found no congregation to hear the sermon; the folk were all out celebrating Robin Hood's Day.[30] Or of the good woman who suffered from insomnia but could always count on having a good nap during the sermon at St. Thomas of Acres.[31] Sometimes, as in the case of the Robin Hood's Day story, he would feel that his own humor was misplaced, and then he would rebuke his auditors for laughing.

A noticeable characteristic of Latimer's style is his gift for the telling phrase. "Purgatory pickpurse," the "Italian bishop yonder," "clawbacks," "Dr. Dubber," strawberry preachers who "come but once a year, and tarry not long"—one could continue with dozens of examples. Most of them strike us as amusing, and it may have been that Latimer's sense of humor was implicit in his style. Certainly we can scarcely refrain from a chuckle as he concludes one of his alliterative periods, such as the following denunciation of worldly bishops: "They be so placed in palaces, couched in courts, ruffling in their rents, dancing in their dominions, burdened with ambassages, pampering of their paunches, like a monk that maketh his jubilee, munching in their mangers, and moiling in their gay manors and mansions, and so troubled with loitering in their lordships, that they cannot attend it." But if we are amused, we are also constantly aware of the preacher's fundamental seriousness.

Another characteristic which sets Latimer's sermons apart from most others of the period is the occasional introduction of bits of autobiography. Actually, there are relatively few of these in the extant sermons, but these few serve to keep the preacher alive in our minds. Readers of the sermons here reprinted will come upon the account of Latimer's yeoman father, who was able to pay for his son's university education and provide ample dowries for his daughters; of the mother who twice a day milked thirty cows;[32] of the preacher's conversion through the instrumentality of "little

[30] See below, p. 105. [31] See below, p. 98. [32] See below, p. 67.

Bilney"; [33] of his encounters with Henry VIII, such as his struggle to persuade a still superstitious king that the shrine of the Blood of Hales must be destroyed.[34] Here is a passage from a sermon not included in the present volume:

I was once called to one of my kinsfolk (it was at that time when I had taken degree at Cambridge and was made master of art) I was called, I say, to one of my kinsfolk which was very sick and died immediately after my coming. Now there was an old cousin of mine which, after the man was dead, gave me a wax candle in my hand and commanded me to make certain crosses over him that was dead, for she thought the devil would run away by and by. Now I took the candle, but I could not cross him as she would have me to do, for I had never seen it afore. Now she, perceiving that I could not do it, with a great anger took the candle out of my hand, saying, "It is pity that thy father spendeth so much upon thee," and so she took the candle and crossed and blessed him, so that he was sure enough.[35]

The story, introduced to deplore superstition, becomes a delightful and revealing bit of autobiography.

Even when he is not openly autobiographical, Latimer's background and life experience are repeatedly reflected in his words. His years as a student at Cambridge, his close association with Henry VIII, his triumphs and trials as a bishop and as a quondam—these and many others might be cited as supplying the foundation materials upon which the theological or moral ideas are grounded. Certainly the yeoman ancestry underlies the following passage from the first Court sermon of 1549:

For if ye bring it to pass that the yeomanry be not able to put their sons to school . . . , I say ye pluck salvation from the people and utterly destroy the realm. For by yeomen's sons the faith of Christ is and hath been maintained chiefly. Is this realm taught by rich men's sons? No, no, read the chronicles. Ye shall find sometime noblemen's

[33] See below, p. 167. [34] See below, pp. 130–131.

[35] "Sermon on the Epistle for the Twenty-first Sunday after Trinity" (*Sermons and Remains,* I, 499).

sons which have been unpreaching bishops and prelates, but ye shall find none of them learned men.[36]

And the following is only one of many passages which have as their background the daily and seasonal round of work on the farm at Thurcaston:

A plowland must have sheep. Yea, they must have sheep to dung their ground for bearing of corn, for if they have no sheep to help to fat the ground, they shall have but bare corn and thin. They must have swine for their food, to make their veneries or bacon of. . . . Bacon is their necessary meat to feed on, which they may not lack. They must have other cattles, as horses to draw their plow and for carriage of things to the markets, and kine for their milk and cheese, which they must live upon and pay their rents. These cattle must have pasture. . . . And pasture they cannot have if the land be taken in and enclosed from them.[37]

One might dwell at length upon other qualities of Latimer's style—his gift for cadence and balance, for example, when he wished to achieve those effects, and his equal facility with intentional cacophony. But if I were constrained to name the one characteristic that has kept these sermons alive for four centuries, it would be the feeling for the identity of the man behind the sermons—the reader's constant awareness of Hugh Latimer, the farm boy who became a bishop and preached before kings, articulate, occasionally raucous, courageous, sometimes foolhardy, sometimes cantankerous, sometimes tender, deeply serious of purpose but not much given to solemnity, a man who set his hand to the plow and in the end did not look back.

Just as any account of Latimer's career as a preacher must begin with an account of his conversion to the cause of Protestantism, so it must end with some account, however brief, of the last act in the drama, which began with the death of Edward VI and the accession of the Catholic Mary Tudor in July, 1553. Immediately the Ed-

[36] See below, p. 68. [37] See below, pp. 149–150.

wardine Book of Common Prayer was banished from the churches and the mass restored. It was evident that those reformers who had denied the doctrine of transubstantiation and the validity of the mass as a propitiatory sacrifice would be called to account. Many of them fled to the Continent, to enter upon a life of exile which, for all they then knew, might last for a generation or more. Others, cast in more heroic mold, chose to stand their ground. Among the latter was Hugh Latimer.

Two months after Mary's accession, an order was issued for Latimer's appearance before the Privy Council.[38] Although the government would have preferred that he flee overseas, he refused to do so, saying to the pursuivant who delivered the summons, "I doubt not but that God, as He hath made me worthy to preach His word before two excellent princes, so will He able me to witness the same unto the third, either to her comfort or discomfort eternally." [39] He appeared for a brief hearing before the Council on September 13, then was sent to the Tower, where he was kept for the next six months. Among his fellow prisoners were Archbishop Cranmer and Nicholas Ridley, the Edwardine Bishop of London. In spite of difficulties the three men managed to confer. Much of their time was spent in searching the scriptures for texts which might guide them in their forthcoming ordeal. "I assure you," said Latimer, "as I will answer at the tribunal throne of God's majesty, we could find in the testament of God's body and blood no other presence but a spiritual presence, nor that the mass was any sacrifice for sins." [40]

Meanwhile the Privy Council was preparing to deal elaborately with these three archheretics.[41] A disputation was to be held at Oxford, with learned divines from both universities present to hear each of the prisoners answer to three propositions—that in the mass

[38] *Acts of the Privy Council of England,* new ser., ed. John E. Dasent (London, 1890–1892), IV, 340.

[39] Foxe, VII, 464. [40] *Sermons and Remains,* II, 259.

[41] The following account of the disputations, trials, and executions is derived from Foxe, VI, 439–536; VII, 406–423, 518–551.

the natural body and blood of Christ are really present, that after the consecration no substance of bread and wine remain, and that the lively sacrifice of the church is in the mass propitiatory. While preparations for the disputation were in train, the three bishops were removed to Oxford and lodged in the notorious prison known as Bocardo. The preliminary hearings were held on April 14, 1554, in the church of St. Mary the Virgin, with thirty-three Doctors of Divinity seated in the choir and members of the University and townspeople crowding the body of the church. Each of the accused was heard separately. Each refused to subscribe affirmatively to the three propositions.

The disputations proper began on April 16 in the Divinity School. On that day Cranmer debated with the doctors for six hours. Ridley's turn came on the seventeenth, Latimer's on the eighteenth. Latimer, old and ill, was unable to debate, but he gave the presiding officer a long written statement of his opinions. He believed, he said, in a real spiritual presence but not in a corporeal presence. He could find no support for transubstantiation in scripture. He believed that Christ had sacrificed Himself on the Cross once and for all. Some of the doctors tried to quiz him, but he skillfully parried or evaded their questions. His examiners urged him to recant. "You shall have no hope in me to turn," he replied. "I pray for the Queen daily, even from the bottom of my heart, that she may turn from this religion." Two days later the three bishops were again brought before the thirty-three divines and solemnly informed that they had been overcome in disputation. They were formally condemned and remanded to ward, Cranmer to Bocardo, Ridley to the house of the sheriff, Latimer to the house of a bailiff.

Although they were condemned, they could not be sentenced, for the old statute for the burning of heretics had been repealed in the reign of Edward and was not re-enacted until December, 1554. Even then, although John Rogers, the Marian protomartyr, and others in ever-increasing numbers perished in the flames, the three bishops remained in confinement. Cranmer suffered agonies of vacillation.

Latimer experienced a breakdown of some sort but recovered. Finally, in September, 1555, the government decided to deal with Latimer and Ridley; Cranmer's case was delayed by reason of technicalities connected with his status as archbishop.

The trial began on September 30 in the Divinity School, before a commission of three bishops appointed by Cardinal Pole, the papal legate. Ridley was heard first and maintained at some length the opinions he had expressed in the disputation eighteen months earlier. Then Latimer was brought in, "his hat in his hand, having a kerchief on his head and a great cap . . . wearing an old threadbare Bristol frieze gown girdled to his body with a penny leather girdle, at the which hanged by a long string of leather his Testament, and his spectacles without case depending upon his neck upon his breast." Like Ridley, he remained intransigent. The formal sentencing came on the following day. The court ordered that Latimer and Ridley be excommunicated, degraded from the degrees of bishop, priest, and all other order, and turned over to the secular arm for punishment according to law.

Fifteen days passed before the execution. Early in the morning on October 15 the prisoners were led to the place of execution, "upon the side of the town in the ditch over against Balliol College," where the whole town and University had turned out to witness the spectacle. Again refusing to recant, the two men were chained to the stake. As the torch was applied and the flames mounted, Latimer spoke his famous words: "Be of good comfort, Master Ridley, and play the man. We shall this day light such a candle, by God's grace, in England as I trust shall never be put out." Ridley's agony was horribly protracted, for the fire failed to burn properly. But Latimer lost consciousness almost immediately and he seemed to suffer not at all.

SELECTED SERMONS

OF

HUGH LATIMER

CONVOCATION SERMON JUNE 9, 1536[1]

THE SERMON THAT THE REVEREND FATHER IN CHRIST HUGH LATIMER, BISHOP OF WORCESTER, MADE TO THE CLERGY IN THE CONVOCATION BEFORE THE PARLIAMENT BEGAN, THE NINTH DAY OF JUNE, THE TWENTY-EIGHTH YEAR OF THE REIGN OF OUR SOVEREIGN LORD KING HENRY VIII. NOW TRANSLATED OUT OF LATIN INTO ENGLISH, TO THE INTENT THAT THINGS WELL SAID TO A FEW MAY BE UNDERSTAND OF MANY AND DO GOOD TO ALL THEM THAT DESIRE TO BE BETTER

Filii hujus seculi, etc. (Luke 16:8)

BRETHREN, ye be come together this day, as far as I perceive, to hear of great and weighty matters. Ye be come together to entreat of

[1] The title page of the Folger Library copy (STC 15286) reads as follows: "The Sermon that the Reuerende father in Christ, Hugh Latimer, byshop of worcester, made to the clergie, in the conuocation, before the Parlyament began, the 9. day of June, the .28. yere of the reigne of our Souerayne lorde kyng Henry the viii. nowe translated out of latyne into englyshe, to the intent, that thingis well said to a fewe, may be understande of many, and do good to al them that desyre to be better."

things that most appertain to the commonwealth. This being thus, ye look, I am assured, to hear of me—which am commanded to make as a preface this exhortation, albeit I am unlearned and unworthy—such things as shall be much meet for this your assembly. I therefore, not only very desirous to obey the commandment of our Primate but also right greatly coveting to serve and satisfy all your expectation, lo, briefly and as plain as I can, will speak of matters both worthy to be heard in your congregation and also of such as best shall become mine office in this place. That I may do this the more commodiously, I have taken that notable sentence in which our Lord was not afraid to pronounce "the children of this world to be much more prudent and politic than the children of light in their generation" (Luke 16:8). Neither I will be afraid, trusting that He will aid and guide me to use this sentence as a ground and foundation of all such things as hereafter I shall speak of.

Now I suppose that you see right well, being men of such learning, for what purpose the Lord said this and that ye have no need to be holpen with any part of my labor in this thing. But yet if ye will pardon me I will wade somewhat deeper in this matter, and as nigh as I can fetch it from the first original beginning. For undoubtedly ye may much marvel at this saying, if ye well ponder both what is said and who saith it. Define me first these three things: what prudence is; what the world; what light; and who be the children of the world, who of the light. See what they signify in scripture. I marvel if by and by ye all agree that the children of the world should be wiser than the children of the light.

To come somewhat nigher the matter, thus the Lord beginneth: "There was a certain rich man that had a steward, which was accused unto him that he had dissipated and wasted his goods. This rich man called his steward to him and said, 'What is this that I

The colophon reads: ¶ Imprinted at London by Thomas Berthelet, printer to the kinges grace. The yere from the byrthe of Christ. 1537. the 23. of Nouember. Cum priuilegio."

hear of thee? Come, make me an account of thy stewardship; thou mayest no longer bear this office'" (Luke 16:1–2).

Brethren, because these words are so spoken in parable and are so wrapped in wrinkles that yet they seem to have a face and similitude of a thing done indeed and like an history, I think it much profitable to tarry somewhat in them. And though we may perchance find in our hearts to believe all that is there spoken to be true, yet I doubt whether we may abide[2] it that these words of Christ do pertain unto us and admonish us of our duty, which do and live after such sort as though Christ, when He spake anything, had, as the time served Him, served His turn and not regarded the time that came after Him, neither provided for us or any matters of ours; as some of the philosophers thought which said that God walketh up and down in heaven and thinketh never a deal of our affairs. But, my good brethren, err not you so; stick not you to such your imaginations. For if ye inwardly behold these words, if ye diligently roll them in your minds and after explicate and open them, ye shall see our time much touched in these mysteries. Ye shall perceive that God by this example shaketh us by the noses and pulleth us by the ears. Ye shall perceive very plain that God setteth before our eyes in this similitude what we ought most to flee and what we ought soonest to follow. For Luke saith, "The Lord spake these words to His disciples." Wherefore let it be out of all doubt that He spake them to us which, even as we will be compted the successors and vicars of Christ's disciples, so we be if we be good dispensers and do our duty. He said these things partly to us, which spake them partly of Himself. For He is that rich man which not only had but hath and shall have evermore, I say not one but many stewards, even to the end of the world.

He is man, seeing that He is God and man. He is rich not only in mercy but in all kind of riches, for it is He that giveth us all things abundantly. It is He of Whose hand we received both our lives and

[2] *Abide:* endure.

other things necessary for the conservation of the same. What man hath anything, I pray you, but he hath received it of His plentifulness? To be short, it is He that "openeth His hand, and filleth all beasts with His blessing" (Psalm 104:28), and not only giveth unto us in most ample wise His benediction. Neither His treasure can be spent, how much soever He lash out;[3] how much soever we take of Him, His treasure tarrieth still, ever taken, never spent.

He is also the good man of the house; the church is His household, which ought with all diligence to be fed with His word and His sacraments. These be His goods most precious, the dispensation and administration whereof He would bishops and curates should have. Which thing St. Paul affirmeth, saying, "Let men esteem us as the ministers of Christ and dispensers of God's mysteries" (I Cor. 4:1). But, I pray you, what is to be looked for in a dispenser? This surely, that he be found faithful and that he truly dispense and lay out the goods of the Lord; that he give meat in time; give it, I say, and not sell it; meat, I say, and not poison. This doth intoxicate and slay the eater; that feedeth and nourisheth him. Finally, let him not slack and defer the doing of his office, but let him do his duty when time is and need requireth it. This is also to be looked for, that he be one whom God hath called and put in office and not one that cometh uncalled, unsent for, not one that of himself presumeth to take honor upon him. What is to be looked for? Surely, if all this that I say be required in a good minister, it is much lighter to require them all in every one than to find one anywhere that hath them all. Who is a true and faithful steward? He is true, he is faithful, that coineth no new money but taketh it ready coined of the goodman of the house, and neither changeth it ne clippeth it, after it is taken to him to spend, but spendeth even the selfsame that he had of his Lord and spendeth it as his Lord's commandment is, neither to his own advantage uttering[4] it nor, as the lewd servant did, hiding it in the ground.

Brethren, if a faithful steward ought to do as I have said, I pray

[3] *Lash out:* squander. [4] *Uttering:* circulating.

you ponder and examine this well, whether our bishops and abbots, prelates and curates, have been hitherto faithful stewards or no. Ponder whether yet many of them be as they should be or no. Go ye to, tell me now as your conscience leadeth you—I will let pass to speak of many other—was there not some that, despising the money of the Lord as copper and not current, either coined new themselves or else uttered abroad newly coined of other; sometime either adulterating the Word of God or else mingling it, as taverners do which brew and utter the evil and good both in a pot; sometime in the stead of God's word blowing out the dreams of men? While they thus preached to the people the redemption that cometh by Christ's death to serve only them that died before His coming, that were in the time of the Old Testament; and that now since, redemption and forgiveness of sins purchased by money and devised of men is of efficacy, and not redemption purchased by Christ. They have a wonderful pretty example to persuade this thing, of a certain married woman which, when her husband was in purgatory, in that fiery furnace that hath burned away so many of our pence, paid her husband's ransom and so of duty claimed him to be set at liberty.

While they thus preached to the people, that dead images (which at the first, as I think, were set up only to represent things absent) not only ought to be covered with gold but also ought of all faithful and Christian people—yea, in this scarceness and penury of all things—to be clad with silk garments and those also laden with precious gems and jewels, and that beside all this they are to be lighted with wax candles both within the church and without the church, yea, at noon days, as who should say, here no cost can be too great, whereas in the mean time we see Christ's faithful and lively images, bought with no less price than with His most precious blood—alas, alas!—to be anhungered, athirst, acold, and to lie in darkness, wrapped in all wretchedness, yea, to lie there until death take away their miseries. While they preached these will-works [5] that come but of our own devotion, although they be not so neces-

[5] *Will-works:* voluntary works, such as pilgrimages and the lighting of votive candles.

sary as the works of mercy and the precepts of God, yet they said, and in the pulpit, that will-works were more principal, more excellent, and—plainly to utter what they mean—more acceptable to God than works of mercy; as though now man's inventions and fancies could please God better than God's precepts, or strange things better than His own. While they thus preached that more fruit, more devotion cometh of the beholding of an image, though it be but a Paternoster while,[6] than is gotten by reading and contemplation in scripture, though ye read and contemplate therein seven years' space. Finally, while they preached thus, souls tormented in purgatory to have most need of our help and that they can have no aid but of us in this world, of the which two, if the one be not false yet at the least it is ambiguous, uncertain, doubtful, and therefore rashly and arrogantly with such boldness affirmed in the audience of people; the other, by all men's opinions, is manifestly false.

I let pass to speak of much other suchlike counterfeit doctrine which hath been blasted and blown out by some for the space of three hours together. Be these the Christian and divine mysteries and not rather the dreams of men? Be these the faithful dispensers of God's mysteries and not rather false dissipators of them, whom God never put in office, but rather the devil set them over a miserable family, over an house miserably ordered and entreated? Happy were the people if such preached seldom. And yet it is a wonder to see these, in their generation, to be much more prudent and politic than the faithful ministers are in their generation, while they go about more prudently to stablish men's dreams than these do to hold up God's commandments.

Thus it cometh to pass that works lucrative, will-works, men's fancies reign; and Christian works, necessary works, fruitful works be trodden under the foot. Thus the evil is much better set out by evil men than is the good by good men, because the evil be more wise than be the good in their generation. These be the false stewards whom all good and faithful men every day accuse unto the

[6] *Paternoster while:* the time it takes to say a Pater Noster.

rich master of the household, not without great heaviness, that they waste his goods, whom he also one day will call to him, and say to them as he did to his steward when he said, "What is this that I hear of thee?" Here God partly wondereth at our ingratitude and perfidy, partly chideth us for them, and, being both full of wonder and ready to chide, asketh us, "What is this that I hear of you?" As though He should say unto us, "All good men in all places complain of you, accuse your avarice, your exactions, your tyranny. They have required in you a long season, and yet require, diligence and sincerity. I commanded you that with all industry and labor ye should feed My sheep; ye earnestly feed yourselves from day to day, wallowing in delights and idleness. I commanded you to teach My commandments and not your fancies, and that ye should seek My glory and My vantage; you teach your own traditions and seek your own glory and profit. You preach very seldom, and when ye do preach ye do nothing but cumber them that preach truly, as much as lieth in you, that it were much better such not to preach at all than so perniciously to preach. Oh, what I hear of you! You that ought to be My preachers, what other thing do you than apply all your study hither to bring all My preachers to envy, shame, contempt? Yea, more than this, ye pull them into perils, into prisons, and, as much as in you lieth, to cruel deaths.

"To be short, I would that Christian people should hear My doctrine, and at their commodity[7] read it also, as many as would. Your care is not that all men may hear it, but all your care is that no layman do read it, surely being afraid lest they by the reading should understand it and, understanding, learn to rebuke your slothfulness. This is your generation, this is your dispensation, this is your wisdom. In this generation, in this dispensation, you be most politic, most witty. These be the things that I hear of your demeanor. I wished to hear better report of you. Have ye thus deceived Me? Or have ye rather deceived yourselves? Where I had but one house, that is to say, the church, and this so dearly beloved of Me that for the

[7] *Commodity:* convenience.

love of her I put Myself forth to be slain and to shed My blood, this church at My departure I committed unto your charge, to be fed, to be nourished, and to be made much of. My pleasure was ye should occupy My place. My desire was ye should have borne like love to this church, like fatherly affection, as I did. I made you My vicars, yea, in matters of most importance.

"For thus I taught openly: 'He that should hear you should hear Me; he that should despise you should despise Me' (Luke 10:16). I gave you also keys, not earthly keys but heavenly. I left My goods that I have evermore most highly esteemed, that is, My word and sacraments, to be dispensed of you. These benefits I gave you. And do you give Me these thanks? Can ye find in your hearts thus to abuse My goodness, My benignity, My gentleness? Have ye thus deceived Me? No, no, ye have not deceived Me, but yourselves. My gifts and benefits toward you shall be to your greater damnation. Because ye have contemned the lenity and clemency of the master of the house, ye have right well deserved to abide the rigor and severity of the judge. Come forth then, let us see accompt of your stewardship. An horrible and fearful sentence: Ye may have no longer My goods in your hands. A voice to weep at and to make men tremble!"

You see, brethren, you see to what evil the evil stewards must come to. Your labor is paid for if ye can so take heed that no such sentence be spoken to you; nay, we must all take heed lest these threatenings one day take place in us. But lest the length of my sermon offend you too sore, I will leave the rest of the parable and take me to the handling of the end of it, that is, I will declare you how the children of this world be more witty, crafty, and subtile, than are the children of the light in their generation. Which sentence would God it lay in my poor tongue to explicate with such light of words that I might seem rather to have painted it before your eyes than to have spoken it, and that you might rather seem to see the thing than to hear it! But I confess plainly this thing to be far above my power. Therefore, this being only left to me, I wish for that I have not, and am sorry that that is not in me which I would so gladly have, that is, power so to handle the thing that I have in hand that all that I say may turn to the glory of God, your souls' health, and the edifying of Christ's body.

Wherefore I pray you all to pray with me unto God, and that in your petition you desire that these two things He vouchsafe to grant us: first, a mouth for me to speak rightly; next, ears for you, that in hearing me ye may take profit at my hand. And that this may come to effect, you shall desire Him unto Whom our master Christ bade we should pray, saying even the same prayer that He Himself did institute, *Pater noster*. Wherein ye shall pray for our most gracious sovereign lord the King, chief and supreme head of the church of England under Christ, and for the most excellent, gracious, and virtuous lady Queen Jane,[8] his most lawful wife, and for all his, whether they be of the clergy or laity, whether they be of the nobility or else other His Grace's subjects, not forgetting those that, being departed out of this thrallsome [9] life, now sleep in the sleep of peace, and rest from their labors in quietness and in peaceable sleep, faithfully, lovingly, and patiently looking for that that they clearly shall see when God shall be so pleased. For all these, and for grace necessary, ye shall say unto God God's prayer, *Pater noster*.[10]

[THE SECOND PART OF THE SERMON BEFORE CONVOCATION]

Filii hujus seculi, etc (Luke 16:8)

Christ in this saying touched the sloth and sluggishness of His and did not allow the fraud and subtility of others, neither was glad that

[8] Jane Seymour, third queen of Henry VIII, whom he had married privately on May 30, 1536, ten days before the date of this sermon. Her predecessor, Anne Boleyn, had been executed May 19.

[9] *Thrallsome:* slavish. The *OED* does not record this attractive word, which in later editions was replaced by *transitory*.

[10] Here, as in many other sermons, Latimer uses the *Pater noster* as the bidding prayer—i.e., a prayer said for persons dead and living whose names were on the list of those to be prayed for.

it was indeed as He had said, but complained rather that it should be so, as many men speak many things, not that they ought to be so, but that they are wont to be so. Nay, this grieved Christ, that the children of this world should be of more policy than the children of light, which thing yet was true in Christ's time and now in our time is most true. Who is so blind but he seeth this clearly, except perchance there be any that cannot discern the children of the world from the children of light? The children of the world conceive and bring forth more prudently, and things conceived and brought forth they nourish and conserve with much more policy than do the children of light. Which thing is as sorrowful to be said as it seemeth absurd to be heard. When ye hear the children of the world, you understand the world as a father. For the world is father of many children, not by first creation and work but by imitation and love. He is not only a father but also the son of another father. If ye know once his father, by and by ye shall know his children. For he that hath the devil to his father must needs have devilish children. The devil is not only taken for father but also for prince of the world, that is, of worldly folk. It is either all one thing, or else not much different, to say "children of the world" and "children of the devil," according to that that Christ said to the Jews, "Ye are of your father the devil" (John 8:44); whereas undoubtedly He spake to children of this world.

Now seeing the devil is both author and ruler of the darkness in the which the children of this world walk or, to say better, wander, they mortally hate both the light and also the children of light. And hereof it cometh that the children of light never, or very seldom, lack persecution in this world unto which the children of the world, that is, of the devil, bringeth them. And there is no man but he seeth that these use much more policy in procuring the hurt and damage of the good than those in defending themselves. Therefore, brethren, gather you the disposition and study of the children by the disposition and study of the fathers. You know this is a proverb much used, "An evil crow, an evil egg." Then the children of this world that are known to have so evil a father, the world, so evil a grandfather, the devil, cannot choose but be evil. Surely the first head of their ancestry was that deceitful serpent the devil, a monster monstrous above all monsters. I cannot wholly express him, I wot not what to call him but a certain thing altogether made of the hatred of God, of mistrust in God, of lyings, deceits, perjuries, discords, manslaughters, and, to say at one word, a thing concrete,[11] heaped up and made of all kind of mischief. But what the devil mean I to go about to describe particularly the devil's nature, when no reason, no power of man's mind can comprehend it? This alonely I can say grossly, and as in a sum, of the which all we—our hurt is the more—have experience, the devil to be a stinking sentine[12] of all vices, a foul filthy channel[13] of all mischiefs, and that this world, his son, even a child meet to have such a parent, is not much unlike his father.

Then, this devil being such one as can never be unlike himself, lo, of Envy, his well-beloved leman,[14] he begat the World, and after left it with Discord at nurse, which World, after that it came to man's state, had of many concubines many sons. He was so fecund a father and had gotten so many children of Lady Pride, Dame Gluttony, Mistress Avarice, Lady Lechery, and of Dame Subtlety[15] that now hard and scant ye may find any corner, any kind of life, where many of his children be not. In court, in cowls, in cloisters, in rochets, be they never so white, yea, where shall ye not find them? Howbeit, they that be secular and laymen are not by and by[16] children of the world, nor they children of light that are called spiritual and of the clergy. No, no, as ye may find among the laity many children of light, so among the clergy—how much soever we arrogate these holy

[11] *Concrete:* compounded of various elements.

[12] *Sentine:* an open sink.

[13] *Channel:* gutter. The *OED* cites this passage to illustrate the meaning "a medium of communication."

[14] *Leman:* paramour.

[15] This kind of personification is in the tradition of the preaching friars. See G. R. Owst, *Literature and Pulpit in Medieval England* (Cambridge, 1933), chap. ii.

[16] *By and by:* for that reason.

titles unto us, and think them only attributed to us, *Vos estis lux mundi, peculium Christi, etc.,* "Ye are the light of the world (Matt. 5:14), the chosen people of Christ, a kingly priesthood, an holy nation (I Peter 2:9), and such other"—ye shall find many children of the world, because in all places the world getteth many children.

Among the lay people the world ceaseth not to bring to pass that as they be called worldly so they are worldly indeed, driven headlong by worldly desires, insomuch that they may right well seem to have taken as well the manners as the name of their father. In the clergy the world also hath learned a way to make of men spiritual worldlings, yea, and there also to form worldly children, where with great pretense of holiness and crafty color of religion they utterly desire to hide and cloak the name of the world, as though they were ashamed of their father, which do execrate and detest the world (being nevertheless their father) in words and outward signs, but in heart and work they coll [17] and kiss him, and in all their lives declare themselves to be his babes; insomuch that in all worldly points they far pass and surmount those that they call seculars, laymen, men of the world. The child so diligently followeth the steps of his father, never destitute of the aid of his grandfather. These be our holy, holy men that say they are dead to the world, when no men be more lively in worldly things than some of them be. But let them be in profession and name most farthest from the world, most alienate from it, yea, so far that they may seem to have no occupying, no kindred, no affinity, nothing to do with it, yet in their life and deeds they show themselves no bastards, but right-begotten children of the world; as the which the world long sithens had by his dear wife Dame Hypocrisy and since hath brought them up and multiplied them to more than a good many; increased them too much, albeit they swear by all he saints, and she saints too, that they know not their father nor mother, neither the world nor hypocrisy, as indeed they can semble and dissemble all things, which thing they might learn wonderful well of their parents.

[17] *Coll:* embrace.

I speak not of all religious men but of those that the world hath fast knit at his girdle even in the midst of their religion, that is, of many and mo than many. For I fear lest in all orders of men the better, I must say the greater, part of them be out of order and children of the world. Many of these might seem ingrate and unkind children, that will no better acknowledge and recognize their parents in words and outward pretense but abrenounce and cast them off, as though they hated them as dogs and serpents. Howbeit they in this wise are most grateful to their parents, because they be most like them, so lively representing them in countenance and conditions that their parents seem in them to be young again, forasmuch as they ever say one and think another. They show themselves to be as sober, as temperate, as Curius [18] the Roman was, and live every day as though all their life were a shroving time.[19] They be like their parents, I say, inasmuch as they in following them seem and make men believe they hate them. Thus Grandfather Devil, Father World, and Mother Hypocrisy have brought them up. Thus good obedient sons have borne away their parents' commandments; neither these be solitary, how religious, how mocking—how monking, I would say—soever they be.

Oh, ye will lay this to my charge, that *monachus* and *solitarius* signifieth all one. I grant this to be so, yet these be so solitary that they be not alone but accompanied with great flocks of fraternities. And I marvel if there be not a great sort of bishops and prelates that are brethren german unto these, and as a great sort, so even as right born and world's children by as good title as they. But because I cannot speak of all, when I say prelates I understand bishops, abbots, priors, archdeacons, deans, and other of such sort that are now called to this Convocation, as I see, to entreat here of nothing but of such matters as both appertain to the glory of Christ and to the wealth of the people of England. Which thing I pray God they do as earnestly

[18] A consul of the third century B.C., a type of the ancient Roman virtue.

[19] *Shroving time:* merrymaking time. Shrove Tuesday, the day before Ash Wednesday, was traditionally a day of revelry.

as they ought to do. But it is to be feared lest, as light hath many her children here, so the world hath sent some of his whelps hither, among the which I know there can be no concord nor unity, albeit they be in one place, in one congregation. I know there can be no agreement between these two as long as they have minds so unlike and so contrary affections, judgments so utterly diverse in all points.

But if the children of this world be either more in number or more prudent than the children of light, what then availeth us to have this Convocation? Had it not been better we had not been called together at all? For as the children of this world be evil, so they breed and bring forth things evil; and yet there be more of them in all places, or at the least they be more politic than the children of light in their generation. And here I speak of the generation whereby they do engender and not of that whereby they are engendered, because it should be too long to entreat how the children of light are engendered and how they come in at the door, and how the children of the world be engendered and come in another way. Howbeit, I think all you that be here were not engendered after one generation, neither that ye all came by your promotions after one manner. God grant that ye, engendered worldly, do not engender worldly. And as now I much pass not how ye were engendered or by what means ye were promoted to those dignities that ye now occupy, so it be honest, good, and profitable that ye in this your consultation shall do and engender.

The end of your Convocation shall show what ye have done; the fruit that shall come of your consultation shall show what generation ye be of. For what have ye done hitherto, I pray you, these seven years[20] and more? What have ye engendered? What have ye brought forth? What fruit is come of your long and great assembly? What one thing that the people of England hath been the better of an hair, or you yourselves either more accepted before God or better discharged toward the people committed unto your cure? For that

[20] The allusion is to the seven years (Nov., 1529, to April, 1536) during which the so-called Reformation Parliament was in session. Convocation sat concurrently.

the people is better learned and taught now, than they were in time past, to whether of these ought we to attribute it, to your industry or to the providence of God and the foreseeing of the King's Grace?[21] Ought we to thank you, or the King's Highness? Whether stirred other first, you the King that he might preach, or he you by his letters that ye should preach ofter? Is it unknown, think you, how both ye and your curates were, in manner, by violence enforced to let books to be made—[not] by you but by profane and lay persons—to let them, I say, be sold abroad and read for the instruction of the people? I am bold with you, but I speak Latin and not English, to the clergy, not to the laity; I speak to you being present and not behind your backs. God is my witness, I speak whatsoever is spoken of the good will that I bear you. God is my witness, Which knoweth my heart and compelleth me to say that I say.

Now I pray you a God's name, what did you, so great fathers, so many, so long a season, so oft assembled together? What went you about? What would you have brought to pass? Two things taken away—the one that ye (which I heard) burned a dead man;[22] the other that ye (which I felt) went about to burn one being alive:[23] him, because he did, I cannot tell how, in his testament withstand your profit; in other points, as I have heard, a very good man, reported to be of an honest life while he lived, full of good works, good both to the clergy and also to the laity; this other, which truly never hurt any of you, ye would have raked in the coals because he would not subscribe to certain articles that took away the supremity of the King. Take away these two noble acts and there is nothing else left that ye went about that I know, saving that I now remem-

[21] Latimer is presumably referring to Henry VIII's letter addressed to each of the bishops in 1536. In it the bishops are enjoined to preach regularly and to see to it that the clergy of their dioceses do the same. A copy of the letter is preserved in MS. Cotton. Cleop. E. V. f. 290. It is reprinted in Wilkins, *Concilia,* III, 825–826.

[22] William Tracy, a justice of the peace, who died in 1530. In his will he forbade the saying of masses for the repose of his soul. The will was pronounced heretical by Convocation and in 1532 Tracy's body was exhumed and burned (Foxe, V, 31–32).

[23] Latimer himself was examined on charges of heresy in 1532.

ber that somewhat ye attempted against Erasmus;[24] albeit as yet nothing is come to light.

Ye have oft sit in consultation, but what have ye done? Ye have had many things in deliberation, but what one is put forth whereby either Christ is more glorified or else Christ's people made more holier? I appeal to your own conscience. How chanced this? How came this thus? Because there were no children of light, no children of God among you which, setting the world at nought, would study to illustrate the glory of God and thereby show themselves children of light? I think not so, certainly I think not so. God forbid that all you which were gathered together under the pretense of light should be children of the world! Then why happened this? Why, I pray you? Perchance either because the children of the world were more in number in this your congregation, as it oft happeneth, or at the least of more policy than the children of light in their generation, whereby it might very soon be brought to pass that those were much more stronger in gendering the evil than these in producing good. The children of light have policy, but it is like the policy of the serpent and is joined with dovish simplicity. They engender nothing but simply, faithfully, and plainly, even so doing all that they do. And therefore they may with more facility be cumbered in their engendering and be the more ready to take injuries. But the children of this world have worldly policy, foxly craft, lionlike cruelty, power to do hurt more than either *aspis* or *basiliscus,* engendering and doing all things fraudulently, deceitfully, guilefully, which as Nimrods[25] and such sturdy and stout hunters, being full of simulation and dissimulation before the Lord, deceive the children of light and cumber them easily. Hunters go not forth in every man's sight but do their affairs closely and with use of guile and deceit wax every day more craftier than other.

[24] Alludes to the attacks on Erasmus' *Novum Testamentum,* perhaps specifically to the charge of Henry Standish, Bishop of St. Asaph, that Erasmus was guilty of heresy in substituting *sermo* for *verbum* in John 1:1.

[25] Gen. 10:8–9.

The children of this world be like crafty hunters; they be misnamed children of light, forasmuch as they so hate light and so study to do the works of darkness. If they were the children of light, they would not love darkness. It is no marvel that they go about to keep other in darkness, seeing they be in darkness, from top to toe overwhelmed with darkness, darker than is the darkness of hell. Wherefore it is well done in all orders of men, but in especial in the order of prelates, to put a difference between children of light and children of the world, because great deceit ariseth in taking the one for the other. Great imposture cometh when they that the common people take for the light go about to take the sun and the light out of the world. But these be easily known, both by the diversity of minds and also their armors. For whereas the children of light are thus minded, that they seek their adversaries' health, wealth, and profit, with loss of their own commodities and ofttimes with jeopardy of their life, the children of the world, contrariwise, have such stomachs that they will sooner see them dead that doth them good than sustain any loss of temporal things.

The armor of the children of light are, first, the Word of God, which they ever set forth and with all diligence put it abroad that, as much as in them lieth, it may bring forth fruit. After this, patience and prayer, with the which in all adversities the Lord comforteth them. Other things they commit to God, unto Whom they leave all revengement. The armor of the children of the world are sometime frauds and deceits, sometime lies and money. By the first they make their dreams, their traditions; by the second they stablish and confirm their dreams, be they never so absurd, never so against scripture, honesty, reason. And if any man resist them, even with these weapons they procure to slay him. Thus they bought Christ's death, the very light itself, and obscured Him after His death. Thus they buy every day the children of light and obscure them, and shall so do until the world be at an end. So that it may be ever true, that Christ said: "The children of the world be wiser," etc.

These worldlings pull down the lively faith and full confidence that men have in Christ and set up another faith, another confidence, of their own making; the children of light contrary. These worldlings set little by such works as God hath prepared for our salvation, but they extol traditions and works of their own invention; the children of light contrary. The worldlings, if they spy profit, gains, lucre in anything, be it never such a trifle, be it never so pernicious, they preach it to the people—if they preach at any time—and these things they defend with tooth and nail. They can scarce disallow the abuses of these, albeit they be intolerable, lest in disallowing the abuse they lose part of their profit. The children of the light, contrary, put all things in their degree, best highest, next next, the worst lowest. They extol things necessary, Christian, and commanded of God. They pull down will-works feigned by men and put them in their place. The abuses of all things they earnestly rebuke. But yet these things be so done on both parties, and so they both do gender, that children of the world show themselves wiser than the children of light, and that frauds and deceits, lies and money, seem evermore to have the upper hand. I hold my peace. I will not say how fat feasts and jolly banquets be jolly instruments to set forth worldly matters withal. Neither the children of the world be only wiser than the children of light, but are also some of them among themselves much wiser than the other in their generation. For albeit as touching the end the generation of them all is one, yet in this same generation some of them have more craftily engendered than the other of their fellows.

For what a thing was that that once every hundred year [26] was brought forth in Rome of the children of this world and with how much policy it was made, ye heard at Paul's Cross [27] in the beginning of the last Parliament. How some brought forth canonizations, some expectations,[28] some pluralities and unions, some totquots [29]

[26] That is, in the jubilee years.

[27] The outdoor pulpit in the yard of St. Paul's cathedral. The Paul's Cross sermons were usually of an official or semiofficial nature. Latimer preached there frequently during his tenure as Bishop of Worcester and later during the reign of Edward VI.

[28] *Expectations:* the sale prospectively of benefices which were not yet vacant.

[29] *Totquots:* dispensations permitting unlimited pluralism.

and dispensations, some pardons, and these of wonderful variety,[30] some stationaries,[31] some jubilaries,[32] some pocularies[33] for drinkers, some manuaries[34] for handlers of relics, some pedaries[35] for pilgrims, some oscularies[36] for kissers. Some of them engendered one, some other such fetures,[37] and every one in that he was delivered of was excellent politic, wise, yea, so wise that with their wisdom they had almost made all the world fools.

But yet they that begot and brought forth that our old ancient purgatory pickpurse; that that was swaged[38] and cooled with a Franciscan's cowl, put upon a dead man's back, to the fourth part of his sins;[39] that that was utterly to be spoiled, and of none other but of our most prudent lord Pope, and of him as oft as him listed;[40]

30 At this point the Latin original reads as follows: *alii indulgentias, et has mira varietate splendidas, nunc stationarias, nunc jubilarias, nunc pocularias, pedarias, et oscularias.* The English should more properly have read, "pardons *for* stationaries . . . *for* jubilaries," etc.

31 *Stationaries:* indulgences granted for attending a "station"—each of a number of holy places visited by pilgrims in fixed succession, especially each of those churches in Rome at which, each on a fixed day, the clergy assemble for litanies and prayers.

32 *Jubilaries:* indulgences granted for having visited Rome or other designated places during a jubilee year.

33 *Pocularies:* indulgences granted for having drunk from a pardon bowl (see note 23 to the "Sermon on the Plowers," p. 46 below).

34 *Manuaries:* indulgences granted for having touched a relic. (In some older dictionaries the meaning "hallowed gloves" is given as a result of the misreading of the Latin.) See note 30 above.

35 *Pedaries:* indulgences for having made a pilgrimage on foot.

36 *Oscularies:* indulgences for having kissed a painted or carved representation of Christ or the Blessed Virgin.

37 *Fetures* (*foetures*): offspring.

38 *Swaged:* assuaged.

39 Clement V, Pope from 1305 to 1314, is said to have promised remission of a fourth part of his sins to anyone who was buried in the habit of the Friars Minor. John Bale writes: "And to be prayed for . . . there must be masses and diriges. . . . He must be buried in St. Francis' gray coat. . . ." See *The Image of Both Churches,* in *Select Works of John Bale,* ed. Henry Christmas (Cambridge: The Parker Society, 1849), p. 329.

40 The sense of this clause is by no means clear. The Latin reads as follows: *Illud non nisi a prudentissimo, domino papa, vel quoties libuerit, in totum spoliandum,* which might be translated "that [purgatory] should not be exploited entirely, and as

that satisfactory,[41] that missal,[42] that scalary [43]—they, I say, that were the wise fathers and genitors of this purgatory were in my mind the wisest of all their generation, and so far pass both the children of light and also the rest of their company that they both are but fools, if ye compare them with these. It was a pleasant fiction and from the beginning so profitable to the feigners of it that almost, I dare boldly say, there hath been no emperor that hath gotten more by taxes and tallages [44] of them that were alive than these, the very and right-begotten sons of the world, got by dead men's tributes and gifts. If there be some in England that would this sweeting [45] of the world to be with no less policy kept still than it was born and brought forth in Rome, who then can accuse Christ of lying? No, no; as it hath been ever true, so it shall be that the children of the world be much wiser not only in making their things but also in conserving them.

I wot not what it is, but somewhat it is I wot, that some men be so loath to see the abuse of this monster purgatory, which abuse is more than abominable; as who should say there is none abuse in it, or else as though there can be none in it. They may seem heartily to love the old thing that thus earnestly endeavor them to restore him his old name. They would not set an hair by the name but for the thing. They be not so ignorant—no, they be crafty—but that they know if the name come again the thing will come after. Thereby it ariseth that some men make their cracks [46] that they, mauger of all men's heads, have found purgatory. I cannot tell what is found. This, to

---

often as possible, except by a most prudent Pope."

41 *Satisfactory:* a mass for the expiation of sins.

42 *Missal* (meaning uncertain).

43 *Scalary:* a mass of the Scala Coeli, one of the three churches of the Abbey of the Tre Fontane, outside Rome, where St. Bernard is said to have had a vision of the heavenly ladder on which the souls of those released from purgatory by his prayers were ascending to heaven. The term was also applied to masses said at altars in England which carried similar indulgences.

44 *Tallages:* levies.

45 *Sweeting:* darling.

46 *Cracks:* boasts.

pray for dead folks, this is not found, for it was never lost. How can that be found that was not lost? O subtle finders, that can find things, an God will, ere they be lost! For that cowlish deliverance, their scalary loosings, their papal spoliations, and other such their figments they cannot find, they cannot find. No, these be so lost, as they themselves grant, that though they seek them never so diligently yet they shall not find them, except perchance they hope to see them come in again with their names, and that then money-gathering may return again and deceit walk about the country and so stablish their kingdom in all kingdoms. But to what end this chiding between the children of the world and the children of light will come only He knoweth that once shall judge them both.

Now to make haste and to come somewhat nigher the end. Go ye to, good brethren and fathers, for the love of God, go ye to; and seeing we are here assembled, let us do something whereby we may be known to be the children of light. Let us do somewhat, lest we which hitherto have been judged children of the world seem even still to be so. All men call us prelates. Then, seeing we be in council, let us so order ourselves that as we be prelates in honor and dignity, so we may be prelates in holiness, benevolence, diligence, and sincerity. All men know that we be here gathered, and with most fervent desire they anheale,[47] breathe, and gape for the fruit of our Convocation. As our acts shall be, so they shall name us, so that now it lieth in us whether we will be called children of the world or children of light.

Wherefore lift up your heads, brethren, and look about with your eyes. Spy what things are to be reformed in the church of England. Is it so hard, is it so great a matter for you to see many abuses in the clergy, many in the laity? What is done in the Arches?[48] Nothing to be amended? What do they there? Do they evermore rid the

[47] *Anheale:* pant for.

[48] *Arches:* the Court of Arches, the chief consistory court of the Archbishop of Canterbury, so called because it formerly convened in the church of St. Mary-le-Bow (*de arcubus*).

people's business and matters, or cumber and ruffle them? Do they evermore correct vice, or else defend it, sometime being well corrected in other places? How many sentences [49] be given there in time, as they ought to be? If men say truth, how many without bribes? Or if all things be well done there, what do men in bishops' consistories? [50] Shall you ofter see the punishments assigned by the laws executed, or else money redemptions used in their stead? How think you by the ceremonies that are in England ofttimes, with no little offense of weak consciences, contemned; more oftener with superstition so defiled and so depraved that you may doubt whether it were better some of them to tarry still or utterly to take them away? Have not our forefathers complained of the number of ceremonies, of the superstition and estimation of them?

Do ye see nothing in our holidays, of the which very few were made at the first, and they to set forth goodness, virtue, and honesty? But sithens, in some places, there is neither mean nor measure in making new holidays, as who should say this one thing is serving of God, to make this law that no man may work. But what doth the people on these holidays? Do they give themselves to godliness or else ungodliness? See ye nothing, brethren? If you see not, yet God seeth. God seeth all the whole holidays to be spent miserably in drunkenness, in glossing,[51] in strife, in envy, in dancing, dicing, idleness, and gluttony. He seeth all this and threateneth punishment for it. He seeth it which neither is deceived in seeing nor deceiveth when He threateneth.

Thus men serve the devil; for God is not thus served, albeit ye say ye serve God. No, the devil hath more service done unto him on one holiday than on many working days. Let all these abuses be compted as nothing, who is he that is not sorry to see in so many holidays rich and wealthy persons to flow in delicates [52] and men that live by their

[49] *Sentences:* judgments.

[50] *Bishops' consistories:* episcopal courts for dealing with ecclesiastical causes.

[51] *Glossing:* gluttony.

[52] *Delicates*: luxuries.

travail, poor men, to lack necessary meat and drink for their wives and their children, and that they cannot labor upon the holidays except they will be cited and brought before our officials?[53] Were it not the office of good prelates to consult upon these matters and to seek some remedy for them? Ye shall see, my brethren, ye shall see once what will come of this our winking.[54]

What think ye of these images that are had more than their fellows in reputation, that are gone unto with such labor and weariness of the body, frequented with such our cost, sought out and visited with such confidence? What say ye by these images that are so famous, so noble, so noted, being of them so many and so divers in England? Do you think that this preferring of picture to picture, image to image, is the right use and not rather the abuse of images? But you will say to me, "Why make ye all these interrogations? And why in these your demands do you let and withdraw the good devotion of the people? Be not all things well done that are done with good intent, when they be profitable to us?" So, surely, covetousness both thinketh and speaketh. Were it not better for us, more for estimation, more meeter for men in our places to cut away a piece of this our profit, if we will not cut away all, than to wink at such ungodliness and so long to wink for a little lucre, specially if it be ungodliness and also seem unto you ungodliness?

These be two things, so oft to seek mere images and sometime to visit the relics of saints. And yet as in those there may be much ungodliness committed, so there may here some superstition be hid, if that sometime we chance to visit pigs' bones instead of saints' relics, as in time past it hath chanced, I had almost said in England. Then this is too great a blindness, a darkness too sensible, that these should be so commended in sermons of some men and preached to be done after such manner, as though they could not be evil done, which notwithstanding are such that neither God nor man commandeth them to be done. No, rather, men commanded them either not

[53] *Officials:* the presiding officers or judges in the ecclesiastical courts.

[54] *Winking:* shutting the eyes.

to be done at all or else more slowlier and seldomer to be done, forasmuch as our ancestors made this constitution: "We command the priests that they oft admonish the people, and in especial women, that they make no vows but after long deliberation, consent of their husbands, and counsel of the priest."[55] The church of England in time past made this constitution. What saw they that made this decree? They saw the intolerable abuses of images. They saw the perils that might ensue of going on pilgrimage. They saw the superstitious difference that men made between image and image. Surely, somewhat they saw.

The constitution is so made that in manner it taketh away all such pilgrimages. For it so plucketh away the abuse of them that it leaveth either none or else seldom use of them. For they that restrain making vows for going of pilgrimage restrain also pilgrimage, seeing that for the most part it is seen that few go on pilgrimage but vow-makers and such as by promise bind themselves to go. And when, I pray you, should a man's wife go on pilgrimage, if she went not before she had well debated the matter with herself and obtained the consent of her husband, being a wise man, and were also counseled by a learned priest so to do? When should she go far off to these famous images? For this the common people of England think to be going on pilgrimage, to go to some dead and notable image out of town, that is to say, far from their house. Now if your forefathers made this constitution and yet thereby did nothing, the abuses every day more and more increased, what is left for you to do? Brethren and fathers, if ye purpose to do anything, what should ye sooner do than to take utterly away these deceitful and juggling images, or else, if ye know any other mean to put away abuses, to show it if ye intend to remove abuses? Methink it should be grateful and pleasant to you to mark the earnest mind of your forefathers and to look upon their desire where they say in their constitution,

[55] *Item, moneat sacerdos mulieres, ne faciant vota, nisi cum magna deliberatione; aut virorum suorum consensu; aut consilio sacerdotum.* This is Item 32 in the Provincial Constitutions of Edmund Rich, Archbishop of Canterbury, ca. 1236 (Wilkins, *Concilia,* I, 838).

"We command you," and not, "We counsel you." How have we been so long acold, so long slack in setting forth so wholesome a precept of the church of England, where we be so hot in all things that have any gains in them, albeit they be neither commanded us nor yet given us by counsel; as though we had lever the abuse of things should tarry still than, it taken away, lose our profit? To let pass the solemn and nocturnal bacchanals, the prescript miracles that are done upon certain days in the west part of England, who hath not heard? I think ye have heard of St. Blesis'[56] heart, which is at Malvern, and of St. Algar's[57] bones, how long they deluded the people, I am afraid to the loss of many souls. Whereby men may well conjecture that all about in this realm there is plenty of such juggling deceits. And yet hitherto ye have sought no remedy. But even still the miserable people is suffered to take the false miracles for the true, and to lie still asleep in all kind of superstition. God have mercy upon us!

Last of all, how think you of matrimony? Is all well here? What of baptism? Shall we evermore in ministering of it speak Latin and not English rather, that the people may know what is said and done? What think ye of these mass priests and of the masses themselves? What say ye? Be all things here so without abuses that nothing ought to be amended? Your forefathers saw somewhat which made this constitution[58] against the venality and sale of masses that under pain of suspending no priest should sell his saying of tricennals[59] or annals.[60] What saw they that made this constitution? What priests saw they? What manner of masses saw they, trow ye? But at the last what became of so good a constitution? God have mercy upon us!

If there be nothing to be amended abroad concerning the whole,

[56] St. Blaise. [57] St. Algar has eluded the hagiologists.

[58] The allusion is to a mandate against the sale of masses issued in 1350 by Archbishop Simon Islip. It was re-enacted by Islip in 1351 and by Archbishop Simon Sudbury in 1378 (Wilkins, *Concilia,* III, 1, 15, 135).

[59] Masses said on thirty consecutive days.

[60] Masses for a dead person said daily for a year.

let every one of us make one better; if there be neither abroad nor at home anything to be amended and redressed, my lords, be ye of good cheer, be merry; and at the least, because we have nothing else to do, let us reason the matter how we may be richer. Let us fall to some pleasant communication. After, let us go home, even as good as we came hither, that is, right-begotten children of the world and utterly worldlings. And while we live here, let us all make bone[61] cheer. For after this life there is small pleasure, little mirth for us to hope for, if now there be nothing to be changed in our fashions. Let us say, not as St. Peter did, "Our end approacheth nigh" (I Peter 4:7); this is an heavy hearing. But let us say as the evil servant said, "It will be long ere my master come" (Matt. 24:48; Luke 12:45). This is pleasant. Let us beat our fellows. Let us eat and drink with drunkards. Surely, as oft as we do not take away the abuse of things, so oft we beat our fellows. As oft as we give not the people their true food, so oft we beat our fellows. As oft as we let them die in superstition, so oft we beat them. To be short, as oft as we blind lead them blind, so oft we beat and grievously strike our fellows. When we welter in pleasures and idleness, then we eat and drink with drunkards.

But God will come, God will come; He will not tarry long away. He will come upon such a day as we nothing look for Him, and at such hour as we know not. He will come and cut us in pieces. He will reward us as He doth the hypocrites. He will set us where wailing shall be, my brethren, where gnashing of teeth shall be, my brethren. And let here be the end of our tragedy, if ye will. These be the delicate dishes prepared for world's well-beloved children. These be the wafers and junkets[62] provided for worldly prelates—wailing and gnashing of teeth. Can there be any mirth where these two courses last all the feast? Here we laugh; there we shall weep. Our teeth make merry here, ever dashing in delicates; there we shall be torn with teeth and do nothing but gnash and grind our own. To

[61] *Bone:* good. [62] *Junkets:* sweetmeats.

what end have we now excelled other in policy? What have we brought forth at the last? Ye see, brethren, what sorrow, what punishment is provided for you if ye be worldlings. If ye will not thus be vexed, be not ye the children of the world. If ye will not be the children of the world, be not stricken with the love of worldly things; lean not upon them. If ye will not die eternally, live not worldly.

Come, go to, my brothers, go to, I say again and once again, go to. Leave the love of your profit. Study for the glory and profit of Christ; seek in your consultations such things as pertain to Christ and bring forth at the last somewhat that may please Christ. Feed ye tenderly, with all diligence, the flock of Christ. Preach truly the Word of God. Love the light, walk in the light. And so be ye the children of light while ye are in this world that ye may shine in the world that is to come bright as the sun, with the Father, the Son, and the Holy Ghost, to Whom be all honor and glory. Amen.

SERMON ON THE PLOWERS JANUARY 18, 1548[1]

A NOTABLE SERMON OF THE REVEREND FATHER MASTER HUGH LATIMER, WHICH HE PREACHED IN THE SHROUDS AT PAUL'S CHURCH IN LONDON, ON THE EIGHTEENTH DAY OF JANUARY, 1548

Quaecumque scripta sunt ad nostram doctrinam scripta sunt
(Romans 15:4)

"All things which are written are written for our erudition and knowledge. All things that are written in God's book, in the Bible

[1] The title page (STC 15291) reads as follows: "A notable Sermon of the reuerende father Maister Hughe Latemer, whiche he preached in the Shrouds at paules churche in London, on the .xviii. daye of January. 1548."

The reference to the "Shrouds" indicates that the sermon was preached in the enclosed place used for the Paul's Cross sermons when the weather was inclement.

The colophon reads: "Imprinted at London by Ihon Day, dwellynge at Aldersgate, and Wylliam Seres, dwellyng in Peter Colledge. These bokes are to be sold at the new shop by the lytle Conduyte in Chepesyde. ¶Cum gratia et Priuilegio ad imprimendum solum."

From the context, as well as from the time and place of its delivery, it is clear that this sermon was preached in support of the Royal Injunctions of July, 1547, which provided, among other things, that each parish should buy a copy of the Great Bible and a copy of Erasmus' *Paraphrase* of the Gospels and Acts; that on Sundays when there was no other sermon the priest should read from one of the Homilies; and that book, in the book of the Holy Scripture, are written to be our doctrine."

I TOLD you in my first sermon, honorable audience, that I purposed to declare unto you two things: the one, what seed should be sown in God's field, in God's plowland; and the other, who should be the sowers, that is to say, what doctrine is to be taught in Christ's church and congregation, and what men should be the teachers and preachers of it. The first part I have told you in the three sermons past, in which I have assayed to set forth my plow, to prove what I could do.

And now I shall tell you who be the plowers, for God's word is a seed to be sown in God's field, that is, the faithful congregation, and the preacher is the sower. And it is in the Gospel: *Exivit qui seminat seminare semen suum,* "He that soweth, the husbandman, the plowman, went forth to sow his seed" (Luke 8:5). So that a preacher is resembled to a plowman; as it is in another place, *Nemo admota aratro manu, et a tergo respiciens, aptus est regno Dei,* "No man that putteth his hand to the plow and looketh back is apt for the kingdom of God" (Luke 9:62). That is to say, let no preacher be negligent in doing his office. Albeit this is one of the places that hath been racked, as I told you of racking scriptures. And I have been one of them myself that hath racked it, I cry God mercy for it, and have been one of them that have believed and have expounded it against religious persons that would forsake their order which they had professed and would go out of their cloister; whereas indeed it toucheth not monkery, nor maketh anything at all for any such matter, but it is directly spoken of diligent preaching of the Word of God.

For preaching of the gospel is one of God's plow works, and the preacher is one of God's plowmen. Ye may not be offended with my similitude in that I compare preaching to the labor and work of

---

every holder of a benefice worth £100 per year was to maintain a student at one of the universities and an additional student for each additional £100 of income.

plowing and the preacher to a plowman; ye may not be offended with this my similitude, for I have been slandered of some persons for such things. It hath been said of me, "Oh, Latimer! nay, as for him I will never believe him while I live nor never trust him, for he likened Our Blessed Lady to a saffron bag." [2] Where indeed I never used that similitude. But it was, as I have said unto you before now, according to that which Peter saw before in the spirit of prophecy and said that there should come afterward men *per quos via veritatis maledictis afficeretur*. There should come fellows "by whom the way of truth should be ill spoken of and slandered" (II Peter 2:2). But in case I had used this similitude, it had not been to be reproved but might have been without reproach. For I might have said thus: as the saffron bag that hath been full of saffron or hath had saffron in it doth ever after savor and smell of the sweet saffron that it contained, so Our Blessed Lady, which conceived and bare Christ in her womb, did ever after resemble the manners and virtues of that precious babe which she bare. And what had Our Blessed Lady been the worse for this or what dishonor was this to Our Blessed Lady?

But as preachers must be ware and circumspect that they give not any just occasion to be slandered and ill spoken of by the hearers, so must not the auditors be offended without cause. For heaven is in the gospel likened to a mustard seed; it is compared also to a piece of leaven; as Christ saith, that at the last day He will come like a thief. And what dishonor is this to God or what derogation is this to heaven? Ye may not then, I say, be offended with my similitude, forbecause I liken preaching to a plowman's labor and a prelate to a plowman. But now you will ask me whom I call a prelate. A prelate is that man, whatsoever he be, that hath a flock to be taught of him, whosoever hath any spiritual charge in the faithful congregation,

[2] The fortieth item among the "Erroneous opinions complained of in convocation" (1536) reads as follows: "Item, that our lady was no better than another woman, and like a bag of pepper or saffron when the spice is out; and that she can do no more with Christ than another sinful woman" (Wilkins, *Concilia,* III, 806).

and whosoever he be that hath cure of soul.[3] And well may the preacher and the plowman be likened together. First, for their labor of all seasons of the year, for there is no time of the year in which the plowman hath not some special work to do, as in my country in Leicestershire the plowman hath a time to set forth and to assay his plow, and other times for other necessary works to be done. And then they also may be likened together for the diversity of works and variety of offices that they have to do. For as the plowman first setteth forth his plow, and then tilleth his land and breaketh it in furrows, and sometime ridgeth it up again and at another time harroweth it and clotteth it, and sometime dungeth it and hedgeth it, diggeth it and weedeth it, purgeth and maketh it clean, so the prelate, the preacher, hath many diverse offices to do. He hath first a busy work to bring his parishioners to a right faith, as Paul calleth it, and not to a swerving faith, but to a faith that embraceth Christ and trusteth to His merits; a lively faith, a justifying faith, a faith that maketh a man righteous without respect of works, as ye have it very well declared and set forth in the Homily.[4] He hath then a busy work, I say, to bring his flock to a right faith and then to confirm them in the same faith; now casting them down with the law and with threatenings of God for sin; now ridging them up again with the gospel and with the promises of God's favor; now weeding them by telling them their faults and making them forsake sin; now clotting them by breaking their stony hearts and by making them supplehearted and making them to have hearts of flesh, that is, soft hearts and apt for doctrine to enter in; now teaching to know God rightly and to know their duty to God and their neighbors; now

[3] This is Latimer's personal definition of *prelate*. The *OED* records no instance of the word in a sense other than that of a cleric of superior rank.

[4] *Certain Sermons, or Homilies, Appointed by the King's Majesty to be declared and read by all parsons, vicars, or curates, every Sunday in their churches, where they have cure* (1547), was an official statement of Anglican doctrine prepared under the supervision of Archbishop Cranmer. The reference is to the Homilies entitled "Of a True, Lively, and Christian Faith" and "Of Good Works Annexed to Faith."

exhorting them, when they know their duty, that they do it and be diligent in it.

So that they have a continual work to do. Great is their business and therefore great should be their hire. They have great labors and therefore they ought to have good livings, that they may commodiously feed their flock; for the preaching of the Word of God unto the people is called meat. Scripture calleth it meat, not strawberries, that come but once a year, and tarry not long but are soon gone.[5] But it is meat; it is no dainties. The people must have meat that must be familiar and continual and daily given unto them to feed upon. Many make a strawberry of it, ministering it but once a year; but such do not the office of good prelates. For Christ saith, *Quis putas est servus prudens et fidelis? Qui dat cibum in tempore,* "Who think you is a wise and a faithful servant? He that giveth meat in due time" (Matt. 24:45). So that he must at all times convenient preach diligently, therefore saith He, "Who trow you is a faithful servant?" He speaketh it as though it were a rare thing to find such a one, and as though He should say there be but a few of them to find in the world. And how few of them there be throughout this realm that give meat to their flock as they should do, the visitors can best tell.[6] Too few, too few. The more is the pity, and never so few as now.

By this then it appeareth that a prelate or any that hath cure of soul must diligently and substantially work and labor. Therefore saith Paul to Timothy, *Qui episcopatum desiderat, hic bonum opus desiderat,* "He that desireth to have the office of a bishop or a prelate, that man desireth a good work" (I Tim. 3:1). Then if it be good work, it is work; ye can make but a work of it. It is God's work, God's plow, and that plow God would have still going. Such then as

[5] Latimer seems to have originated this metaphor, which was used by a number of later preachers and writers.

[6] The reference is to the general visitation of all churches ordered by Protector Somerset in 1547. The work was assigned to thirty visitors, ten of them clerics and the rest laymen. See Walter H. Frere, *Visitation Articles and Injunctions of the Period of the Reformation* (London, 1910), II, 114.

loiter and live idly are not good prelates or ministers. And of such as do not preach and teach nor do not their duties, God saith by His prophet Jeremiah, *Maledictus qui facit opus Dei fradulenter* (Jer. 48:10)—"guilefully or deceitfully." Some books have it *negligenter,* "negligently or slackly." How many such prelates, how many such bishops, Lord, for Thy mercy, are there now in England? And what shall we in this case do? Shall we company with them? O Lord, for Thy mercy! Shall we not company with them? O Lord, whither shall we flee from them? But "cursed be he that doth the work of God negligently or guilefully." A sore word for them that are negligent in discharging their office or have done it fraudulently, for that is the thing that maketh the people ill.

But true it must be that Christ saith, *Multi sunt vocati, pauci vero electi,* "Many are called but few are chosen" (Matt. 22:14). Here have I an occasion by the way somewhat to say unto you, yea, for the place I alleged unto you before out of Jeremiah, the forty-eighth chapter. And it was spoken of a spiritual work of God, a work that was commanded to be done; and it was of shedding blood and of destroying the cities of Moab. For, saith He, "Cursed be he that keepeth back his sword from shedding of blood" (Jer. 48:10). As Saul, when he kept back the sword from shedding of blood at what time he was sent against Amalek, was refused of God for being disobedient to God's commandments, in that he spared Agag the king. So that that place of the prophet was spoken of them that went to the destruction of the cities of Moab, among the which there was one called Nebo, which was much reproved for idolatry, superstition, pride, avarice, cruelty, tyranny, and for hardness of heart, and for these sins was plagued of God and destroyed.

Now what shall we say of these rich citizens of London? What shall I say of them? Shall I call them proud men of London, malicious men of London, merciless men of London? No, no, I may not say so; they will be offended with me then. Yet must I speak. For is there not reigning in London as much pride, as much covetousness, as much cruelty, as much oppression, and as much superstition as was in Nebo? Yes, I think, and much more, too. Therefore I say, repent, O London; repent; repent. Thou hearest thy faults told thee; amend them; amend them. I think if Nebo had had the preaching that thou hast they would have converted. And you rulers and officers, be wise and circumspect, look to your charge, and see you do your duties; and rather be glad to amend your ill living than to be angry when you are warned or told of your fault. What ado was there made in London at a certain man because he said—and indeed at that time on a just cause—"Burgesses!" quoth he, "nay, butterflies." Lord, what ado there was for that word! And yet would God they were no worse than butterflies! Butterflies do but their nature. The butterfly is not covetous, is not greedy of other men's goods, is not full of envy and hatred, is not malicious, is not cruel, is not merciless. The butterfly glorieth not in her own deeds nor preferreth the traditions of men before God's word; it committeth not idolatry nor worshipeth false gods. But London cannot abide to be rebuked; such is the nature of man. If they be pricked, they will kick; if they be rubbed on the gall, they will wince; but yet they will not amend their faults; they will not be ill spoken of.

But how shall I speak well of them? If you could be content to receive and follow the Word of God and favor good preachers, if you could bear to be told of your faults, if you could amend when you hear of them, if you would be glad to reform that is amiss, if I might see any such inclination in you that leave to be merciless and begin to be charitable, I would then hope well of you. I would then speak well of you. But London was never so ill as it is now. In times past men were full of pity and compassion, but now there is no pity. For in London their brother shall die in the streets for cold; he shall lie sick at their door between stock and stock,[7] I cannot tell what to call it, and perish there for hunger. Was there any more unmercifulness in Nebo? I think not. In times past, when any rich man died in London, they were wont to help the poor scholars of the universities

[7] *Between . . . stock:* between posts, i.e., in a doorway.

with exhibition.[8] When any man died, they would bequeath great sums of money toward the relief of the poor. When I was a scholar in Cambridge myself, I heard very good report of London and knew many that had relief of the rich men of London. But now I can hear no such good report, and yet I inquire of it and hearken for it. But now charity is waxed cold; none helpeth the scholar nor yet the poor. And in those days what did they when they helped the scholars? Marry, they maintained and gave them livings that were very papists and professed the Pope's doctrine. And now that the knowledge of God's word is brought to light, and many earnestly study and labor to set it forth, now almost no man helpeth to maintain them.

O London, London! Repent, repent, for I think God is more displeased with London than ever He was with the city of Nebo. Repent therefore, repent, London, and remember that the same God liveth now that punished Nebo, even the same God and none other; and He will punish sin as well now as He did then; and He will punish the iniquity of London as well as He did them of Nebo. Amend therefore. And ye that be prelates, look well to your office, for right prelating is busy laboring and not lording. Therefore preach and teach, and let your plow be doing. Ye lords, I say, that live like loiterers, look well to your office; the plow is your office and charge. If you live idle and loiter, you do not your duty, you follow not your vocation. Let your plow therefore be going and not cease, that the ground may bring forth fruit.

But now methinketh I hear one say unto me, "Wot you what you say? It is a work. It is a labor. How then hath it happened that we have had so many hundred years so many unpreaching prelates, lording loiterers, and idle ministers?" Ye would have me here to make answer and to show the cause thereof. Nay, this land is not for me to plow; it is too stony, too thorny, too hard for to plow. They have so many things that make for them, so many things to lay for

[8] *Exhibition:* subvention for the maintenance of a student.

themselves, that it is not for my weak team to plow them. They have to lay for themselves long customs, ceremonies, and authority, placing in Parliament, and many things more. And I fear me this land is not yet ripe to be plowed; for, as the saying is, it lacketh weathering;[9] this gear lacketh weathering; at least way it is not for me to plow. For what shall I look for among thorns but pricking and scratching? What among stones but stumbling? What—I had almost said—among serpents but stinging? But this much I dare say, that since lording and loitering hath come up, preaching hath come down, contrary to the apostles' times. For they preached and lorded not, and now they lord and preach not. For they that be lords will ill go to plow; it is no meet office for them; it is not seeming for their estate. Thus came up lording loiterers; thus crept in unpreaching prelates; and so have they long continued. For how many unlearned prelates have we now at this day! And no marvel. For if the plowmen that now be were made lords, they would clean give over plowing; they would leave off their labor, and fall to lording outright, and let the plow stand. And then, both plows not walking, nothing should be in the commonweal but hunger. For ever since the prelates were made lords and nobles, the plow standeth; there is no work done; the people starve. They hawk, they hunt, they card, they dice; they pastime in their prelacies with gallant gentlemen, with their dancing minions,[10] and with their fresh companions, so that plowing is set aside. And by the lording and loitering, preaching and plowing is clean gone. And thus if the plowmen of the country were as negligent in their office as prelates be, we should not long live, for lack of sustenance. And as it is necessary for to have this plowing for the sustentation of the body, so must we have also the other for the satisfaction of the soul, or else we cannot live long ghostly. For as the body wasteth and consumeth away for lack of bodily meat, so doth the soul pine away for default of ghostly meat.

[9] *Weathering:* beneficial action of the weather on the soil.

[10] *Minions:* favorites, paramours.

But there be two kinds of enclosing[11] to let or hinder both these kinds of plowing; the one is an enclosing to let or hinder the bodily plowing, and the other to let or hinder the holy day plowing, the church plowing. The bodily plowing is taken in and enclosed through singular commodity.[12] For what man will let go or diminish his private commodity for a commonwealth? And who will sustain any damage for the respect of a public commodity? The other plow also no man is diligent to set forward, nor no man will hearken to it. But to hinder and let it all men's ears are open; yea, and a great many of this kind of plowmen, which are very busy and would seem to be very good workmen. I fear me some be rather mock gospelers than faithful plowmen. I know many myself that profess the gospel and live nothing thereafter. I know them and have been conversant with some of them. I know them, and—I speak it with an heavy heart—there is as little charity and good living in them as in any other. According to that which Christ said in the Gospel to the great number of people that followed Him, as though they had had an earnest zeal to His doctrine whereas indeed they had it not, *Non quia vidistis signa, sed quia comedistis de panibus*. "Ye follow me," saith He, "not because ye have seen the signs and miracles that I have done; but because ye have eaten the bread and refreshed your bodies, therefore you follow Me" (John 6:26). So that I think many one nowadays professeth the gospel for the living's sake, not for the love they bear to God's word. But they that will be true plowmen must work faithfully for God's sake, for the edifying of their brethren. And as diligently as the husbandman ploweth for the sustentation of the body, so diligently must the prelates and ministers labor for the feeding of the soul. Both the plows must still be doing, as most necessary for man. And wherefore

[11] *Enclosing:* the practice of converting plowland to pasture for sheep. Because it led to widespread unemployment of farm laborers, it was under constant attack by the reformers.

[12] *Singular commodity:* private profit.

are magistrates ordained, but that the tranquillity of the commonweal may be confirmed, limiting [13] both plows?

But now for fault of unpreaching prelates, methink I could guess what might be said for excusing of them. They are so troubled with lordly living, they be so placed in palaces, couched in courts, ruffling in their rents, dancing in their dominions, burdened with ambassages, pampering of their paunches, like a monk that maketh his jubilee, munching in their mangers, and moiling in their gay manors and mansions, and so troubled with loitering in their lordships, that they cannot attend it. They are otherwise occupied, some in the King's matters, some are ambassadors, some of the Privy Council, some to furnish the Court, some are lords of the Parliament, some are presidents, and some comptrollers of mints.[14] Well, well!

Is this their duty? Is this their office? Is this their calling? Should we have ministers of the church to be comptrollers of the mints? Is this a meet office for a priest that hath cure of souls? Is this his charge? I would here ask one question. I would fain know who comptrolleth the devil at home at his parish, while he comptrolleth the mint? If the apostles might not leave the office of preaching to be deacons, shall one leave it for minting? I cannot tell you; but the saying is that, since priests have been minters, money hath been worse than it was before. And they say that the evilness of money hath made all things dearer. And in this behalf I must speak to England. "Hear, my country, England," as Paul said in his first epistle to the Corinthians, the sixth chapter; for Paul was no sitting bishop but a walking and a preaching bishop. But when he went from them, he left there behind him the plow going still, for he

[13] *Limiting:* controlling, regulating.

[14] This would seem to be an attack upon Cuthbert Tunstall, the conservative Bishop of Durham, who was President of the Council of the North and master of the episcopal mint at Durham until its discontinuance in 1547. The episcopal mints at Canterbury, York, and Durham dated from the thirteenth century.

wrote unto them and rebuked them for going to law and pleading their causes before heathen judges. "Is there," saith he, "utterly among you no wise man to be an arbitrator in matters of judgment? What, not one of all that can judge between brother and brother, but one brother go to law with another, and that under heathen judges? *Constituite contemptos qui sunt in ecclesia, etc.* 'Appoint them judges that are most abject and vile in the congregation'" (I Cor. 6:4–6). Which he speaketh in rebuking them; "For," saith he, *ad erubescentiam vestram dico*—'I speak it to your shame.'" So, England, I speak it to thy shame. Is there never a nobleman to be a lord president but it must be a prelate? Is there never a wise man in the realm to be a comptroller of the mint? "I speak it to your shame, I speak it to your shame." If there be never a wise man, make a water-bearer, a tinker, a cobbler, a slave, a page, comptroller of the mint. Make a mean gentleman, a groom, a yeoman, make a poor beggar lord president.

Thus I speak, not that I would have it so, but to your shame, if there be never a gentleman meet nor able to be lord president. For why are not the noblemen and young gentlemen of England so brought up in knowledge of God and in learning that they may be able to execute offices in the commonweal? The King hath a great many of wards, and I trow there is a Court of Wards.[15] Why is there not a school for the wards as well as there is a court for their lands? Why are they not set in schools where they may learn? Or why are they not sent to the universities that they may be able to serve the King when they come to age? If the wards and young gentlemen were well brought up in learning and in the knowledge of God, they would not when they come to age so much give themselves to other vanities. And if the nobility be well trained in godly learning, the people would follow the same train. For truly, such as the

[15] Minors of superior rank were legally the wards of the Crown, and the income from their estates contributed substantially to the royal revenue. An act of 1540 established the Court of Wards to manage their affairs.

noblemen be, such will the people be. And now the only cause why noblemen be not made lord presidents is because they have not been brought up in learning.

Therefore for the love of God appoint teachers and schoolmasters, you that have charge of youth. And give the teachers stipends worthy their pains, that they may bring them up in grammar, in logic, in rhetoric, in philosophy, in the civil law, and in that which I cannot leave unspoken of, the Word of God. Thanks be unto God, the nobility otherwise is very well brought up in learning and godliness, to the great joy and comfort of England; so that there is now good hope in the youth that we shall another day have a flourishing commonwealth, considering their godly education. Yea, and there be already noblemen enough, though not so many as I would wish, able to be lord presidents, and wise men enough for the mint. And as unmeet a thing it is for bishops to be lord presidents or priests to be minters as it was for the Corinthians to plead matters of variance before heathen judges. It is also a slander to the noblemen, as though they lacked wisdom and learning to be able for such offices, or else were no men of conscience, or else were not meet to be trusted and able for such offices. And a prelate hath a charge and cure otherwise; and therefore he cannot discharge his duty and be a lord president too. For a presidentship requireth a whole man, and a bishop cannot be two men. A bishop hath his office, a flock to teach, to look unto, and therefore he cannot meddle with another office which alone requireth a whole man. He should therefore give it over to whom it is meet, and labor in his own business; as Paul writeth to the Thessalonians, "Let every man do his own business, and follow his calling" (I Thess. 4:11). Let the priest preach and the noblemen handle the temporal matters. Moses was a marvelous man, a good man. Moses was a wonderful fellow, and did his duty, being a married man. We lack such as Moses was. Well, I would all men would look to their duty, as God hath called them, and then we should have a flourishing Christian commonweal.

And now I would ask a strange question. Who is the most

Sermon Sleevers

diligent bishop and prelate in all England, that passeth all the rest in doing his office? I can tell, for I know him who it is; I know him well. But now I think I see you listing and hearkening that I should name him. There is one that passeth all the other and is the most diligent prelate and preacher in all England. And will ye know who it is? I will tell you; it is the devil. He is the most diligent preacher of all other; he is never out of his diocese; he is never from his cure; ye shall never find him unoccupied; he is ever in his parish; he keepeth residence at all times; ye shall never find him out of the way; call for him when you will, he is ever at home. The diligentest preacher in all the realm, he is ever at his plow; no lording nor loitering can hinder him; he is ever applying his business; ye shall never find him idle, I warrant you.

And his office is to hinder religion, to maintain superstition, to set up idolatry, to teach all kind of popery. He is ready as can be wished for to set forth his plow, to devise as many ways as can be to deface and obscure God's glory. Where the devil is resident and hath his plow going, there away with books and up with candles; away with Bibles and up with beads; away with the light of the gospel and up with the light of candles, yea, at noondays. Where the devil is resident, that he may prevail, up with all superstition and idolatry: censing, painting of images, candles, palms, ashes, holy water, and new service of men's inventing;[16] as though man could invent a better way to honor God with than God Himself hath appointed. Down with Christ's Cross, up with purgatory pickpurse, up with him, the popish purgatory, I mean. Away with clothing the naked, the poor and impotent; up with decking of images and gay garnishing of stocks and stones; up with man's traditions and his laws, down with God's traditions and His most holy word. Down with the old honor due to God, and up with the new god's honor. Let all things be done in Latin. There must be nothing but Latin, not as much as *Memento, homo, quod cinis es, et in cinerem reverteris,*

[16] Probably any ceremony which lacked scriptural authority.

"Remember, man, that thou art ashes, and into ashes thou shalt return" (Gen. 3:19), which be the words that the minister speaketh to the ignorant people when he giveth them ashes upon Ash Wednesday. But it must be spoken in Latin; God's word may in no wise be translated into English.

Oh, that our prelates would be as diligent to sow the corn of good doctrine as Satan is to sow cockle and darnel! And this is the devilish plowing, the which worketh to have things in Latin and letteth [17] the fruitful edification. But here some man will say to me, "What, sir, are ye so privy of the devil's counsel that ye know all this to be true?" Truly I know him too well and have obeyed him a little too much in condescending to some follies; and I know him as other men do, yea, that he is ever occupied and ever busy in following his plow. I know by St. Peter, which saith of him, *Sicut leo rugiens circuit quaerens quem devoret,* "He goeth about like a roaring lion, seeking whom he may devour" (I Peter 5:8). I would have this text well viewed and examined, every word of it. *Circuit,* he goeth about in every corner of his diocese; he goeth on visitation daily, he leaveth no place of his cure unvisited. He walketh round about from place to place and ceaseth not. *Sicut leo,* "as a lion," that is, strongly, boldly and proudly, straitly and fiercely, with haughty looks, with his proud countenances, with his stately braggings. *Rugiens,* "roaring," for he letteth not slip any occasion to speak or to roar out when he seeth his time. *Quaerens,* "he goeth about seeking," and not sleeping, as our bishops do; but he seeketh diligently, he searcheth diligently all corners whereas he may have his prey. He roveth abroad in every place of his diocese. He standeth not still; he is never at rest, but ever in hand with his plow, that it may go forward.

But there was never such a preacher in England as he is. Who is able to tell his diligent preaching, which every day and every hour laboreth to sow cockle and darnel, that he may bring out of form [18]

[17] *Letteth:* hinders. [18] *Form:* customary use.

and out of estimation and room[19] the institution of the Lord's Supper and Christ's Cross? For there he lost his right. For Christ said, *Nunc judicium est mundi, princeps seculi hujus ejicietur foras. Et sicut exaltavit Moses serpentem in deserto, ita exaltari oportet Filium hominis. Et cum exaltatus fuero a terra, omnia traham ad meipsum,* "Now is the judgment of this world, and the prince of this world shall be cast out." "And as Moses did lift up the serpent in the wilderness, so must the Son of man be lift up." "And when I shall be lift up from the earth, I will draw all things unto Myself" (John 12:31; 3:14; 12:32). For the devil was disappointed of his purpose, for he thought all to be his own; and when he had once brought Christ to the cross, he thought all cocksure. But there lost he all his reigning; for Christ said, *Omnia traham ad meipsum,* "I will draw all things to Myself." He meaneth drawing of man's soul to salvation. And that He said He would do *per semetipsum,* by His own self, not by any other body's sacrifice. He meant by His own sacrifice on the cross, where He offered Himself for the redemption of mankind, and not the sacrifice of the mass to be offered by another. For who can offer Him but Himself? He was both the offerer and the offering. And this is the prick, this is the mark at the which the devil shooteth, to evacuate[20] the Cross of Christ and to mingle[21] the institution of the Lord's Supper. The which although he cannot bring to pass, yet he goeth about by his sleights and subtile means to frustrate the same; and these fifteen hundredth years he hath been a doer, only purposing to evacuate Christ's death and to make it of small efficacy and virtue. For whereas Christ, according as the serpent was lift up in the wilderness, so would He Himself to be exalted, that thereby as many as trusted in Him should have salvation; but the devil would none of that. They would have us

[19] *Room:* place.

[20] *Evacuate:* make worthless. (According to the *OED* this is the earliest sense of the word in English.)

[21] *Mingle:* confuse, confound.

saved by a daily oblation propiatory, by a sacrifice expiatory or remissory.

Now if I should preach in the country, among the unlearned, I would tell what "propitiatory," "expiatory," and "remissory" is. But here is a learned auditory, yet for them that be unlearned I will expound it. "Propitiatory," "expiatory," "remissory," or "satisfactory," for they signify all one thing in effect, and is nothing else but a thing whereby to obtain remission of sins and to have salvation. And this way the devil used to evacuate the death of Christ, that we might have affiance in other things, as in the daily sacrifice of the priest, whereas Christ would have us to trust in His only sacrifice. So He was, *Agnus occisus ab origine mundi,* "The Lamb that hath been slain from the beginning of the world" (Rev. 13:8); and therefore He is called *juge sacrificium,* "a continual sacrifice" (Dan. 8:11, 12); and not for the continuance of the mass, as the blanchers[22] have blanched it and wrested it and as I myself did once mistake it. But Paul saith, *per semetipsum purgatio facta,* "by Himself," and by none other, Christ "made purgation" (Heb. 1:3) and satisfaction for the whole world.

Would Christ this word "by Himself" had been better weighed and looked upon, and *in sanctificationem,* "to make them holy," for He is *juge sacrificium,* "a continual sacrifice," in effect, fruit and operation; that like as they which seeing the serpent hang up in the desert were put in remembrance of Christ's death, in whom as many as believed were saved, so all men that trusted in the death of Christ shall be saved, as well they that were before as they that came after. For He was a continual sacrifice, as I said, in effect, fruit, operation, and virtue; as though He had from the beginning of the world, and continually should to the world's end, hang still on the cross. And He is as fresh hanging on the cross now, to them that believe and trust in Him, as He was fifteen hundredth years ago, when He was crucified.

[22] *Blanchers:* perverters.

Then let us trust upon His only death, and look for none other sacrifice propitiatory than the same bloody sacrifice, the lively sacrifice, and not a dry sacrifice but a bloody sacrifice. For Christ Himself said, *consummatum est:* "It is perfectly finished. I have taken at my Father's hand the dispensation of redeeming mankind; I have wrought man's redemption and have dispatched the matter." Why then mingle ye Him? Why do ye divide Him? Why make you of Him mo sacrifices than one? Paul saith, *Pascha nostrum immolatus est Christus,* "Christ our passover is offered" (I Cor. 5:7); so that the thing is done, and Christ hath done it, and He hath done it *semel,* "once for all"; and it was a bloody sacrifice, not a dry sacrifice. Why, then, it is not the mass that availeth or profiteth for the quick and the dead.

Woe worth thee, O devil, woe worth thee, that hast prevailed so far and so long, that thou hast made England to worship false gods, forsaking Christ their Lord. Woe worth thee, devil, woe worth thee, devil, and all thine angels. If Christ by His death draweth all things to Himself, and draweth all men to salvation and to heavenly bliss that trust in Him, then the priests at the mass, at the popish mass, I say, what can they draw, when Christ draweth all but lands and goods from the right heirs? The priests draw goods and riches, benefices and promotions to themselves; and such as believed in their sacrifice they draw to the devil. But Christ it is that draweth souls unto Him by His bloody sacrifice. What have we to do then but *epulari in Domino,* "to eat in the Lord" at His supper? What other service have we to do to Him and what other sacrifice have we to offer but the mortification of our flesh? What other oblation have we to make but of obedience, of good living, of good works, and of helping our neighbors? But as for our redemption, it is done already, it cannot be better; Christ hath done that thing so well that it cannot be amended. It cannot be devised how to make that any better than He hath done it.

But the devil, by the help of that Italian bishop yonder, his chaplain, hath labored by all means that he might to frustrate the death of Christ and the merits of His Passion. And they have devised for that purpose to make us believe in other vain things by his pardons, as to have remission of sins for praying on hallowed beads, for drinking of the bakehouse bowl. As a canon of Waltham Abbey once told me that whensover they put their loaves of bread into the oven, as many as drank of the pardon bowl[23] should have pardon for drinking of it. A mad thing, to give pardon to a bowl! Then to Pope Alexander's holy water,[24] to hallowed bells, palms, candles, ashes, and what not? And of these things, every one hath taken away some part of Christ's sanctification; every one hath robbed some part of Christ's Passion and Cross and hath mingled Christ's death and hath been made to be propitiatory and satisfactory and to put away sin. Yea, and Alexander's holy water yet at this day remaineth in England and is used for a remedy against spirits and to chase away devils. Yea, and I would this had been the worst. I would this were the worst. But woe worth thee, O devil, that hast prevailed to evacuate Christ's Cross and to mingle the Lord's Supper. These be the Italian bishop's devices, and the devil hath pricked at this mark to frustrate the Cross of Christ. He shot at this mark long before Christ came; he shot at this prick four thousand years before Christ hanged on the cross or suffered His Passion.

For the brazen serpent was set up in the wilderness to put men in remembrance of Christ's coming, that like as they which beheld the brazen serpent were healed of their bodily diseases, so they that looked spiritually upon Christ that was to come in Him should be

[23] A bowl regarded as the relic of a saint. Thomas Becon, a younger contemporary of Latimer, speaks of the "synagogue of Satan [which] knoweth none other relics of saints than rotten bones . . . worm-eaten bowls" (*A Comfortable Epistle to the Afflicted People of God,* in *Prayers and Other Pieces of Thomas Becon,* ed. John Ayre [Cambridge: The Parker Society, 1844], p. 198). Bale speaks of "pardon masers, or drinking dishes, as St. Benet's bowl, St. Edmund's bowl, St. Blyth's bowl, and Westminster bowl, with other such holy relics" (*The Image of Both Churches,* p. 527).

[24] Alexander I (Pope, ca. 105–ca. 115) is said to have introduced the use of holy water mixed with salt to rid Christian homes of evil spirits.

saved spiritually from the devil. The serpent was set up in memory of Christ to come; but the devil found means to steal away the memory of Christ's coming and brought the people to worship the serpent self, and to cense him, to honor him and to offer to him, to worship him and to make an idol of him. And this was done by the market men that I told you of.[25] And the clerk of the market did it for the lucre and advantage of his master that thereby his honor might increase, for by Christ's death he could have but small worldly advantage. And even now so hath he certain blanchers longing to the market, to let and stop the light of the gospel and to hinder the King's proceedings in setting forth the word and glory of God. And when the King's Majesty, with the advice of his honorable Council, goeth about to promote God's word and to set an order in matters of religion,[26] there shall not lack blanchers that will say, "As for images, whereas they have been used to be censed and to have candles offered unto them, none be so foolish to do it to the stock or stone or to the image itself, but it is done to God and His honor before the image."

And though they should abuse it, these blanchers will be ready to whisper the King in the ear and to tell him that this abuse is but a small matter, and that the same, with all other like abuses in the church, may be reformed easily. "It is but a little abuse," say they, "and it may be easily amended. But it should be not taken in hand at the first, for fear of trouble or further inconveniences. The people will not bear sudden alterations; an insurrection may be made after sudden mutation, which may be to the great harm and loss of the realm. Therefore all things shall be well, but not out of hand for fear of further business." These be the blanchers that hitherto have stopped the Word of God and hindered the true setting forth of the same. There be so many put-offs, so many put-bys, so many respects

[25] Evidently in one of the earlier sermons in this series which have not been preserved.

[26] The Royal Injunctions of 1547 (Frere, *Visitation Articles,* II, 114–130). See also note 1, pp. 28–29.

and considerations of worldly wisdom. And I doubt not but there were blanchers in the old time to whisper in the ear of good King Hezekiah for the maintenance of idolatry done to the brazen serpent,[27] as well as there hath been now of late, and be now, that can blanch the abuse of images and other like things. But good King Hezekiah would not be so blinded; he was like to Apollos, "fervent in spirit."[28] He would give no ear to the blanchers; he was not moved with these worldly respects, with these prudent considerations, with these policies. He feared not insurrections of the people. He feared not lest his people would not bear the glory of God. But he, without any of these respects or policies or considerations, like a good king, for God's sake and for conscience sake by and by[29] plucked down the brazen serpent and destroyed it utterly and beat it to powder. He out of hand did cast down all images; he destroyed all idolatry and clearly did extirpate all superstition. He would not hear these blanchers and worldly-wise men, but without delay followeth God's cause and destroyeth all idolatry out of hand. Thus did good King Hezekiah; for he was like Apollos, fervent in spirit and diligent to promote God's glory.

And good hope there is that it shall be likewise here in England; for the King's Majesty is so brought up in knowledge, virtue, and godliness that it is not to be mistrusted but that we shall have all things well and that the glory of God shall be spread abroad throughout all parts of the realm, if the prelates will diligently apply their plow and be preachers rather than lords. But our blanchers, which will be lords and no laborers, when they are commanded to go and be resident upon their cures and preach in their benefices, they would say, "What? I have set a deputy there; I have a deputy that looketh well to my flock and the which shall discharge my duty." "A deputy," quoth he! I looked for that word all this while. And what a deputy must he be, trow ye? Even one like himself. It must be a canonist, that is to say, one that is brought up in the study

[27] II Kings 18:1–5. [28] Acts 12:24–28. [29] *By and by:* immediately.

of the Pope's laws and decrees, one that will set forth papistry as well as himself will do, and one that will maintain all superstition and idolatry, and one that will nothing at all, or else very weakly, resist the devil's plow. Yea, happy it is if he take no part with the devil; and where he should be an enemy to him, it is well if he take not the devil's part against Christ.

But in the meantime the prelates take their pleasures. They are lords and no laborers. But the devil is diligent at his plow. He is no unpreaching prelate; he is no lordly loiterer from his cure but a busy plowman; so that among all the prelates and among all the pack of them that have cure the devil shall go for my money, for he still applieth his business. Therefore, ye unpreaching prelates, learn of the devil; to be diligent in doing of your office, learn of the devil; and if you will not learn of God nor good men, for shame learn of the devil. *Ad erubescentiam vestram dico,* "I speak it for your shame." If you will not learn of God nor good man to be diligent in your office, learn of the devil. Howbeit there is now very good hope that the King's Majesty, being by the help of good governance of his most honorable counselors he is trained and brought up in learning and knowledge of God's Word, will shortly provide a remedy and set an order herein. Which thing that it may so be, let us pray for him. Pray for him, good people, pray for him. Ye have great cause and need to pray for him.

Finis

FIRST SERMON BEFORE KING EDWARD VI MARCH 8, 1549[1]

THE FIRST SERMON OF MASTER HUGH LATIMER, WHICH HE PREACHED BEFORE THE KING'S MAJESTY WITHIN HIS GRACE'S PALACE AT WESTMINSTER. M.D.XLIX. THE EIGHTH OF MARCH

Quaecumque scripta sunt ad nostram doctrinam scripta sunt
(Romans 15:4)
"Whatsoever things are written aforetime are written for our learning, that we through patience and comfort of scriptures might have hope."

IN TAKING this part of scripture, most noble audience, I play as a truant which, when he is at school, will choose a lesson wherein he is perfect, because he is loath to take pain in studying a new lesson, or

[1] The title page of the Folger copy of STC 15271 reads as follows: "¶The fyrste Sermon of Mayster Hughe Latimer, whiche he preached before the Kinges Maiestie wythin his graces palayce at Westminster M.D. XLIX. the. viii. of March. Cum gratia et Priuilegio ad imprimendum solum."

The colophon reads: "Imprinted at London by Iohn Day, dwellynge ouer Aldersgate, and William Seres, dwellyng in Peter Colledge. Cum priuilegio ad imprimendum solum."

else feareth stripes for his slothfulness. In like manner I might seem, now in my old age, to some men to take this part of scripture because I would wade easily away therewith and drive my matter at my pleasure and not to be bound unto a certain theme. But ye shall consider that the foresaid words of Paul are not to be understand of all scriptures, but only of those which are of God written in God's book; and all things which are therein are written for our learning. The excellency of this word is so great and of high dignity that there is no earthly thing to be compared unto it. The author thereof is great, that is, God Himself, eternal, almighty, everlasting. The scripture, because of Him, is also great, eternal, most mighty, and holy. There is no king, emperor, magistrate, and ruler, of what state soever they be, but are bound to obey this God and to give credence unto His holy word in directing their steps ordinately according unto the same word.

Yea, truly, they are not only bound to obey God's book but also the minister of the same, "for the word's sake," so far as he speaketh "sitting in Moses' chair," that is, if his doctrine be taken out of Moses' law. For in this world God hath two swords; the one is a temporal sword, the other a spiritual. The temporal sword resteth in the hands of kings, magistrates, and rulers under him, whereunto all subjects, as well the clergy as the laity, be subject and punishable for any offense contrary to the same book. The spiritual sword is in the hands of the ministers and preachers; whereunto all kings, magistrates, and rulers ought to be obedient, that is, to hear and follow so long as the ministers sit in Christ's chair, that is, speaking out of Christ's book. The king correcteth transgressors with the temporal sword and the preacher also, if he be an offender. But the preacher cannot correct the king, if he be a transgressor of God's word, with the temporal sword; but he must correct and reprove him with the spiritual sword, fearing no man, setting God only before his eyes, under Whom he is a minister, to supplant and root up all vice and mischief by God's word. Whereunto all men ought to be obedient, as is mentioned in many places of scripture, and amongst many this is one, *Quaecumque jusserint vos servare, servate, et facite,* "Whatsoever they bid you observe, that observe and do" (Matt. 23:3). Therefore let the preacher teach, improve, amend, and instruct in righteousness with the spiritual sword, fearing no man, though death should ensue. Thus Moses, fearing no man, with this sword did reprove King Pharaoh at God's commandment.[2]

Micaiah the prophet also did not spare to blame King Ahab for his wickedness, according to God's will, and to prophesy of his destruction, contrary unto many false prophets.[3] These foresaid kings, being admonished by the ministers of God's word because they would not follow their godly doctrine and correct their lives, came unto utter destruction. Pharaoh giving no credit unto Moses, the prophet of God, but appliant unto the lusts of his own heart, what time he heard of the passage of God's people, having no fear or remembrance of God's work, he did prosecute after, intending to destroy them, and was drowned in the Red Sea. King Ahab also, because he would not hearken unto Micaiah, was killed with an arrow. Likewise also the house of Jeroboam, with other many, came unto destruction because he would not hear the ministers of God's word and correct his life according unto His will and pleasure. Let the preacher therefore never fear to declare the message of God unto all men. And if the king will not hear them, then the preachers may admonish and charge them with their duties and so leave them unto God and pray for them. But if the preachers digress out of Christ's chair and shall speak their own fantasies, then instead of *Quaecumque jusserint vos facere, facite et servate,* "Whatsoever they bid you observe, that observe and do" (Matt. 23:3), change it into these words following, *Cavete vero vobis a pseudo-prophetis, qui veniunt ad vos, etc.,* "Beware of false prophets, which come unto you in sheep's clothing, but inwardly they are ravening wolves: ye shall know them by their fruits" (Matt. 7:15–16). Yea, change

[2] Exodus 5, 6, 7. [3] I Kings 22.

Quaecumque jusserint, if their doctrine be evil, into *Cavete a fermento Pharisaeorum, etc.,* that is, "Take heed and beware of the leaven of the Pharisees and of the Sadducees" (Matt. 16:6).

In teaching evil doctrine all preachers are to be eschewed and in no wise to be hearkened unto; in speaking truth they are to be heard. All things written in God's book are most certain, true, and profitable for all men, for in it is contained meet matter for kings, princes, rulers, bishops, and for all estates. Wherefore it behooveth every preacher somewhat to appoint and accommodate himself and his matter agreeable unto the comfort and amendment of the audience unto the which he declareth the message of God. If he preach before a king, let his matter be concerning the office of a king; if before a bishop, then let him treat of bishoply duties and orders: and so forth in other matters, as time and audience shall require.

I have thought it good to entreat upon these words following which are written in the seventeenth chapter of Deuteronomy, *Cum veneris in terram quam Dominus Deus dat tibi possederisque eam, etc.,* that is, "When thou art come unto the land which the Lord thy God giveth thee and enjoyest it and dwellest therein, if thou shalt say 'I will set a king over me, like unto all the nations that are about me,' then thou shalt make him king over thee whom the Lord thy God shall choose. One of thy brethren must thou make king over thee and mayest not set a stranger over thee which is not of thy brethren. But in any wise let him not hold too many horses, that he bring not the people again to Egypt through the multitude of horses, forasmuch as the Lord hath said unto you, 'Ye shall henceforth go no more again that way.' Also he shall not have too many wives, lest his heart turn away; neither shall he gather him silver and gold too much" (Deut. 17:14–17).

As in divers other places of scripture is meet matter for all estates, so in this foresaid place is described chiefly the doctrine fit for a king. But who is worthy to utter this doctrine before our most noble King? Not I, God knoweth, which am through age both weak in body and oblivious. Unapt I am, not only because of painful study but also for the short warning.[4] Well, unto God I will make my moan, who never failed me. *Auxiliator in necessitatibus,* "God is my helper in all my necessities"; to Him alone will I make my petition. To pray unto saints departed I am not taught; to desire like grace of God as they had, right godly it is; or to believe God to be no less merciful unto us, being faithful, than He was unto them, greatly comfortable it is. Therefore only unto God let us lift up our hearts and say the Lord's Prayer.[5]

"Cum veneris, etc.—When thou art come unto the land which the Lord, etc. Thou shalt appoint him king," etc.

1. "One of thy brethren must thou make king over thee, and must not set a stranger over thee which is not of thy brethren.

2. "But in any wise let not such one prepare unto himself many horses, that he bring not, etc.

3. "Furthermore, let him not prepare unto himself many wives, lest his heart recede from God.

4. "Nor he shall not multiply unto himself too much gold and silver."

As the text doth rise, I will touch and go a little in every place until I come unto "too much." I will touch all the foresaid things, but not "too much." The text is, "When thou shalt come into the land," etc. To have a king the Israelites did with much importunity call unto God, and God long before promised them a king, and were fully certified thereof that God had promised that thing. For unto Abraham He said, *Ego crescere te faciam vehementer, ponamque te in gentes, sed et reges ex te prodibunt:* that is, "I will multiply thee exceedingly, and will make nations of thee; yea, and kings shall spring out of thee" (Gen. 17:6). These words were spoken long before the children of Israel had any king. Notwith-

[4] I.e., he is preaching on short notice.

[5] Here again Latimer uses the Lord's Prayer as the bidding prayer.

standing, yet God prescribed unto them an order how they should choose their king and what manner a man he should be, where he saith, "When thou shalt come into the land," etc. As who should say, "O ye children of Israel, I know your nature right well, which is evil and inclined unto all evils. I know that thou wilt choose a king to reign over thee and to appear glorious in the face of the world after the manner of gentiles. But because thou art stiff-necked, wild, and art given to walk without a bridle and line, therefore now I will prevent [6] thy evil and beastly manners; I will hedge strongly thy way; I will make a durable law which shall compel thee to walk ordinately and in a plain way; that is, thou shalt not choose thee a king after thy will and fantasy, but after Me thy Lord and God."

Thus God conditioned with the Jews, that their king should be such a one as He Himself would choose them. And was not much unlike the bargain that I heard of late should be betwixt two friends for a horse. The owner promised the other should have the horse if he would; the other asked the price; he said twenty nobles. The other would give him but four pound. The owner said he should not have him then. The other claimed the horse because he said he should have him if he would. Thus this bargain became a Westminster matter.[7] The lawyers got twice the valor of the horse; and when all came to all, two fools made an end of the matter. Howbeit the Israelites could not go to law with God for choosing their king; for would they, nill they, their king should be of His choosing, lest they should walk inordinately in a deceivable way unto their utter loss and destruction. For, as they say commonly, *Qui vadit plane, vadit sane:* that is, "He that walketh plainly, walketh safely." [8]

As the Jews were stiff-necked and were ever ready to walk inordinately, no less are we Englishmen given to untowardness and inordinate walking after our own fantasies and brains. We will walk

[6] *Prevent:* anticipate. [7] Westminster Hall as a court of law.

[8] "A common saying," according to a marginal note in the text. In Thomas Fuller's *Gnomologia* (1732) it takes the form "Keep the common road and thou'rt safe."

without the limits of God's word; we will choose a king at our own pleasure. But let us learn to frame our lives after the noble King David, which, when he had many occasions given of King Saul to work evil for evil, yea, and having many times opportunity to perform mischief and to slay King Saul, nevertheless, yet fearing, would not follow his fleshly affections and walk inordinately without the will of God's word, which he confessed always to be his direction, saying, *Lucerna pedibus meis verbum tuum et lumen semitis meis,* "Thy word, O Lord, is a lantern unto my feet and a light unto my steps" (Psalm 119:105). Thus, having in mind to walk ordinately, he did always avoid to do evil. For when King Saul was in a cave without any man, David and his men sitting by the sides of the cave, yea, and David's men moving him to kill Saul, David made answer and said unto them, *Servet me Dominus, ne rem istam, etc., contra dominum meum Messiam, etc.:* that is, "The Lord keep me from doing this thing unto my master, that is the Lord's anointed" (I Sam. 24:6). At another time also, moved by Abishai to kill Saul sleeping, David said, *Ne interficias eum; quis enim impune manum suam inferret uncto Domino, etc.:* that is, "Destroy him not; for who can lay his hands on the Lord's anointed and be guiltless?" etc. (I Sam. 26:9).

I would God we would follow King David, and then we should walk ordinately and yet do but that we are bound of duty to do; for God saith, *Quod ego precipio, hoc tantum facito,* "That thing which I command, that only do" (Deut. 12:32). There is a great error risen nowadays among many of us which are vain and newfangled men, climbing beyond the limits of our capacity and wit, in wrenching this text of scripture hereafter following after their own fantasy and brain. Their error is upon this text, *Audi vocem populi in omnibus quae dicunt tibi; non enim te reprobant, sed me reprobarunt ne regnem super eos:* that is, "Hear the voice of the people in all that they say unto thee; for they have not cast thee away, but me" (I Sam. 8:7). They wrench these words awry after their own fantasies, and make much doubt as touching a king and his godly name. They that so do walketh inordinately; they walk not directly and plainly but delight in balks[9] and stubble way.[10]

It maketh no matter by what name the rulers be named, if so be they shall walk ordinately with God and direct their steps with God. For both patriarchs, judges, and kings had and have their authority of God, and therefore godly. But this ought to be considered which God saith, *Non praeficere tibi potes hominem alienum:* that is, "Thou must not set a stranger over thee." It hath pleased God to grant us a natural liege king and lord of our own nation, an Englishman, one of our own religion. God hath given him unto us, and [he] is a most precious treasure; and yet many of us do desire a stranger to be king over us. Let us no more desire to be bywalkers,[11] but let us endeavor to walk ordinately and plainly after the Word of God. Let us follow David. Let us not seek the death of our most noble and rightful king, our own brother both by nativity and godly religion. Let us pray for his good state, that he live long among us.

Oh, what a plague were it that a strange king, of a strange land and of a strange religion, should reign over us! Where now we be governed in the true religion, he should extirp and pluck away altogether and then plant again all abomination and popery. God keep such a king from us! Well, the King's Grace hath sisters, my lady Mary and my lady Elizabeth, which by succession and course are inheritors to the crown, who if they should marry with strangers, what should ensue God knoweth. But God grant they never come unto coursing nor succeeding.[12] Therefore, to avoid this plague, let us amend our lives, and put away all pride, which doth drown men in this realm at these days; all covetousness, wherein the magistrates

[9] *Balks:* stumbling blocks. [10] *Stubble way:* rough way.

[11] *Bywalkers:* walkers on bypaths. The 1549 text reads *bankers,* which the editor has regretfully emended.

[12] There is little doubt that this sentence accurately reports Latimer's sentiments in 1549. But the editions of the sermons published in the reign of Elizabeth I prudently add the words "if they so do, whereby strange religion cometh in" after "But God grant. . . ."

and rich men of this realm are overwhelmed; all lechery and other excessive vices, provoking God's wrath (were He not merciful) even to take from us our natural king and liege lord, yea, and to plague us with a strange king for our unrepentant heart. Wherefore if, as ye say, ye love the King, amend your lives, and then ye shall be a mean that God shall lend him us long to reign over us. For undoubtedly sins provoke much God's wrath. Scripture saith, *Dabo tibi regem in furore meo:* that is, "I will give thee a king in my wrath" (Hos. 13:11). Now we have a lawful king, a godly king: nevertheless, yet many evils do reign. Long time the ministers appointed hath studied to amend and redress all evils; long time before this, great labor hath been about this matter; great cracks [13] hath been made that all should be well. But when all came to all, for all their boasts, little or nothing was done, in whom these words of Horace may well be verified, saying, *Parturiunt montes, nascitur ridiculus mus,* "The mountains swelleth up, the poor mouse is brought out." [14] Long before this time many hath taken in hand to bring many things unto pass, but finally their works came unto small effect and profit.

Now I hear say all things are ended after a godly manner, or else shortly shall be. Make haste, make haste; and let us learn to convert, to repent, and amend our lives. If we do not, I fear, I fear lest for our sins and unthankfulness an hypocrite shall reign over us. Long we have been servants and in bondage, serving the Pope in Egypt. God hath given us a deliverer, a natural king. Let us seek no stranger of another nation, no hypocrite which shall bring in again all papistry, hypocrisy, and idolatry, no diabolical minister which shall maintain all devilish works and evil exercises. But let us pray that God maintain and continue our most excellent king here present, true inheritor of this our realm both by nativity and also by the special gift and ordinance of God. He doth us rectify in the liberty of the gospel; in that therefore let us stand. *State ergo in libertate qua*

[13] *Cracks:* boasts. [14] *Ars poetica,* l. 139.

Christus nos liberavit, "Stand ye in the liberty wherewith Christ hath made us free" (Gal. 5:1). In Christ's liberty we shall stand, if we so live that we profit, if we cast away all evil, fraud, and deceit, with such other vices contrary to God's word. And in so doing we shall not only prolong and maintain our most noble king's days in prosperity, but also we shall prosper our own lives, to live not only prosperously but also godly.

"In any wise, let not such a one prepare unto himself many horses," etc. In speaking these words, ye shall understand that I do not intend to speak against the strength, policy, and provision of a king, but against excess and vain trust that kings have in themselves more than in the living God, the author of all goodness and giver of all victory. Many horses are requisite for a king; but he may not exceed in them nor triumph in them more than is needful for the necessary affairs and defense of the realm. What meaneth it that God hath to do with the king's stable but only He would be master of his horses? The scripture saith, *In altis habitat,* "He dwelleth on high." It followeth, *Humilia respicit,* "He looketh on low things" (Psalm 113:5–6); yea, upon the king's stables, and upon all the offices in his house. God is [the] great Grandmaster [15] of the king's house, and will take accompt of everyone that beareth rule therein for the executing of their offices, whether they have justly and truly served the king in their offices or no. Yea, God looketh upon the king himself, if he worketh well or not. Every king is subject unto God, and all other men are subjects unto the king. In a king God requireth faith, not excess of horses. Horses for a king be good and necessary, if they be well used, but horses are not to be preferred above poor men.

I was once offended with the King's horses and thereof took occasion to speak in the presence of the King's Majesty that dead is, when abbeys stood. Abbeys were ordained for the comfort of the

[15] I.e., the Lord Chamberlain, or possibly the Lord Great Chamberlain. In either case, the metaphor is unfortunate.

poor. Wherefore I said it was not decent that the King's horses should be kept in them,[16] as many were at that time, the living of poor men thereby minished and taken away.[17] But afterward a certain nobleman said to me, "What hast thou to do with the King's horses?" I answered and said, "I speak my conscience, as God's word directeth me." He said, "Horses be the maintenances and part of a king's honor and also of his realm; wherefore, in speaking against them, ye are against the King's honor." I answered, "God teacheth what honor is decent for the King and for all other men according unto their vocations. God appointeth every king a sufficient living for his state and degree, both by lands and other customs; and it is lawful for every king to enjoy the same goods and possessions. But to extort and take away the right of the poor is against the honor of the King. An you do move the King to do after that manner, then you speak against the honor of the King." For I full certify you, extortioners, violent oppressors, engrossers[18] of tenements and lands, through whose covetousness villages decay and fall down, the King's liege people for lack of sustenance are famished and decayed—they be those which speak against the honor of the King. God requireth in the King and all magistrates a good heart, to walk directly in His ways, and in all subjects an obedience due unto a king. Therefore I pray God both the King and also we his people may endeavor diligently to walk in His ways, to His great honor and our profit.

"Let him not prepare unto himself too many wives," etc. Al-

[16] Latimer probably refers to the fact that horses were put to pasture on abbey lands which had formerly been under cultivation. There is no evidence that horses were stabled in the abbey churches.

[17] At the time of the suppression Latimer had urged that the larger abbeys be reformed but continued as "places of study and good letters and to the continual relief of the poor." During his tenure as Bishop of Worcester he was not in favor of the government's policy of complete dissolution. See A. G. Chester, *Hugh Latimer, Apostle to the English* (Philadelphia, 1954), chap. xvii.

[18] *Engrossers:* monopolists who bought up land in order to control the supply and price of food, especially grain.

though we read here that the kings amongst the Jews had liberty to take more wives than one, we may not therefore attempt to walk inordinately and to think that we may take also many wives. For Christ hath forbidden this unto us Christians. And let us not impute sin unto the Jews because they had many wives, for they had a dispensation so to do. Christ limiteth one wife unto us only, and it is a great thing for a man to rule one wife rightly and ordinately. For a woman is frail and proclive unto all evils; a woman is a very weak vessel and may soon deceive a man and bring him unto evil. Many examples we have in Holy Scripture. Adam had but one wife, called Eve, and how soon had she brought him to consent unto evil and to come to destruction! How did wicked Jezebel prevent King Ahab's heart from God and all godliness, and finally unto destruction! It is a very hard thing for a man to rule well one woman. Therefore let our king, what time His Grace shall be so minded to take a wife, to choose him one which is of God, that is, which is of the household of faith. Yea, let all estates be no less circumspect in choosing her, taking great deliberation, and then [they] shall not need divorcements and such mischiefs, to the evil example and slander of our realm. And that she be one as the King can find in his heart to love and lead his life in pure and chaste espousage; and then shall he be the more prone and ready to advance God's glory, punish and extirp the great lechery used in this realm.

Therefore we ought to make a continual prayer unto God for to grant our King's Grace such a mate as may knit his heart and hers, according to God's ordinance and law; and not consider and cleave only to a politic matter or conjunction for the enlarging of dominions, for surety and defense of countries, setting apart the institution and ordinance of God. We have now a pretty little shilling, indeed a very pretty one. I have but one, I think, in my purse; and the last day I had put it away almost for an old groat,[19] and so I trust some

[19] In 1549 shillings of two different standards were struck. One of them, although it was of finer silver than the other, was unpopular because it was only slightly larger than a groat.

will take them. The fineness of the silver I cannot see, but therein is printed a fine sentence, that is, *Timor Domini Fons Vitae Vel Sapientiae,*[20] "The fear of the Lord is the fountain of life or wisdom" (Prov. 14:27). I would God this sentence were always printed in the heart of the King in choosing his wife and in all his officers. For like as the fear of God is *fons sapientiae* or *vitae,* so the forgetting of God is *fons stultitiae,* the fountain of foolishness or of death, although it be never so politic, for upon such politic matters death doth ensue and follow, all their divorcements and other like conditions, to the great displeasure of Almighty God. Which evils, I fear me, is much used at these days in the marriage of noblemen's children for joining lands to lands, possessions to possessions, neither the virtuous education nor living being regarded; but in the infancy such marriages be made, to the displeasure of God and breach of epousals.[21]

Let the King therefore choose unto him a godly wife, whereby he shall the better live chaste; and in so living all godliness shall increase and righteousness be maintained. Notwithstanding, I know hereafter some will come and move Your Grace towards wantonness and to the inclination of the flesh and vain affections. But I would Your Grace should bear in memory an history of a good king called Louis,[22] that traveled towards the Holy Land—which was a great matter in those days—and by the way sickened, being long absent from his wife. And upon this matter the physicians did agree that it was for lack of a woman and did consult with the bishops therein, who did conclude that because of the distance of his wife (being in another country) he should take a wench. This good king, hearing their conclusion, would not consent thereunto, but said he had

[20] The legend reads *Timor Domine Fons Vite. Vel Sapientiae* was Latimer's addition.

[21] Many instances might be cited, but a conspicuous case with literary associations is the marriage, a generation after Latimer's time, of Penelope Devereux, daughter of the Earl of Oxford, and Lord Rich.

[22] Louis IX of France, "St. Louis."

rather be sick even unto death than he would break his espousals.[23] Woe worth such counselors! Bishops! Nay, rather buzzards.

Nevertheless, if the King should have consented to their conclusion and accomplished the same, if he had not chanced well, they would have excused the matter; as I have heard of two that have consulted together, and according to the advice of his friend the one of them wrought where the succession was not good; the other imputed a piece of reproach to him for his such counsel given. He excused the matter, saying that he gave him none other counsel but if it had been his cause he would have done likewise. So I think the bishops would have excused the matter if the King should have reproved them for their counsel. I do not read that the King did rebuke them for their counsel; but if he had, I know what would have been their answer. They would have said, "We give you no worse counsel than we would have followed ourselves if we had been in like case."

Well, sir, this king did well and had the fear of God before his eyes. He would not walk in bywalks, where are many balks. Amongst many balkings is much stumbling, and by stumbling it chanceth many times to fall down to the ground. And therefore let us not take any bywalks, but let God's word direct us. Let us not walk after nor lean to our own judgments and proceedings of our forefathers, nor seek not what they did but what they should have

[23] This narrative was drastically bowdlerized in the Parker Society edition of the sermons, but the editor, in a note, did call attention to the fact that Latimer's "memory" had failed him. As a matter of fact, the preacher altered the story quite irresponsibly in order to attack Louis's bishops. As reported by Gaufridus de Bello-Loco, these virtuous sentiments were expressed by Louis's pious and strong-willed mother, Blanche of Castile, in an entirely different context. She had heard rumors of her son's youthful profligacy but pretended to disbelieve them. "If her son the king [she said], whom she loved above all other mortal creatures, were sick unto death and she were to be told that he might be made well by sinning with a woman not his wife, she would rather allow him to die than have him offend his Creator by even once committing a mortal sin" (*Sancti Ludovici . . . Vita . . . per F. Gaufridum de Bello-loco,* ed. Claudii Menardi [Paris, 1617], pp. 7–8).

done. Of which thing scripture admonisheth us, saying *Ne inclinemus praeceptis et traditionibus patrum, neque faciamus quod videtur rectum in oculis nostris,* "Let us not incline ourselves unto the precepts and traditions of our fathers; nor let us do that seemeth right in our eyes." [24] But surely we will not exchange our fathers' doings and traditions with scripture, but chiefly lean unto them and to their prescription and do that seemeth good in our own eyes. But surely that is going down the ladder. *Scala coeli,* as it was made by the Pope, came to be a mass; [25] but that is a false ladder to bring men to heaven. The true ladder to bring a man to heaven is the knowledge and following of scripture. Let the King therefore choose a wife which feareth God; let him not seek a proud wanton and one full of rich treasures and worldly pomp.

"He shall not multiply unto himself too much gold and silver." Is there too much, think you, for a king? God doth allow much unto a king, and it is expedient that he should have much; for he hath great expenses and many occasions to spend much for the defense and surety of his realm and subjects. And necessary it is that a king have a treasure always in a readiness for that and such other affairs as be daily in his hands; the which treasure, if it be not sufficient, he may lawfully and with a safe conscience take taxes of his subjects. For it were not meet the treasure should be in the subjects' purses when the money should be occupied,[26] nor it were not best for themselves; for the lack thereof it might cause both it and all the rest that they have should not long be theirs. And so for a necessary and expedient occasion it is warranted by God's word to take of the subjects. But if there be sufficient treasures, and the burdening of subjects be for a vain thing, so that he will require thus much or so much of his subjects, which perchance are in great necessity and penury, then this covetous intent and the request thereof is "too

24 Probably Deut. 12:6. But neither the Latin nor the English corresponds very closely to the ordinary versions.

25 See note 43 to the "Convocation Sermon," p. 20 above.

26 *Occupied:* invested, or spent usefully.

much," which God forbiddeth the king here in this place of scripture to have.

But who shall see this "too much" or tell the King of this "too much"? Think you, any of the King's privy chamber? No, for fear of loss of favor. Shall any of his sworn chaplains? No, they be of the closet and keep close such matters. But the King himself must see this "too much"; and that shall he do by no means with the corporal eyes. Wherefore he must have a pair of spectacles which shall have two clear sights in them: that is, that one is faith, not a seasonable faith which shall last but a while, but a faith which is continuing in God; the second clear sight is charity, which is fervent towards his Christian brother. By them two must the King see ever when he hath too much. But few there be that useth these spectacles, the more is their damnation. Not without cause Chrysostom with admiration saith, *Miror si aliquis rectorum potest salvari,* "I marvel if any ruler can be saved." [27] Which words he speaketh not of an impossibility but of a great difficulty, for that their charge is marvelous great, and that none about them dare show them the truth of the thing how it goeth.

Well, then, if God will not allow a king too much, whether will he allow a subject too much? No, that he will not. Whether hath any man here in England too much? I doubt most rich men have too much, for without too much we can get nothing. As for example, the physician: if the poor man be diseased, he can have no help without too much. And of the lawyer, the poor man can get no counsel, expedition, nor help in his matter except he give him too much. At merchants' hands no kind of wares can be had except we give for it too much. You landlords, you rent raisers—I may say you step-lords, you unnatural lords—you have for your possessions yearly too much. For that herebefore went for twenty or forty pound by year, which is an honest portion to be had gratis in one lordship of another man's sweat and labor, now is it let for fifty or a hundred

[27] *Epistola ad Hebraeos,* cap. 13, hom. XXXIV (J.-P. Migne, *Patrologiae Graecae,* ser. 2, LXIII, col. 233).

pound by year. Of this "too much" cometh this monstrous and portentous dearth made by man, notwithstanding God doth send us plentifully the fruits of the earth, mercifully, contrary unto our deserts. Notwithstanding, "too much," which these rich men have, causeth such dearth that poor men which live of their labor cannot with the sweat of their face have a living, all kind of victuals is so dear—pigs, geese, capons, chickens, eggs, etc. These things with other are so unreasonably enhanced; and I think verily that if yet this continue, we shall at length be constrained to pay for a pig a pound.

I will tell you, my lords and masters, this is not for the King's honor. Yet some will say, "Knowest thou what belongeth unto the King's honor better than we?" I answer that the true honor of a king is most perfectly mentioned and painted forth in the scriptures, of which if ye be ignorant for lack of time that ye cannot read it, albeit that your counsel be never so politic, yet is it not for the King's honor. What his honor meaneth, ye cannot tell. It is the King's honor that his subjects be led in the true religion, that all his prelates and clergy be set about their work in preaching and studying and not to be interrupted from their charge. Also it is the King's honor that the commonwealth be advanced, that the dearth of these foresaid things be provided for and the commodities of this realm so employed as it may be to the setting his subjects on work and keeping them from idleness. And herein resteth the King's honor and his office. So doing, his accompt before God shall be allowed and rewarded.

Furthermore, if the King's honor, as some men say, standeth in the great multitude of people, then these graziers, enclosers, and rent rearers are hinderers of the King's honor. For whereas have been a great many of householders and inhabitants, there is now but a shepherd and his dog. So they hinder the King's honor most of all. My lords and masters, I say also that all such proceedings which are against the King's honor—as I have a part declared before, and as far as I can perceive—do intend plainly to make the yeomanry slavery and the clergy shavery. For such works are all singular, private wealth and commodity. We of the clergy had too much, but that is taken away and now we have too little. But for mine own part I have no cause to complain, for I thank God and the King I have sufficient; and, God is my judge, I came not to crave of any man anything. But I know them that have too little. There lieth a great matter by these appropriations.[28] Great reformations is to be had in them. I know where is a great market town, with divers hamlets and inhabitants, where do rise yearly of their labors to the value of fifty pound, and the vicar that serveth, being so great a cure, hath but twelve or fourteen marks by year, so that of this pension he is not able to buy him books nor give his neighbor drink. All the great gain goeth another way.

My father was a yeoman and had no lands of his own, only he had a farm of three or four pound by year at the uttermost, and hereupon he tilled so much as kept half a dozen men. He had walk for a hundred sheep, and my mother milked thirty kine. He was able, and did find [29] the King a harness,[30] with himself and his horse, while he came to the place that he should receive the King's wages. I can remember that I buckled his harness when he went unto Blackheath field.[31] He kept me to school, or else I had not been able to have preached before the King's Majesty now. He married my sisters with five pound or twenty nobles apiece, so that he brought them up in godliness and fear of God. He kept hospitality for his poor neighbors, and some alms he gave to the poor. And all this did he of the said farm, where he that now hath it payeth sixteen pound by year or more and is not able to do anything for his prince, for himself, nor for his children, or give a cup of drink to the poor.

Thus all the enhancing and rearing goeth to your private com-

[28] *Appropriations:* transfer of the temporal interests of benefices to laymen.

[29] *Find:* provide. [30] *Harness:* armor.

[31] The open common to the southeast of London where, in June, 1497, the forces of Henry VII defeated the Cornish rebels who had risen in protest against heavy taxation.

modity and wealth. So that where ye had a single "too much," you have that and since the same ye have enhanced the rent, and so have increased another "too much." So now ye have a double "too much," which is too-too much. But let the preacher preach till his tongue be worn to the stumps, nothing is amended. We have good statutes made for the commonwealth, as touching commoners, enclosers,[32] many meetings and sessions, but in the end of the matter there cometh nothing forth. Well, well, this is one thing I will say unto you. From whence it cometh I know, even from the devil. I know his intent in it. For if ye bring it to pass that the yeomanry be not able to put their sons to school—as indeed universities do wondrously decay already—and that they be not able to marry their daughters, to the avoiding of whoredom, I say ye pluck salvation from the people and utterly destroy the realm. For by yeomen's sons the faith of Christ is and hath been maintained chiefly. Is this realm taught by rich men's sons? No, no, read the chronicles. Ye shall find sometime noblemen's sons which have been unpreaching bishops and prelates, but ye shall find none of them learned men. But verily they that should look to the redress of these things be the greatest against them. In this realm are a great many of folks, and amongst many I know but one of tender zeal at the motion of his poor tenants hath let down his lands to the old rents for their relief. For God's love let not him be a phoenix, let him not be alone, let him not be an hermit closed in a wall; some good man follow him and do as he giveth example.

Surveyors[33] there be that greedily gorge up their covetous guts—hand makers,[34] I mean, honest men I touch not—but all such as so survey, they make up their mouths, but the commons be utterly undone by them, whose bitter cry ascending up to the ears of the God of Sabaoth, the greedy pit of hellburning fire, without great repentance, do tarry and look for them. A redress God grant! For surely, surely, but that two things do comfort me I would despair of

[32] *Commoners, enclosers:* enclosers of common lands.

[33] *Surveyors:* tax collectors. [34] *Hand makers:* profiteers.

the redress in these matters. One is that the King's Majesty, when he cometh to age, will see a redress of these things so out of frame, giving example by letting down his own lands first, and then enjoin his subjects to follow him. The second hope I have is, I believe that the general accompting day is at hand, the dreadful day of judgment, I mean, which shall make an end of all these calamities and miseries. For, as the scriptures be, *Cum dixerint, Pax, pax,* "When they shall say, Peace, peace," (Jer. 6:14), *Omnia Tuta,* "All things are sure," then is the day at hand. A merry day, I say, for all such as do in this world study to serve and please God, and continue in His faith, fear, and love; and a dreadful horrible day for them that decline from God, walking in their own ways, to whom, as it is written in the twenty-fifth of Matthew, is said, *Ite, maledicti, in ignem aeternum,* "Go, ye cursed, into everlasting punishment, where shall be wailing and gnashing of teeth" (Matt. 25:41). But unto the other He shall say, *Venite, benedicti,* "Come, ye blessed children of my Father, possess ye the kingdom prepared for you from the beginning of the world" (Matt. 25:34). Of the which God make us all partakers! Amen.

SECOND SERMON BEFORE KING EDWARD VI MARCH 15, 1549[1]

THE SECOND SERMON OF MASTER HUGH LATIMER, WHICH HE PREACHED BEFORE THE KING'S MAJESTY WITHIN HIS GRACE'S PALACE AT WESTMINSTER THE FIFTEENTH DAY OF MARCH, 1549

Quaecumque scripta sunt ad nostram doctrinam, etc.
(Romans 15:4)
"All things that are written in God's book, in the Holy Bible, they were written before our time, but yet to continue from age to age, as long as the world doth stand."

IN THIS book is contained doctrine for all estates, even for kings. A king herein may learn how to guide himself. I told you in my last sermon much of the duty of a king, and there is one place behind

[1] The title page of the volume (STC 15274) containing this and the two sermons following reads as follows: "The seconde Sermon of Master Hughe Latemer, whych he preached before the Kynges maiestie, within hys graces Palayce at Westminster the. xv. day of Marche. M.ccccc. xlix. Cum gracia et priuilegio ad imprimendum solum."
The colophon reads: "Imprinted at London by Ihon Daye, dwellinge at Aldersgate, and William Seres, dwellinge in Peter Colledge. These bokes are to be sold at the new

yet, and it followeth in the text: *Postquam autem sederit in solio regni sui, etc.,* "And when the king is set in the seat of his kingdom, he shall write him out a book and take a copy of the priests or Levites" (Deut. 17:18). He shall have the book with him. And why? "To read in it all the days of his life, to learn to fear God and learn His laws," and other things, as it followeth in the text, with the appurtenances and hangings-on "that he turn not from God, neither to the right hand nor to the left." And wherefore shall he do this? "That he may live long, he and his children" (Deut. 17:19–20).

Hitherto goeth the text. That I may declare this the better, to the edifying of your souls and the glory of God, I shall desire you to pray, etc.

Et postquam sederit, etc. Before I enter into this place, right honorable audience, to furnish it accordingly, which by the grace of God I shall do at leisure, I would repeat the place I was in last and furnish it with a story or two which I left out in my last sermon. I was in a matter concerning the sturdiness of the Jews, a froward and stiff-necked kind of people, much like our Englishmen nowadays, that in the minority of a king take upon them to break laws and to go byways. For when God had promised them a king, when it came to point they refused him. These men walked bywalks. And the saying, is "Many bywalks, many balks"; many balks much stumbling; and where much stumbling is there is sometime a fall. Howbeit there were some good walkers among them that walked in the king's highway ordinarily, uprightly, plain Dunstable way;[2] and for this purpose I would show you an history which is written in the third of the Kings.

King David being in his childhood, an old man in his second

shop by the litle Conduite in Chepeside. Cum gracia et priuilegio ad imprimendum solum."

Although the title page names only the second sermon, this volume contains also the third, fourth, fifth, sixth, and seventh sermons before Edward VI.

[2] *Dunstable way:* originally the road (part of the Roman Watling Street) from London to Dunstable, notable for its directness and evenness; hence, plain, straightforward.

childhood—for all old men are twice children, as the proverb is, *Senex bis puer,* "an old man twice a child" [3]—it happened with him as it doth oftentimes when wicked men of a king's childhood take occasion of evil. This King David, being weak of nature and impotent, insomuch that when he was covered with clothes he could take no heat, was counseled of his servants to take a fair young maid to nourish him and to keep him warm in his body. I suppose she was his wife. Howbeit he had no bodily company with her, and well she might be his wife. For though the scripture doth say, *Non cognovit eam,* "He knew her not" (I Kings 1:4), he had no carnal copulation with her, yet it saith not, *Non duxit eam uxorem,* "He married her not." And I cannot think that King David would have her to warm his bosom in bed except she had been his wife, having a dispensation of God to have as many wives as he would, for God had dispensed with them to have many wives.

Well, what happened to King David in his childhood by the child of the devil? Ye shall hear. King David had a proud son, whose name was Adonijah, a man full of ambition, desirous of honor, always climbing, climbing. Now whiles the time was of his father's childhood, he would depose his father, not knowing of his father's mind, saying, *Ego regnabo,* "I will reign, I will be king" (*ibid.,* 1:5). He was a stout-stomached child, a bywalker, of an ambitious mind. He would not consent to his father's friends but gat him a chariot and men to run before it, and divers other adherents to help him forward, worldly-wise men such as had been before of his father's counsel, great men in the world. And some, no doubt of it, came of good will, thinking no harm. For they would not think that he did it without his father's will, having such great men to set him forth. For every man cannot have access at all times to the king, to know his pleasure. Well, algates [4] he would be king and makes a great

[3] In one form or another this proverb goes back to the Greek of the fifth century B.C. Latimer was probably recalling the form it takes in the *Adagia* of Erasmus: *Bis pueri senes.*

[4] *Algates:* in any event.

feast, and thither he called Joab, the ringleader of his father's army, a worldly-wise man, a bywalker that would not walk the king's highway, and one Abiathar, the high priest—for it is marvel if any mischief be in hand if a priest be not at some end of it. They took him as king and cried, *Vivat rex Adonias,* "God save King Adonijah." David suffered all this and let him alone, for he was in his childhood, a bedrid man.

But see how God ordered the matter. Nathan the prophet and Zadoc, a priest, and Benaiah and [the] Cherethites and Pelethites, the King's guard, they were not called to the feast. These were good men and would not walk byways. Therefore it was folly to break the matter to them; they were not called to counsel. Therefore Nathan, when he heard of this, he cometh to Bathsheba, Solomon's mother, and saith, "Hear ye not how Adonijah the son of Haggith reigneth king, David not knowing?" (I Kings 1:11). And he bade her put the King in mind of his oath that he sware that her son Solomon should be king after him. This was wise counsel, according to the proverb, *Qui vadit plane, vadit sane,* "He that walketh in the high, plain way, walketh safely."

Upon this she went and brake the matter to David and desired him to show who should reign after him in Jerusalem, adding that if Adonijah were king, she and her son, after his death, should be destroyed, saying, *Nos erimus peccatores,* "We shall be sinners (*ibid.,* 1:21). We shall be taken for traitors; for though we meant no harm but walked uprightly, yet because we went not the byway with him, he, being in authority, will destroy us." And by and by cometh in Nathan and taketh her tale by the end, and showeth him how Adonijah was saluted king and that he had bid to dinner the King's servants—all saving him and Zadoc and Benaiah—and all his brethren, the King's sons, save Solomon.

King David, remembering himself, swore, "As sure as God liveth, Solomon my son shall reign after me," and by and by commanded Nathan and Zadoc and his guard, the Cherethites and Pelethites, to take Solomon his son and set him upon his mule and anoint him king. And so they did, crying, *Vivat Salomon Rex* (*ibid.*, 1:34). Thus was Solomon throned by the advice and will of his father. And though he were a child, yet was his will to be obeyed and fulfilled, and they ought to have known his pleasure.

Whiles this was adoing, there was such a joy and outcry of the people for their new king and blowing of trumpets that Joab and the other company, being in their jollity and keeping good cheer, heard it and suddenly asked, "What is this ado?" And when they perceived that Solomon by the advice of his father was anointed king, by and by there was all whisht.[5] All their good cheer was done; and all that were with Adonijah went away and let him reign alone, if he would. And why? He walked a byway, and God would not prosper it.

God will not work with private authority nor with anything done inordinately. When Adonijah saw this, that he was left alone, he took sanctuary and held by the horns of the altar and sware that he would not depart thence till Solomon would swear that he should not lose his life.

Here is to be noted the notable sentence and great mercy of King Solomon. "Let him," saith he, "order himself like a quiet man, and there shall not one hair fall from his head. *Sed si inventum fuerit malum in eo,* 'But if there shall be any evil found in him,' if he hath gone about any mischief, he shall die for it" (*ibid.*, 1:52). Upon this he was brought into Solomon; and as the book saith, he did homage unto him. And Solomon said to him, *Vade in domum tuam,* "Get thee into thy house" (*ibid.*, 1:53). Belike he meant to ward, and there to see his wearing.[6] As if he should say, "Show thyself without gall of ambition, to be a quiet subject, and I will pardon thee for this time, but I will see the wearing of thee." Here we may see the wonderful great mercy of Solomon for this notorious treason that Adonijah had committed. It was a plain matter, for he suffered himself to be called king. It hung not of[7] vehement suspi-

[5] *All whisht:* dead silence. [6] *Wearing:* future behavior.

[7] *Hung . . . of:* did not depend upon.

cion or conjecture, nor sequel or consequent; yet notwithstanding Solomon for that present forgave him, saying, "I will not forget it utterly, but I will keep it in suspense. I will take no advantage of thee at this time." This Adonijah and Absalom were brethren and came both of a strange mother; and Absalom likewise was a traitor and made an insurrection against his father. Beware therefore these mothers; and let kings take heed how they marry, in what houses, in what faith. For strange bringing-up bringeth strange manners.

Now giveth David an exhortation to Solomon and teacheth him the duty of a king and giveth him a lesson, as it followeth at large in the book, and he that list to read it may see it there at full. But what doth Adonijah all this while? He must yet climb again; the gall of ambition was not out of his heart. He will now marry Abishag, the young queen that warmed King David's bosom, as I told you, and cometh me to Bathsheba, desiring her to be a mean to Solomon her son that he might obtain his purpose, and bringeth me out a couple of lies at a clap, and committeth me two unlawful acts. For first he would have been king without his father's consent, and now he will marry his father's wife. And the two lies are these. First, said he to Bathsheba, "Thou knowest that the kingdom belongeth to me, for I am the elder; the kingdom was mine" (I Kings 2.15). He lied falsely; it was none of his. Then said he, "All the eyes of Israel were cast upon me" (*ibid.*). That is to say, all Israel consented to it. And there he lied falsely, for Nathan, Zadoc, and other wise men never agreed to it. Here was a great enterprise of Adonijah; he will be climbing still.

Well, Bathsheba went at his request to her son Solomon and asked a boon, and he granted her whatsoever she did ask. Notwithstanding, he brake his promise afterward, and that right well. For all promises are not to be kept, specially if they be against the Word of God, or not standing with a common profit. And therefore as soon as Solomon heard that Adonijah would have married the young Queen Abishag, "Nay, then let him be king too," said he. "I perceive now that he is a naughty man, a proud-hearted fellow; the gall of ambition is not yet out of his heart"; and so commanded him to be put to death. Thus was Adonijah put to execution, whereas, if he had kept his house and not broken his injunction, he might have lived still. Abiathar, what became of him? The King, because he had served his father before him, would not put him to death, but made him as it were a quondam.[8] "Because thou hast been with my father," said he, "and didst carry the ark before him, I will not kill thee. But I will promise thee thou shalt never minister any more; *vade in agrum tuum,* 'get thee to thy land,' and live there" (I Kings 2:26). A great matter of pity and compassion! So God grant us all such mercy!

And here was the end of Eli's stock, according to the promise and threatening of God. As for the Pelethites, we do not read that they were punished. Marry, Shimei transgressed his injunction, for he kept not his house but went out of Jerusalem to seek two servants of his that had run from him; and when it came to Solomon's ear, it cost him his life.

I have ripped the matter now to the pill[9] and have told you of plain walkers and of bywalkers, and how a king in his childhood is a king as well as in any other age. We read in scripture of such as were but twelve or eight years old,[10] and yet the word of the Holy Ghost called them kings, saying, *Coepit regnare,* "He began to reign," or he began to be king. Here is of bywalkers. This history would be remembered. The proverb is, *Felix quem faciunt aliena pericula cautum,* "Happy is he that can beware by another man's jeopardy."[11] For if we offend not as other do, it is our deserts. If we fall not, it is God's preservation. We are all offenders; for either

[8] *Quondam:* the technical term for an ecclesiastical or civil official who had been removed from or had resigned his office. After his forced resignation from his bishopric Latimer often applied the term to himself ironically.

[9] *Ripped . . . pill:* laid it bare to the skin.

[10] For example, Joash at the age of seven (II Kings 11:21) and Josiah at the age of eight (II Kings 22:1).

[11] Latimer would have found this proverb also in Erasmus' *Adagia.*

we may do, or have done, or shall do (except God preserve us) as evil as the worst of them. I pray God we may all amend and repent! But we will all amend now, I trust. We must needs amend our lives every man. The Holy Communion is at hand, and we may not receive it unworthily.

Well, to return to my history. King David, I say, was a king in his second childhood. And so young kings, though they be children, yet are they kings notwithstanding. And though it be written in scripture, *Vae tibi, O terra, ubi puer est rex,* "Woe to thee, O land, where the king is a child" (Eccles. 10:16), it followeth in another place, *Beata terra ubi rex nobilis,* "Blessed is the land where there is a noble king" (*ibid.,* 10:17). Where kings be no banqueters, no players, and they spend not the time in hawking and hunting. And when had the King's Majesty a Council that took more pain both night and day for the setting forth of God's word and profit of the commonwealth? And yet there be some wicked people[12] that will say, "Tush, this gear will not tarry; it is but my Lord Protector's[13] and my Lord of Canterbury's[14] doing; the King is a child; he knoweth not of it." Jesu mercy! How like are we Englishmen to the Jews, ever stubborn, stiff-necked, and walking of byways! Yea, I think no Jew would at any time say, "This gear will not tarry." I never heard nor read at any time that they said, "These laws were made in such a king's days when he was but a child; let us alter them." O Lord, what pity is this that we should be worse than the Jews!

"Blessed be the land," saith the Word of God, "where the king is noble." What people are they that say, "The King is but a child"? Have we not a noble king? Was there ever king so noble, so godly, brought up with so noble counselors, so excellent and well-learned

[12] The allusion is probably to Edmund Bonner, Bishop of London, who in the preceding September had refused to assert the King's prerogative in a sermon which he had been ordered to preach for that purpose at Paul's Cross. He was imprisoned in the Marshalsea and subsequently deprived of his bishopric.

[13] Edward Seymour, Duke of Somerset.

[14] Archbishop Cranmer.

schoolmasters? I will tell you this, and I speak it even as I think. His Majesty hath more godly wit and understanding, more learning and knowledge at this age than twenty of his progenitors that I could name had at any time of their life.

I told you in my last sermon of ministers, of the King's people, and had occasion to show you how few noblemen were good preachers. And I left out an history then which I will now tell you.[15] There was a Bishop of Winchester in King Henry the Sixth's days, which king was but a child, and yet were there many good acts made in his childhood, and I do not read that they were broken. This bishop was a great man born and did bear such a stroke that he was able to shoulder the Lord Protector. Well, it chanced that the Lord Protector and he fell out; and the Bishop would bear nothing at all with him, but played me the *satrapa,*[16] so that the Regent of France was fain to be sent for from beyond the seas, to set them at one and to go between them. For the Bishop was as able and ready to buckle[17] with the Lord Protector as he was with him. Was not this a good prelate? He should have been at home apreaching in his diocese in a wanion.[18]

This Protector was so noble and godly a man that he was called of every man the "good Duke Humphrey." He kept such a house as never was kept since in England, without any enhancing of rents, I warrant you, or any such matter. And the Bishop, for standing so stiffly by the matter and bearing up the order of our mother, the Holy Church, was made cardinal at Calais; and thither the Bishop of Rome sent him a cardinal's hat. He should have had a Tyburn tippet,[19] a halfpenny halter. And all such proud prelates! These Romish hats never brought good into England.

[15] In the following account of the rivalry between Henry Cardinal Beaufort and Humphrey Duke of Gloucester Latimer follows the "received" Tudor version.

[16] *Satrapa:* ruler, with the imputation of tyranny and luxuriousness.

[17] *Buckle:* grapple. [18] *In a wanion:* with a vengeance.

[19] *Tyburn tippet:* hangman's noose.

Upon this the Bishop goeth me to the Queen Margaret,[20] the King's wife, a proud woman and a stout, and persuaded her that if the Duke were in such authority still and lived, the people would honor him more than they did the King and the King should not be set by. And so between them, I cannot tell how it came to pass, but at St. Edmundsbury, in a Parliament, the good Duke Humphrey was smothered.

But now to return to my text and to make further rehearsal of the same. The matter beginneth thus: *Et postquam sederit rex,* "And when the king is set in the seat of his kingdom . . . ," what shall he do? Shall he dance and dally, banquet, hawk, and hunt? No, forsooth, sir. For as God set an order in the king's stable, as I told you in my last sermon, so will He appoint what pastime a king shall have. What must he do then? He must be a student; he must write God's book himself, not thinking, because he is a king, he hath license to do what he will, as these worldly flatterers are wont to say. "Yea, trouble not yourself, sir, ye may hawk and hunt and take your pleasure. As for the guiding of your kingdom and people, let us alone with it." These flattering clawbacks are original roots of all mischief. And yet a king may take his pastime in hawking or hunting or suchlike pleasures. But he must use them for recreation, when he is weary of weighty affairs, that he may return to them the more lusty. And this is called pastime with good company.[21] "He must write out a book himself." He speaketh of writing because printing was not used at that time. And shall the king write it out himself? He meaneth he shall see it written and, rather than he should be without it, write it himself. Jesus mercy! Is God so chary with a king to have him well brought up and instructed? Yea, forsooth, for if the king be well ordered, the realm is well ordered.

[20] The text reads Katherine, a palpable error. Henry VI's queen was the formidable Margaret of Anjou.

[21] *Pastime . . . company:* the first line of a song written by Henry VIII. Such lines as "For my pastance,/Hunt, sing, and dance,/My heart is set" indicate the ironic nature of Latimer's allusion.

Where shall he have a copy of this book? Of the Levites. And why? Because it shall be a true copy, not falsified. Moses left the book in an old chest, and the Levites had it in keeping. And because there should be no error, no addition nor taking away from it, he biddeth him fetch the copy of the Levites.

And was not here a great miracle of God, how this book was preserved? It had lain hid many years, and the Jews knew not of it. Therefore at length, when they had found it and knew it, they lamented for their ignorance that had so long been without it, and rent their clothes, repenting their unfaithfulness.[22] And so the Holy Bible, God's book that we have among us, it hath been preserved hitherto by a wonderful miracle of God, though the keepers of it were never so malicious. First, ever sith the Bishop of Rome was first in authority, they have gone about to destroy it. But God worketh wonderfully; He hath preserved it, mauger [23] their beards. And yet are we unthankful that we cannot consider it. I will tell you what a bishop of this realm said once to me. He sent for me and marveled that I would not consent to such traditions as were then set out. And I answered him that I would be ruled by God's book, and rather than I would dissent one jot from it I would be torn with wild horses. And I chanced in our communication to name the Lord's Supper.[24] "Tush," saith the bishop, "what do ye call the Lord's Supper? What new term is that?" There stood by him a dubber,[25] one Doctor Dubber; he dubbed him by and by and said that this term was seldom read in the doctors. And I made answer that I would rather follow Paul in using his terms than them, though they had all the doctors on their side. "Why," said the bishop, "cannot we without scriptures order the people? How did they before the scripture was first written and copied out?" But God

[22] Here the preacher jumps to the account, in II Kings 22, of the discovery of the book of the law by Hilkiah the High Priest in the reign of Josiah (638?–608? B.C.).

[23] *Mauger:* in spite of.

[24] This term for the Eucharist was given prominence among the reformers by the publication of Tyndale's *The Supper of the Lord* in 1533.

[25] *Dubber:* a renovator of old clothes.

knoweth, full ill yet would they have ordered them; for, seeing that having it they have deceived us, in what case should we have been now without it? But thanks be to God that by so wonderful a miracle He hath preserved the book still.

It followeth in the text: *Habebit secum, etc.,* "He shall have it with him." In his progress he must have a man to carry it, that when he is hawking and hunting or in any pastime he may always commune with them of it. He shall read in it, not once a year for a time, or for his recreation when he is weary of hawking or hunting, but *cunctis diebus vitae suae,* "all the days of his life." Where are those worldlings now, these bladder-puffed-up wily men? Woe worth them that ever they were about any king! But how shall he read this book? As the Homilies are read.[26] Some call them homelies, and indeed so they may be well called, for they are homely handled. For though the priest read them never so well, yet if the parish like them not there is such talking and babbling in the church that nothing can be heard. And if the parish be good and the priest naught, he will so hack it and chop it that it were as good for them to be without it for any word that shall be understand. And yet, the more pity, this is suffered of Your Grace's bishops in their dioceses unpunished. But I will be a suitor to Your Grace that ye will give your bishops charge ere they go home, upon their allegiance, to look better to their flock and to see Your Majesty's Injunctions [27] better kept. And send your visitors in their tails; and if they be found negligent or faulty in their duties, out with them. I require it in God's behalf; make them quondams, all the pack of them.

But peradventure ye will say, "Where shall we have any to put in their rooms?" Indeed I were a presumptuous fellow to move Your Grace to put them out if there were not other to put in their places. But Your Majesty hath divers of your chaplains, well-learned men and of good knowledge. And yet ye have some that be bad enough,

[26] The Royal Injunctions of 1547 provided that one of the Homilies (see p. 31, note 4 to the "Sermon on the Plowers") should be read when there was no other sermon.

[27] See note 1 to the "Sermon on the Plowers," pp. 28–29.

hangers-on of the Court; I mean not those. But if Your Majesty's chaplains and my Lord Protector's be not able to furnish their places, there is in this realm—thanks be to God—a great sight of laymen well learned in the scriptures and of virtuous and godly conversation, better learned than a great sight of us of the clergy. I can name a number of them that are able and would be glad, I dare say, to minister the function if they be called to it. I move it of conscience to Your Grace, let them be called to it orderly; let them have institution and give them the name of the clergy. I mean not the name only, but let them do the function of a bishop, and live of the same, not as it is in many places that one should have the name and eight other the profit. For what an enormity is this in a Christian realm, to serve in a civility,[28] having the profit of a provostship and a deanery and a parsonage![29] But I will tell you what is like to come of it: it will bring the clergy shortly into a very slavery.

I may not forget here my *scala coeli* that I spoke of in my last sermon. I will repeat it now again, desiring Your Grace in God's behalf that ye will remember it. The Bishop of Rome had a *scala coeli*,[30] but his was a mass matter. This *scala coeli* is the true ladder that bringeth a man to heaven. The top of the ladder, or first grece,[31] is this: "Whosoever calleth upon the name of the Lord shall be saved." The second step: "How shall they call upon Him in Whom they have no belief?" The third stair is this: "How shall they believe in Him of Whom they never heard?" The fourth step: "How shall they hear without a preacher?" Now the nether end of the ladder is: "How shall they preach except they be sent?" (Romans 10:13–15). This is the foot of the ladder, so that we may go backward now and use the school argument *a primo ad ultimum:* take away preaching,

[28] *Civility:* secular office.

[29] Canon Corrie, the editor of the Parker Society edition of the sermons, suggests that this passage refers to Sir Thomas Smith, Secretary of State during Somerset's protectorate, who was also Provost of Eton and Dean of Carlisle.

[30] See note 43 to the "Convocation Sermon," p. 20 above.

[31] *Grece:* step.

take away salvation. But I fear one thing; and it is lest for a safety of a little money you will put in chantry priests, to save their pensions. But I will tell you, Christ bought souls with His blood. And will ye sell them for gold or silver? I would not that ye should do with chantry priests as ye did with the abbots, when abbeys were put down. For when their enormities were first read in the Parliament House,[32] they were so great and abominable that there was nothing but "down with them." But, within a while after, the same abbots were made bishops, as there be some of them yet alive,[33] to save and redeem their pensions. O Lord! think ye that God is a fool and seeth it not? And if He see it, will He not punish it? And so now for safety of money I would not that ye should put in chantry priests. I speak not now against such chantry priests as are able to preach. But those that are not able, I will not have them put in; for if ye do this, ye shall answer for it.[34]

It is in the text that a king ought to fear God: "He shall have the dread of God before his eyes." Work not by worldly policy, for worldly policy feareth not God. Take heed of these clawbacks, these venomous people that will come to you, that will follow like gnathos[35] and parasites. If you follow them, you are out of your book. If it be not according to God's word that they counsel you, do it not for any worldly policy, for then ye fear not God.

[32] A summary of the reports of the visitors to the religious houses was presented to Parliament in February, 1536.

[33] Among those still living in 1549 were the following: John Capon (or Salcot), Abbot of Hyde, who became successively Bishop of Bangor and Bishop of Salisbury; John Chambers, Abbot of Peterborough, who became Bishop of Peterborough; William Rugg (or Repps), Abbot of St. Bennet's, Hulme, who became Bishop of Norwich; John Wakeman, Abbot of Tewkesbury, who became the first Bishop of Gloucester.

[34] Modern historians, less emotional about the matter than Latimer, are agreed that the government's treatment of the displaced religious was humane and generous. See Geoffrey Baskerville, *English Monks and the Suppression of the Monasteries* (London, 1937).

[35] *Gnathos:* Gnatho is the parasite in Terence's *Eunuchus.* Latimer here uses the word as a generic noun, synonymous with *parasites.*

It followeth in the text: *ut non elevetur cor ejus,* "that he be not proud above his brethren." A king must not be proud, for God might have made him a shepherd when he made him a king and done him no wrong. There be many examples of proud kings in scripture. As Pharaoh, that would not hear the message of God. Herod, also, that put John Baptist to death and would not hear him; he told him that it was not lawful for him to marry his brother's wife. Jeroboam also was a proud king. Another king there was that worshiped strange gods and idols of those men whom he had overcome before in battle; and when a prophet told him of it, what said he? "Who made you one of my council?" [36] These were proud kings; their ensamples are not to be followed.

But wherefore shall a king "fear God, and turn neither to the right hand nor to the left?" Wherefore shall he do all this? *Ut longo tempore regnet ipse et filii ejus,* "That he may reign long, he and his children." Remember this, I beseech Your Grace. And when these flatterers and flibbergibs another day shall come and claw you by the back and say, "Sir, trouble not yourself. What should you study? Why should you do this or that?" Your Grace may answer them thus and say, "What, sirrah? I perceive you are weary of us and our posterity. Doth not God say in such a place that a king should write out a book of God's law and read it, learn to fear God? And why? That he and his might reign long. I perceive now thou art a traitor." Tell him this tale once and I warrant you he will come no more to you, neither he nor any other after such a sort. And thus shall Your Grace drive these flatterers and clawbacks away.

And I am afraid I have troubled you too long; therefore I will furnish [37] the text now with an history or two, and then I will leave you to God. Ye have heard how a king ought to pass the time. He must read the book of God; and it is not enough for him to read, but he must be acquainted with all scripture. He must study and he must pray. And how shall he do both these? He may learn at

[36] The reference is evidently to Amaziah, King of Judah (II Chron. 25:14–16).

[37] *Furnish:* illustrate.

Solomon. God spake unto Solomon when he was made a king and bade him ask of Him what he would, and he should have it. "Make thy petition," said God, "and thou shalt obtain." Now mark Solomon's prayer. *Domine, O Domine Deus,* said he, "O Lord God, it is Thou that hast caused me to reign and hast set me in my father's seat (I Kings 3:7), for Thou God only dost make kings." Thus should kings praise God and thank God, as Solomon did. But what was his petition? "Lord," said he, *da mihi cor docile.* He asked "a docible heart, a wise heart, and wisdom to go in and to go out" (*ibid.,* 3:9). That is, "to begin all mine affairs well, and to bring them to good effect and purpose, that I may learn to guide and govern my people."

When he had made his petition, it pleased God well that Solomon asked wisdom and neither riches nor long life; and therefore God made him this answer, "Because thou hast chosen wisdom above all things, I will give thee it, and thou shalt be the wisest king that ever was before thee" (*ibid.,* 3:11–12). And so he was, and the wisest in all kinds of knowledge that ever was sith. And though he did not ask riches, yet God gave him both riches and honor, more than ever any of his ancestors had. So Your Grace must learn how to do of Solomon. Ye must make your petition; now study, now pray. They must be yoked together; and this is called pastime with good company.

Now when God had given Solomon wisdom, He sent him by and by occasion to occupy his wit. For God gave never a gift but He sent occasion, at one time or another, to show it to God's glory. As, if He sent riches, He sendeth poor men to be helped with it. But now must men occupy their goods otherways. They will not look on the poor; they must help their children and purchase them more land than ever their grandfather had before them. But I shall tell you what Christ said: "He that loveth his child better than me is not worthy to be my disciple" (Matt. 10:37). I cannot see how ye shall stand before God at the later day when this sentence shall be laid against you.

But to return to my purpose. There were two poor women came before Solomon to complain. They were two harlots and dwelled together in one house, and it chanced within two days they childed both. The one of these women by chance in the night had killed her child and rose privily and went to the other woman and took her live child away and left her dead child in his place. Upon that they came both before Solomon to have the matter judged whose the child was. And the one said, "It is my child." "Nay," saith the other, "it is mine." So there was yea and nay between them, and they held up the matter with scolding after a womanly fashion. At length Solomon repeated their tale as a good judge ought to do and said to the one woman, "Thou sayest the child is thine." "Yea," said she. "And thou sayest it is thine," to the other. "Well, fetch me a sword," said he; for there was no way now to try which was the true mother but by natural inclination. And so he said to one of his servants, "Fetch me a sword and divide the child between them." When the mother of the child that accused the other heard him say so, "Nay, for God's sake," said she, "let her have the whole child and kill it not." "Nay," quoth the other, "neither thine nor mine, but let it be divided." Then said Solomon, "Give this woman the child; this is the mother of the child." What came of this? *Audivit omnes Israel,* "When all Israel heard of this judgment, they feared the king" (I Kings 3:27). It is wisdom and godly knowledge that causeth a king to be feared.

One word note here, for God's sake, and I will trouble you no longer. Would Solomon, being so noble a king, hear two poor women? They were poor, for, as the scripture saith, they were together alone in a house; they had not so much as one servant between them both. Would King Solomon, I say, hear them in his own person? Yea, forsooth. And yet I hear of many matters before my Lord Protector and my Lord Chancellor [38] that cannot be heard. I must desire my Lord Protector's Grace to hear me in this matter,

[38] Sir Richard Rich, created Baron Rich in 1547.

that Your Grace would hear poor men's suits yourself. Put it to none other to hear; let them not be delayed. The saying is now that money is heard everywhere; if he be rich, he shall soon have an end of his matter. Other are fain to go home with weeping tears for any help they can obtain at any judge's hand. Hear men's suits yourself, I require you in God's behalf, and put it not to the hearing of these velvet coats, these upskips. Now a man can scarce know them from an ancient knight of the country.[39] I cannot go to my book, for poor folks come unto me, desiring me that I will speak that their matters may be heard. I trouble my Lord of Canterbury;[40] and, being at his house, now and then I walk in the garden looking in my book, as I can do but little good at it.[41] But something I must needs do to satisfy this place. I am no sooner in the garden and have read awhile but by and by cometh there some or other knocking at the gate. Anon cometh my man and saith, "Sir, there is one at the gate would speak with you." When I come there, then is it some or other that desireth me that I will speak that his matter might be heard, and that he hath lain this long at great costs and charges and cannot once have his matter come to the hearing. But among all other, one especially moved me at this time to speak. This it is, sir. A gentlewoman came to me and told me that a great man keepeth certain lands of hers from her and will be her tenant in the spite of her teeth, and that in a whole twelvemonth she could not get but one day for the hearing of her matter. And the same day when the matter should be heard the great man brought on his side a great sight of lawyers for his counsel. The gentlewoman had but one man of law, and the great man shakes him so that he cannot tell what to do. So that when the matter came to the point, the judge was a mean to the gentlewoman that she would let the great man have a quietness in her land.

[39] Evidently the allusion is to the country justices of the peace, many of whom were also knights of the shire. Although not all of them were of Justice Shallow's kidney, there is abundant testimony to their general incompetence in this period.

[40] *Trouble:* reside at Lambeth Palace and hence inconvenience the Archbishop.

[41] *I . . . it:* I have little to do.

I beseech Your Grace that ye will look to these matters. Hear them yourself. View your judges, and hear poor men's causes. And you, proud judges, hearken what God saith in His holy book: *Audite illos, ita parvum ut magnum.* "Hear them," saith He, "the small as well as the great, the poor as well as the rich." Regard no person, fear no man. Why? *Quia Domini judicium est,* "The judgment is God's" (Deut. 1:17). Mark this saying, thou proud judge. The devil will bring this sentence at the day of doom. Hell will be full of these judges if they repent not and amend. They are worse than the wicked judge that Christ speaketh of that neither feared God nor the world. There was a certain widow that was a suitor to a judge, and she met him in every corner of the street, crying, "I pray you, hear me, I beseech you, hear me; I ask nothing but right." When the judge saw her so importunate, "Though I fear neither God," saith he, "nor the world, yet because of her importunateness I will grant her request" (Luke 18:4–5). But our judges are worse than this judge was, for they will neither hear men for God's sake, nor fear of the world, nor importunateness, nor anything else. Yea, some of them will command them to ward if they be importunate. I heard say that when a suitor came to one of them he said, "What fellow is it that giveth these folk counsel to be so importunate? He would be punished and committed to ward." Marry, sir, punish me then; it is even I that gave them counsel; I would gladly be punished in such a cause. And if ye mend not, I will cause them to cry out upon you still, even as long as I live. I will do it indeed. But I have troubled you long. As I began with this sentence: *Quaecumque scripta sunt, etc.,* so will I end now with this text: *Beati qui audiunt verbum Dei, et custodiunt illud,* "Blessed are they that hear the word of God and keepeth it" (Luke 11:28).

There was another suit and I had almost forgotten it. There is a poor woman that lieth in the Fleet [42] and cannot come by any means that she can make to her answer and would fain be bailed, offering

[42] The notorious debtors' prison.

to put in sureties worth a thousand pound. And yet she cannot be heard. Methink this is a reasonable cause; it is great pity that such things should so be. I beseech God that He will grant that all that is amiss may be amended, that we may hear His word and keep it, that we may come to the eternal bliss. To the which bliss I beseech God to bring both you and me. Amen.

SIXTH SERMON BEFORE KING EDWARD VI APRIL 12, 1549

THE SIXTH SERMON OF MASTER HUGH LATIMER, WHICH HE PREACHED BEFORE THE KING'S MAJESTY WITHIN HIS GRACE'S PALACE AT WESTMINSTER THE TWELFTH DAY OF APRIL

Quaecumque scripta sunt ad nostram doctrinam scripta sunt
(Romans 15:4)
"All things that are written, are written to be our doctrine."

WHAT doctrine is written for us in the eighth chapter of the first book of the Kings[1] I did partly show unto you, most honorable audience, this day sennight, of that good man, father Samuel, that good judge, how good a man he was, what helpers and coadjutors he took unto him to have his office well discharged. I told you also of the wickedness of his sons, how they took bribes and lived wickedly, and by that means brought both their father and themselves to deposition; and how the people did offend God in asking a king in father Samuel's time; and how father Samuel was put from his

[1] I Samuel in the usual terminology of Protestant Bibles.

office, who deserved it not. I opened to you also how father Samuel clears himself, that he knew not the faults of his sons. He was no bearer with his sons; he was sorry for it when he heard it, but he would not bear with them in their wickedness. *Filii mei vobiscum sunt,* "My sons are with you" (I Sam. 12:2), saith he, "do with them according to their deserts. I will not maintain them nor bear with them." After that, he clears himself at the King's feet, that the people had nothing to burden him withal, neither money nor money worth.

In treating of that part I chanced to show you what I heard of a man that was slain, and I hear say it was not well taken.[2] Forsooth, I intend not to impair any man's estimation or honesty, and they that enforce it to that enforce it not to my meaning. I said I heard but of such a thing, and took occasion by that that I heard to speak against the thing that I knew to be naught, that no man should bear with any man to the maintenance of voluntary and prepensed murder. And I hear say since the man was otherwise an honest man, and they that spake for him are honest men. I am inclinable enough to credit it. I spoke not because I would have any man's honesty impaired. Only I did as St. Paul did, who, hearing of the Corinthians that there should be contentions and misorder among them, did write unto them that he heard; and thereupon by occasion of hearing he set forth the very wholesome doctrine of the Supper of the Lord. We might not have lacked that doctrine, I tell you. Be it so, the Corinthians had no such contentions among them as Paul wrote of; be it so, they had not misordered themselves. It was neither off nor on to that that Paul said; the matter lay in that, that upon hearing he would take occasion to set out the good and true doctrine.

So I did not affirm it to be true that I heard; I spake it to advertise you to beware of bearing with willful and prepensed murder. I would have nothing enforced against any man; this was mine intent

[2] In the preceding sermon Latimer had spoken of several instances of murderers who went unpunished.

and meaning. I do not know what ye call chance-medley[3] in the law; it is not for my study. I am a scholar in scripture, in God's book; I study that. I know what voluntary murder is before God. If I shall fall out with a man, he is angry with me and I with him, and, lacking opportunity and place, we shall put it off for that time; in the mean season I prepare my weapon and sharp it against another time; I swell and boil in this passion towards him; I seek him, we meddle together; it is my chance, by reason my weapon is better than his and so forth, to kill him; I give him his death stroke in my vengeance and anger: this call I voluntary murder in scripture. What it is in the law I cannot tell. It is a great sin, and therefore I call it voluntary.

I remember what a great clerk writeth of this: *Omne peccatum adeo est voluntarium, ut nisi sit voluntarium non sit peccatum.* "Every sin," saith he, "is so voluntary that if it be not voluntary it cannot be called sin."[4] Sin is no actual sin if it be not voluntary. I would we would all know our faults and repent. That that is done, is done; it cannot be called back again. God is merciful; the King is merciful. Here we may repent; this is the place of repentance. When we are gone hence, it is too late then to repent. And let us be content with such order as the magistrates shall take. But sure it is a perilous thing to bear with any such matter. I told you what I heard say; I would have no man's honesty impaired by my telling. I heard say since of another murder, that a Spaniard should kill an Englishman and run him through with his sword; they say he was a tall man. But I hear it not that the Spaniard was hanged for his labor; if I had, I would have told you it too.

They fell out, as the tale goeth, about a whore. O Lord, what whoredom is used nowadays, as I hear by the relation of honest

[3] *Chance-medley:* accident or casualty not purely accidental (as in "manslaughter by chance-medley").

[4] St. Augustine, *De vera religione* (ed. William Green, *Corpus Scriptorum Latinorum,* vol. LXXVII, Vienna, 1961), cap. XIV, p. 20. As usual, Latimer quotes with abandon. The text reads: *Nunc vero usque adeo peccatum voluntarium malum est, ut nullo modo sit peccatum si non sit voluntarium.*

men, which tell it not after a worldly sort, as though they rejoiced at it, but heavily, with heavy hearts, how God is dishonored by whoredom in this city of London; yea, the Bank [5] when it stood was never so common! If it be true that is told, it is marvel that it doth not sink and that the earth gapeth not and swalloweth it up. It is wonderful that the city of London doth suffer such whoredom unpunished. God hath suffered long of His great lenity, mercy, and benignity; but He will punish sharply at length if we do not repent. There is some place in London, as they say, "Immunity, impunity." [6] What should I call it? A privileged place for whoredom. The Lord Mayor hath nothing to do there; the sheriffs they cannot meddle with it; and the quest they not inquire of it. And there men do bring their whores, yea, other men's wives, and there is no reformation of it.

There is such dicing houses also, they say, as hath not been wont to be, where young gentlemen dice away their thrift. And where dicing is, there are other follies also. For the love of God let remedy be had; let us wrestle and strive against sin. Men of England, in times past, when they would exercise themselves—for we must needs have some recreation; our bodies cannot endure without some exercise—they were wont to go abroad in the fields ashooting; but now is turned into glossing,[7] gulling, and whoring within the house. The art of shooting hath been in times past much esteemed in this realm. It is a gift of God that He hath given us to excel all other nations withal; it hath been God's instrument whereby He hath given us many victories against our enemies. But now we have taken up whoring in towns instead of shooting in the fields. A wondrous thing, that so excellent a gift of God should be so little esteemed! I

[5] The borough of Southwark, commonly called the Bankside. Latimer is referring specifically to the houses of prostitution (the "stews") which were "privileged," with some attempt at regulation, until they were suppressed in 1546. See John Stow, *A Survey of London,* ed. C. L. Kingsford (Oxford, 1908), II, 54–55.

[6] Apparently the reference is to the notorius abuses of the privilege of sanctuary which had long been attached to the collegiate church and parish of St. Martin-le-Grand. The privilege was abolished in the reign of James I (Stow, I, 307–309).

[7] *Glossing:* gluttony.

desire you, my lords, even as ye love the honor and glory of God and intend to remove His indignation, let there be sent forth some proclamation, some sharp proclamation to the justices of peace, for they do not their duty. Justices now be no justices. There be many good acts made for this matter already. Charge them upon their allegiance that this singular benefit of God may be practiced and that it be not turned into bolling,[8] glossing, and whoring within the towns; for they be negligent in executing these laws of shooting. In my time my poor father was as diligent to teach me to shoot as to learn any other thing; and so I think other men did their children. He taught me how to draw, how to lay my body in my bow and not to draw with strength of arms, as other nations do, but with strength of the body. I had my bows bought me according to my age and strength; as I increased in them, so my bows were made bigger and bigger. For men shall never shoot well except they be brought up in it. It is a goodly art, a wholesome kind of exercise, and much commended in physic.

Marcilius Ficinus, in his book *De triplici vita*[9]—it is a great while since I read him now—but I remember he commendeth this kind of exercise and saith that it wrestleth against many kinds of diseases. In the reverence of God let it be continued; let a proclamation go forth charging the justices of peace that they see such acts and statutes kept as were made for this purpose.

I will to my matter. I intend this day to entreat of a piece of scripture written in the beginning of the fifth chapter of Luke. I am occasioned to take this place by a book[10] sent to the King's Majesty that dead is by Master Pole. It is a text that he doth greatly abuse for the supremity; he racks it and violents it to serve for the maintenance of the Bishop of Rome. And as he did enforce the tother place that I

[8] *Bolling:* boozing.

[9] This work was published at Strasbourg, probably in 1506. Ficino alludes in several places to the value of physical exercise, but I have found no specific references to the virtue of archery.

[10] *Pro ecclesiasticae unitatis defensione* (sometimes cited as *De unione ecclesiasticae*), 1537. It is a vigorous defense of papal supremacy.

entreated of last, so did he enforce this also to serve his matter. The story is this. Our Saviour Christ was come now to the bank of the water of Gennesaret. The people were come to Him and flocked about Him to hear Him preach. And Jesus took a boat that was standing at the pool (it was Simon's boat) and went into it. And sitting in the boat He preached to them that were on the bank. And when He had preached and taught them, He spake to Simon and bade him launch out further into the deep and loose his nets to catch fish. And Simon made answer and said, "Master, we have labored all night, but we caught nothing; howbeit at Thy commandment, because Thou biddest us, we will go to it again" (Luke 5:5). And so they did and caught a great draught, a miraculous draught, so much that the net brake; and they called to their fellows that were by—for they had two boats—to come to help them; and they came and filled both their boats so full that they were nigh drowning.

This is the story. That I may declare this text so that it may be to the honor of God and edification of your souls and mine both, I shall desire you to help me with your prayer, in the which, etc.

Factum est autem (saith the text) *cum turba irrueret in eum.* St. Luke tells the story, "And it came to pass when the people pressed upon Him" (Luke 5:1), so that He was in peril to be cast into the pond, they rushed so fast upon Him and made such throng to Him. A wondrous thing! What a desire the people had in those days to hear our Saviour Christ preach! And the cause may be gathered of the latter end of the chapter that went before. Our Saviour Christ had preached unto them and healed the sick folks of such diseases and maladies as they had, and therefore the people would have retained Him still. But He made them answer and said, *Et aliis civitatibus oportet me evangelizare regnum Dei, nam in hoc missus sum,* "I must preach the kingdom of God to other cities also; I must show them My Father's will, for I came for that purpose; I was sent to preach the Word of God" (Luke 4:43). Our Saviour Christ said how He must not tarry in one place, for He was sent to the world to preach everywhere.

Is it not a marvelous thing that our unpreaching prelates can read this place and yet preach no more than they do? I marvel that they can go quietly to bed and see how He allureth them with His example to be diligent in their office. Here is a godly lesson also how our Saviour Christ fled from glory. If these ambitious parsons that climb to honor by bywalks inordinately would consider this example of Jesus Christ, they should come to more honor than they do; for when they seek honor by such bywalks, they come to confusion. Honor followeth them that flee from it. Our Saviour Christ gat Him away early in the morning and went unto the wilderness. I would they would follow this example of Christ and not seek honor by such bywalks as they do. But what did the people when He had hid Himself? They smelled Him out in the wilderness and came unto Him by flocks and followed Him a great number. But where read you that a great number of scribes and Pharisees and bishops followed Him?

There is a doctor that writeth of this place; his name is Doctor Gorham, Nicholas Gorham. I knew him to be a school doctor a great while ago, but I never knew him to be an interpreter of scripture till now of late. He saith thus: *Major devotio in laicis vetulis quam in clericis, etc.* "There is more devotion," saith he, "in lay folk and old wives, these simple folk, the vulgar people, than in the clerks."[11] They be better affect to the word of God than those that be of the clergy. I marvel not at the sentence, but I marvel to find such a sentence in such a doctor. If I should say so much, it would be said to me that it is an evil bird that defiles his own nest; and, *Nemo laeditur nisi a seipso,* "There is no man hurt but of his own self." There was verified the saying of our Saviour Christ which He spake in another place: *Ubicumque fuerit cadaver, ibi congregabuntur aquilae,* "Wheresoever a dead carrion is, thither will

[11] The exact reading of the sentence is as follows: *Nam in laicis & vetulis quamque major reperitur deuotio quam in clericis* (*Commentaria Nicolai Gorrani in quatuor Evangelia* [Cologne, 1537], f. 327). Gorranus was a Dominican theologian of the thirteenth century.

the eagles gather" (Matt. 24:28). Our Saviour Christ compares Himself to a dead carrion, for where the carrion is there will the eagles be. And though it be an evil smell to us and stinks in a man's nose, yet it is a sweet smell to the eagles; they will seek it out. So the people sought out Christ; they smelt His savor; He was a sweet smell to them. He is *odor vitae ad vitam,* "the smell of life to life." They flocked about Him like eagles. Christ was the carrion and the people were the eagles. They had no pleasure to hear the scribes and the Pharisees; they stank in their nose; their doctrine was unsavory; it was but of lolions,[12] of decimations, of aniseed and cummin,[13] and such gear. There was no comfort in it for sore consciences; there was no consolation for wounded souls. There was no remedy for sins as was in Christ's doctrine. His doctrine eased the burden of the soul; it was sweet to the common people and sour to the scribes. It was such comfort and pleasure to them that they came flocking about Him.

Wherefore came they? *Ut audirent verbum Dei* (Luke 5:1). It was a good coming; they came to hear the word of God. It was not to be thought that they came all of one mind to hear the word of God. It is likely that in so great a multitude some came of curiosity to hear some novels; and some came smelling a sweet savor, to have consolation and comfort of God's word. For we cannot be saved without hearing of the word; it is a necessary way to salvation. We cannot be saved without faith, and faith cometh by hearing of the word. *Fides ex auditu.* "And how shall they hear without a preacher?" (Romans 10:14). I tell you it is the footsteps[14] of the

[12] *Lolions:* included in the *OED* list of spurious words, with the suggestion that it may be a misprint for *lotions* in the sense of ablutions. If so, the allusion is probably to Matt. 23:25: "Woe be to you, scribes and Pharisees, hypocrites, for ye make clean the utter side of the cup and of the platter, but within they are full of bribery and excess" (Tyndale, 1525). Cf. the next note.

[13] *Decimations . . . cummin:* cf. Matt. 23:23: "Woe be to you, scribes and Pharisees, dissemblers, which tithe mint, anise, and cummin, and leave the weightier matters of the law undone: judgment, mercy, and faith" (Tyndale, 1525).

[14] *Footsteps:* the bottom steps.

ladder of heaven, of our salvation. There must be preachers if we look to be saved. I told you of this gradation before in the tenth to the Romans; consider it well. I had rather ye should come of a naughty mind to hear the word of God for novelty or for curiosity to hear some pastime than to be away. I had rather ye should come as the tale is by the gentlewoman of London. One of her neighbors met her in the street and said, "Mistress, whither go ye?" "Marry," said she, "I am going to St. Thomas of Acres[15] to the sermon; I could not sleep all this last night, and I am going now thither; I never failed of a good nap there."

And so I had rather ye should go anapping to the sermons than not to go at all. For with what mind soever ye come, though ye come for an ill purpose, yet peradventure ye may chance to be caught ere ye go; the preacher may chance to catch you on his hook. Rather than ye should not come at all, I would have you come of curiosity, as St. Augustine came to hear St. Ambrose. When St. Augustine came to Milan (he tells the story himself, in the end of his book of Confessions), he was very desirous to hear St. Ambrose, not for any love he had to the doctrine that he taught, but to hear his eloquence, whether it was so great as the speech was and as the bruit went. Well, before he departed St. Ambrose caught him on his hook and converted him,[16] so that he became of a Manichee[17] and of a Platonist[18] a good Christian, a defender of Christ's religion and of

[15] A hospital and chapel in Cheapside endowed by Thomas, son of Theobald of Halles, and his wife Agnes, the sister of Thomas à Becket. "They gave to the master and brethren the lands with the appurtenances that sometime were Gilbert Becket's, father to the said Thomas, in the which he was born, there to make a church." After the surrender it was sold to the Mercers' Company (Stow, I, 269; II, 144). It is possible that Latimer was making a sly allusion to a particular preacher.

[16] St. Augustine, *Confessions,* lib. V, cap. xiii–xiv (Loeb Classical Library, [London, 1912], I, 254–259).

[17] A believer in the doctrines of Manes, a Persian of the third century, who taught a dualistic system according to which the soul, the child of the kingdom of light, seeks to escape from the body, the kingdom of darkness. Manes, a Zoroastrian who became a Christian, attempted to unite Zoroastrian dualism with Christian soteriology.

[18] A follower of the Alexandrian school of neo-Platonism.

the faith afterward. So I would have you come to sermons. It is declared in many mo places of scripture how necessary preaching is, as this, *Evangelium est potentia Dei ad sa[lutem] omni credenti,* "The preaching of the gospel is the power of God to every man that doth believe" (Romans 1:16). He means God's word opened; it is the instrument and the thing whereby we are saved.

Beware, beware ye diminish not this office, for if ye do ye decay God's power to all that do believe. Christ saith, consonant to the same, *Nisi quis renatus fuerit e supernis, non potest videre regnum Dei,* "Except a man be born again from above, he cannot see the kingdom of God" (John 3:3). He must have a regeneration. And what is this regeneration? It is not to be christened in water, as these firebrands expound it, and nothing else. How is it to be expounded then? St. Peter showeth that one place of scripture declareth another. It is the circumstance and collation of places that make scripture plain. *Regeneramur autem,* saith St. Peter, "and we be born again." How? *Non ex semine mortali, sed immortali,* "Not by a mortal seed, but by an immortal." What is this immortal seed? *Per sermonem Dei viventis,* "By the word of the living God" (I Peter 1:23). By the Word of God preached and opened. Thus cometh in our new birth.

Here you may see how necessary this office is to our salvation. This is the thing that the devil wrestleth most against; it hath been all his study to decay this office. He worketh against it as much as he can; he hath prevailed too much, too much in it. He hath set up a state of unpreaching prelacy in this realm this seven hundred year, a state of unpreaching prelacy. He hath made unpreaching prelates; he hath stirred up by heaps to persecute this office in the title of heresy. He hath stirred up the magistrates to persecute it in the title of sedition; and he hath stirred up the people to persecute it with exprobations[19] and slanderous words, as by the name of "new learning," "strange preaching." And with impropriations he hath

[19] *Exprobations:* (variant of *exprobrations*) reproaches, upbraidings.

turned preaching into private masses. If a priest should have left mass undone on a Sunday within these ten years, all England should have wondered at it; but they might have left off the sermon twenty Sundays and never have been blamed. And thus by these impropriations private masses were set up and preaching of God's word trodden under foot. But what doth he now? What doth he now? He stirs men up to outrageous rearing of rents, that poor men shall not be able to find [20] their children at the school to be divines.

What an unreasonable devil is this! He provides a great while beforehand for the time that is to come. He hath brought up now of late the most monstrous kind of covetousness that ever was heard of. He hath invented fee farming [21] of benefices, and all to decay this office of preaching, insomuch that when any man hereafter shall have a benefice he may go where he will, for any house he shall have to dwell upon or any glebe land to keep hospitality withal. But he must take up a chamber in an alehouse and there sit and play at the tables all the day. A goodly curate! He hath caused also, through this monstrous kind of covetousness, patrons to sell their benefices. Yea, what doth he more? He gets him to the university and causeth great men and squires to send their sons thither and put out poor scholars that should be divines, for their parents intend not they shall be preachers but that they may have a show of learning. Tut, it were too long to declare unto you what deceit and means the devil hath found to decay the office of salvation, this office of regeneration.

But to return to my matter. The people came to hear the word of God. They heard Him with silence. I remember now a saying of St. Chrysostom, and peradventure it might come hereafter in better place, but yet I will take it whilst it cometh to my mind. The saying is this, *Et loquentem eum audierunt in silentio, seriem locutionis non interrumpentes.* "They heard Him," saith he, "in silence, not

[20] *Find:* provide for.

[21] *Fee farming:* the practice whereby the patron of the benefice retained a part of the income for himself.

interrupting the order of his preaching."[22] He means they heard him quietly, without any shuffling of feet or walking up and down. Surely it is an ill misorder that folk shall be walking up and down in the sermon time, as I have seen in this place this Lent; and there shall be such huzzing and buzzing in the preacher's ear that it maketh him oftentimes to forget his matter. Oh, let us consider the King's Majesty's goodness! This place was prepared for banqueting of the body; and His Majesty hath made it a place for the comfort of the soul and to have the Word of God preached in it, showing hereby that he would have all his subjects at it if it might be possible.

Consider what the King's Majesty hath done for you; he alloweth you all to hear with him. Consider where ye be. First, ye ought to have a reverence to God's word; and though it be preached by poor men, yet it is the same word that our Saviour spake. Consider also the presence of the King's Majesty, God's high vicar in earth. Having a respect to his personage, ye ought to have reverence to it and consider that he is God's high minister and yet alloweth you all to be partakers with him of the hearing of God's word. This benefit of his would be thankfully taken, and it would be highly esteemed. Hear in silence, as Chrysostom saith. It may chance that some in the company may fall sick or be diseased; if there be any such, let them go away with silence; let them leave their salutations till they come in the Court; let them depart with silence. I took occasion of Chrysostom's words to admonish you of this thing.

What should be the cause that our Saviour Christ went into the boat? The scripture calleth it *navis* or *navicula,* but it was no ship. It was a fisher's boat; they were not able to have a ship. What should be the cause why He would not stand on the bank and preach there, but He desired Peter to draw the boat somewhat from the shore into

[22] "For when He spake, they used to listen in silence, not making any intrusions, nor breaking in upon the train of His thought" (*In Matthaeum Homilia XXV,* cap. 5, Migne, *Patrologiae Graecae,* ser. 2, vol. LVII, col. 327).

the midst of the water? What should be the cause? What should be the cause? One cause was for that He might sit there more commodiously than on the bank. Another cause was for that He was like to be thrust into the pond of the people that came unto Him. Why, our Saviour Christ might have withstood them; He was strong enough to have kept Himself from thrusting into the water. He was stronger than they all, and if He had listed He might have stood on the water as well as He walked on the water. Truth it is, so might He have done indeed. But as it was sometime His pleasure to show the power of His Godhead, so He declared now the infirmity and imbecility of His manhood.

Here He giveth us an example what we shall do. We must not tempt God by any miracles, so long as we may walk by ordinary ways. As our Saviour Christ, when the devil had Him on the top of the temple and would have had Him cast Himself down, He made him this answer, *Non tentabis Dominum Deum tuum,* "Thou shalt not tempt thy Lord God" (Luke 4:12). As if He should have said, "We may not tempt God at all." It is no time now to show any miracles; there is another way to go down by grecings.[23] Thus He did to show us an example that we must not tempt God, except it be in extreme necessity, and when we cannot otherways remedy the matter to leave it all to God. Else we may not tempt the majesty of His Deity. Beware tempting of God.

Well, He comes to Simon's boat. And why rather to Simon's boat than another? I will answer as I find in experience in myself. I came hither today from Lambeth [24] in a wherry; and when I came to take my boat, the watermen came about me, as the manner is, and he would have me, and he would have me. I took one of them. Now ye will ask me why I came in that boat rather than in another? Because I would go into that that I see stand next me; it stood more

[23] *Grecings:* a flight of steps.

[24] The official London residence of the archbishops of Canterbury. When he was in London during the reign of Edward VI, Latimer made his home there with Archbishop Cranmer.

commodiously for me. And so did Christ by Simon's boat; it stood nearer for Him; He saw a better seat in it. A good natural reason. Now come the papists and they will make a mystery of it; they will pick out the supremacy of the Bishop of Rome in Peter's boat. We may make allegories enough of every place in scripture, but surely it must needs be a simple matter that stands on so weak a ground.

But ye shall see further. He desired Peter to thrust out his boat from the shore. He desired him. Here was a good lesson for the Bishop of Rome and all his College of Cardinals to learn humility and gentleness. *Rogabat eum,* "He desired him" (Luke 4:3). It was gently done of Him, without any austerity, but with all urbanity, mildness and softness, and humility. What an example is this that He gives them here! But they spy it not. They can see nothing but the supremacy of the Bishop of Rome. A wondrous thing, what sight they have; they see nothing but the supremacy of the Bishop of Rome! *Imperabatis ovibus meis,* saith Ezekiel, *cum avaritia et austeritate, et dispersae sunt absque pastore,* "Ye have ruled my sheep, and commanded them with great lordliness, austerity, and power; and thus ye have dispersed my sheep abroad" (Ezek. 34:4–5). And why? There was no shepherd. They had wanted one a great while. Rome hath been many hundred years without a good shepherd. They would not learn to rule them gently; they had rule over them, but it was with cursings, excommunications, with great austerity and thunderbolts and the devil and all, to maintain their unpreaching prelacy. I beseech God open their eyes that they may see the truth and not be blinded with those things that no man can see but they.

It followeth in the text, *Sedens docebat de navi,* "He taught sitting" (Luke 5:3). Preachers, belike, were sitters in those days. As it is written in another place, *Sedent in cathedra Moysi,* "They sit in the chair of Moses" (Matt. 23:2). I would our preachers would preach sitting or standing, one way or other. It was a godly pulpit that our Saviour Christ had gotten Him here, an old rotten boat, and yet He preached His Father's will, His Father's message, out of this pulpit. He regarded the people more than the pulpit. He cared not for the pulpit so He might do the people good. Indeed, it is to be commended for the preacher to stand or sit, as the place is. But I would not have it so superstitiously esteemed but that a good preacher may declare the Word of God sitting on a horse or preaching in a tree. And yet if this should be done, the unpreaching prelates would laugh it to scorn. And though it be good to have the pulpit set up in churches, that the people may resort thither, yet I would not have it so superstitiously used but that in a profane place the Word of God might be preached sometimes; and I would not have the people offended withal, no more than they be with our Saviour Christ's preaching out of a boat. And yet to have pulpits in churches, it is very well done to have them, but they would be occupied; for it is a vain thing to have them as they stand in many churches.

I heard of a bishop of England that went on visitation, and, as it was the custom, when the bishop should come and be rung into the town, the great bell's clapper was fallen down; the tyall[25] was broken, so that the bishop could not be rung into the town. There was a great matter made of this, and the chief of the parish were much blamed for it in the visitation. The bishop was somewhat quick with them and signified that he was much offended. They made their answers and excused themselves as well as they could. "It was a chance," said they, "that the clapper brake, and we could not get it amended by and by. We must tarry till we can have done it; it shall be amended as shortly as may be." Among the other, there was one wiser than the rest and he comes me to the bishop. "Why, my lord," saith he, "doth Your Lordship make so great matter of the bell that lacketh his clapper? Here is a bell," saith he, and pointed to the pulpit, "that hath lacked a clapper this twenty years. We have a parson that fetcheth out of this benefice £50 every year, but we never see him." I warrant you the bishop was an unpreaching

[25] *Tyall* (variant of *tial*): the rope or chain by which the clapper was suspended.

prelate. He could find fault with the bell that wanted a clapper to ring him into the town, but he could not find any fault with the parson that preached not at his benefice. Ever this office of preaching hath been least regarded; it hath scant had the name of God's service. They must sing *Salve festa dies*[26] about the church, that no man was the better for it but to show their gay coats and garments.

I came once myself to a place, riding on a journey homeward from London, and I sent word overnight into the town that I would preach there in the morning, because it was holiday and methought it was an holiday's work. The church stood in my way, and I took my horse and my company and went thither. I thought I should have found a great company in the church, and when I came there the church door was fast locked. I tarried there half an hour and more. At last the key was found, and one of the parish comes to me and says, "Sir, this is a busy day with us. We cannot hear you; it is Robin Hood's Day.[27] The parish are gone abroad to gather for Robin Hood. I pray you let them not." I was fain there to give place to Robin Hood. I thought my rochet should have been regarded, though I were not; but it would not serve, it was fain to give place to Robin Hood's men. It is no laughing matter, my friends; it is a weeping matter, a heavy matter; a heavy matter, under the pretense for gathering for Robin Hood, a traitor and a thief, to put out a preacher, to have his office less esteemed, to prefer Robin Hood before the ministration of God's word. And all this hath come of unpreaching prelates. This realm hath been ill provided for, that it hath had such corrupt judgments in it to prefer Robin Hood to God's word. If the bishops had been preachers, there should never have been any such thing. But we have a good hope of better. We have had a good beginning. I beseech God to continue it! But I tell you, it is far wide that the people have such judgments; the bishops they could laugh at it. What was that to them? They would have

[26] Presumably the refrain of a medieval hymn sung in processionals on festal days.

[27] May 1. Attacks on the Robin Hood ballads and the festivities associated with Robin Hood's Day occur frequently in the utterances of the reformers.

them continue in their ignorance still and themselves in unpreaching prelacy.

Well, sitting, sitting. "He sat down and taught." The text doth tell us that He taught, but it doth not tell us what He taught. If I were a papist, I could tell what He said; I would, in the Pope's judgment, show what He taught. For the Bishop of Rome hath *in scrinio pectoris sui* the true understanding of scriptures. If he call a council of College of Cardinals, he hath authority to determine the supper of the Lord, as he did at the Council of Florence! [28] And Pope Nicholas [29] and Bishop Lanfranc [30] shall come and expound this place and say that our Saviour Christ said thus: "Peter, I do mean this by sitting in thy boat, that thou shalt go to Rome and be bishop there five-and-twenty years after mine ascension; and all thy successors shall be rulers of the universal church after thee."

Here would I place also holy water and holy bread and all unwritten verities, if I were a papist, and that scripture is not to be

[28] The council convened in 1438 by Pope Eugenius IV in opposition to the Council of Basel, which was still in session. The allusion is to the third part of the fifth decretal promulgated at that council, which asserts the doctrine of transubstantiation with great precision. It insists also on the importance of mixing water with the wine: *Non enim debet in calicem aut vinum solum aut aqua sola offeri, sed utrumque permixtum: quia utrumque id est, sanguis et aqua, ex latere Christi profluxisse legitur* (*Sacrorum Conciliorum Nova et Amplissima Collectio*, ed. G. D. Mansi *et al.*, XXXI [Venice, 1798], col. 1056–1057; facsimile repr. [Paris, 1906]). The passage is of interest in connection with the following statement in Latimer's "Third Sermon before Edward VI": "I remember how scrupulous I was in my time of blindness and ignorance. When I should say mass, I have put in water twice or thrice for failing, insomuch that when I have been at my *memento* I have had a grudge in my conscience, fearing I had not put in water enough."

[29] Titulus V among the decretals of Pope Nicholas I (858–867) contains eleven items all of which in one way or another assert the supremacy of Rome (*Sacrorum Conciliorum*, XV, cols. 436–437). It is possible, however, that the allusion is to Nicholas V, the successor of Eugenius IV, during whose pontificate the conciliar movement collapsed and the papal authority was firmly established.

[30] Lanfranc, Archbishop of Canterbury from 1070 to 1089. In a controversy with the Archbishop of York in 1072 he vigorously affirmed the primacy of Rome on the basis of *Tu es Petrus*. But he made no reference to Peter's boat (*Beati Lanfranci . . . Opera omnia* [Paris, 1648], p. 378).

expounded by any private interpretation but by our holy father and his College of Cardinals. This is a great deal a better place than *Duc in altum* (Luke 5:4). But what was Christ's sermon? It may soon be gathered what it was. He is always like Himself. His first sermon was, *Paenitentiam agite,*[31] "Do penance; your living is naught; repent." Again, at Nazareth, when He read in the temple and preached remission of sins and healing of wounded consciences, and in the long Sermon in the Mount, He was always like Himself. He never dissented from Himself.

Oh, there is a writer hath a jolly text here, and his name is Dionysius.[32] I chanced to meet with his book in My Lord of Canterbury's library. He was a monk of the Charterhouse. I marvel to find such a sentence in that author. What taught Christ in this sermon? Marry, saith he, it is not written. And he addeth more unto it: *Evangelistae tantum scripserunt de sermonibus et miraculis Christi quantum cognoverunt, inspirante Deo, sufficere ad aedificationem ecclesiae, ad confirmationem fidei, et ad salutem animarum.*[33] It is true. It is not written. All His miracles were not written, so neither were all His sermons written; yet for all that the evangelists did write so much as was necessary. "They wrote so much of the miracles and sermons of Christ as they knew by God's inspiration to be sufficient for the edifying of the church, the confirmation of our faith, and the health of our souls." If this be true, as it is indeed, where be [un]written verities? I marvel not at the sentence, but to find it in such an author. Jesus! what authority he gives to God's word! But God would that such men should be witness with the authority of His book, will they nill they.

Now to draw towards an end. It followeth in the text, *Duc in altum*. Here comes in the supremity of the Bishop of Rome. When our Saviour Christ had made an end of His sermon and had fed

[31] Apparently the reference is to Mark 1:14–15, but the Latin is that of Matt. 3:2.

[32] Dionysius Carthusianus (Denis le Chartreux), d. 1471.

[33] *In quatuor Evangelistae Enarrationes* (Cologne, 1533), *In Evangelium Lucae,* cap. V, art xii, sig. b6.

their souls, He provided for their bodies. First He began with the soul; Christ's word is the food of it. Now He goeth to the body. He hath charge of them both; He giveth food for them both. We must commit the feeding of the body and of the soul to Him. Well, He saith to Peter, *Duc in altum;* "Launch into the depth; put forth thy boat farther into the deep of the water; loose your nets; now fish" (Luke 5:4). As who would say, "Your souls are now fed; I have taught you My doctrine; now I will confirm it with a miracle." Lo, sir, here is *Duc in altum*. Here Peter was made a great man, say the papists, and all his successors after him. And this is derived of these few words, "Launch into the deep." And their argument is this: He spake to Peter only, and He spake to him in the singular number; *ergo,* He gave him such a pre-eminence above the rest. A goodly argument! I ween it be a syllogismus, *in quem terra pontus*.[34]

I will make a like argument. Our Saviour Christ said to Judas, when he was about to betray Him, *Quod facis fac citius* (John 13:27). Now when He spake to Peter there were none of His disciples by but James and John, but when He spake to Judas they were all present. Well, He said unto him, *Quod facis fac citius,* "Speed thy business that thou hast in thy head; do it."[35] He gave him here a secret monition that He knew what he intended, if Judas had had grace to have taken it and repented. He spake in the singular number to him; *ergo,* He gave him some pre-eminence. Belike He made him a cardinal; and it might full well be, for they have followed Judas ever since. Here is as good a ground for the College of Cardinals as the other is for the supremity of the Bishop of Rome. "Our Saviour Christ," say they, "spake only to Peter for pre-eminence because he was chief of the apostles, and you can show none other cause; *ergo,* this is the cause why He spake to him in the singular number." I daresay there is never a wherryman at Westminster Bridge but he can answer to this and give a natural reason of it. He knoweth that one man is able to shove the boat, but one man was not able to cast out the nets. And therefore He said in the

[34] I.e., a foolish syllogism.

[35] Later editions omit the two sentences which follow.

plural number, *Laxate retia,* "Loose your nets" (Luke 5:4). And He said in the singular number to Peter, "Launch out the boat." Why? Because he was able to do it. But He spake the other in the plural number because he was not able to convey the boat and cast out the nets too. One man could not do it.[36] This would the wherryman say, and that with better reason than to make such a mystery of it as no man can spy but they. And the cause why He spake to all was to show that He will have all Christian men to work for their living. It is He that sends food both for the body and soul, but He will not send it without labor. He will have all Christian people to labor for it; He will use our labor as a mean whereby He sendeth our food.

This was a wondrous miracle of our Saviour Christ, and did it not only to allure them to His discipleship but also for our commodity. It was a seal to seal His doctrine withal. Now ye know that such as be keepers of seals, as my Lord Chancellor and such other, whatsoever they be, they do not always seal; they have a sealing time. For I have heard poor men complain that they have been put off from time to time of sealing to another, till all their money were spent. And as they have times to seal in, so our Saviour Christ had His time of sealing. When He was here in earth with His apostles, and in the time of the primitive church, Christ's doctrine was sufficiently sealed already with seals of His own making. What should our seals do? What need we to seal His seal? It is a confirmed doctrine already.

Oh, Luther, when he came into that world first and disputed against the Decretals,[37] the Clementines,[38] Alexandrines,[39] Extrava-

[36] Although he claimed not to have read Dionysius Carthusianus for a long time, Latimer seems to have had a pretty clear recollection of the following: *Ait autem singulariter Petro, Duc, quia ab solo fieri quivit. Pluraliterque adjungit, Laxate, quia hoc a pluribus fiere aptius potuit* (*loc. cit.*).

[37] The second division of the canon law, consisting of letters and decretals of various Popes from ca. 1148 to ca. 1300.

[38] Part of the third division of the canon law. It includes the constitutions of Clement V and the decrees of the Council of Vienne (1311).

[39] The *Summa* of Pope Alexander III, an important early commentary on the *Decretum Gratiani* (Part I of the canon law).

gantines,[40] what ado had he! But ye will say, "Peradventure he was deceived in some things." I will not take upon me to defend him in all points. I will not stand to it that all that he wrote was true; I think he would not so himself. For there is no man but he may err. He came to further and further knowledge, but surely he was a goodly instrument. Well, I say, when he preached first, they called upon him to do miracles. They were wrought before,[41] and so we need to do no miracles. Indeed, when the popish prelates preached first they had need of miracles, and the devil wrought some in the preaching of purgatory. But what kind of miracles these were all England doth know. But it will not know. A wonderful thing that the people will continue in their blindness and ignorance still! We have great utility of the miracles of our Saviour Jesus Christ. He doth signify unto us by this wonderful work that He is Lord as well of the water as of the land. A good comfort for those that be on the water, when they be in any tempest or danger, to call upon Him.

The fish here came at His commandment. Here we may learn that all things in the water are subject to Christ. Peter said, "Sir, we have labored all night and have not caught one fin; howbeit at your word we will to it afresh" (Luke 5:5). By this it appeareth that the gain, the lucre, the revenues that we get must not be imputed to our labor; we may not say, "Gramercy,[42] labor." It is not our labor; it is our Saviour Christ that sendeth us living. Yet must we labor, for He that said to Peter, "Labor," and He that bade the fishers labor, bids all men to labor in their business. There be some people that ascribe their gains, their increase gotten by any faculty, to the devil. Is there any, trow ye, in England would say so? Now if any man should come to another and say he gat his living by the devil, he would fall out with him. There is not a man in England that so saith, yet is

[40] Part of the third division of the canon law. It consists of twenty decretals and epistles of John XXII and seventy-three others ranging from Boniface VIII to Sixtus IV (1294–1484).

[41] *They . . . before:* i.e., all the necessary miracles were recorded in scripture.

[42] *Gramercy:* thank you (Fr. *grand-merci*).

there some that think it. For all that get it with false buying and selling, with circumvention, with usury, impostures, mixed wares, false weights, deceiving their lords and masters—all those that get their goods on this fashion, what do they think but that the devil sends them gains and riches? For they be his, being unlawfully gotten. What is this to say but that the devil is author of their gains when they be so gotten? For God inhibits them. *Deus non volens iniquitatem tu es,* "God will no iniquity." These folk are greatly deceived.

There be some, again, impute all to their labors and works. Yea, on the holy day they cannot find in their hearts to come to the temple to the blessed Communion; they must be working at home. These are wide again on the other side. And some there be that think if they work nothing at all they shall have enough. They will have no good exercise, but gape and think that God will send meat into their mouths. And these are far wide. They must work. He bade the fishers work; our Saviour Christ bade Peter work; and He that said so to them says the same to us, every man in his art. *Benedictio Dei facit divitem,* "The blessing of God maketh a man rich" (Prov. 10:22). He lets His sun shine upon the wicked, as well as upon the good; He sends riches both to good and bad. But this blessing turns to them into a malediction and a curse; it increaseth their damnation. St. Paul, writing to the Thessalonians, did put an order how every man should work in his vocation: *Cum essemus apud vos, hoc praecipiebamus vobis, ut si quis nollet operari is nec edat.* "When I was among you," saith he, "I made this ordinance, that whosoever would not do the work of his vocation should have no meat" (II Thess. 3:10). It were a good ordinance in a commonweal that every man should be set on work, every man in his vocation. "Let him have no meat."

Now he saith, furthermore, *Audivimus quosdam inter vos versantes inordinate nihil operis facientes,* "I hear say there is some amongst you that lives inordinately" (*ibid.,* 3:11). What is that word "inordinately"? Idly, giving themselves to no occupation for their living; *curiose agentes,* curious men, given to curiosity, to searching what other men do. St. Paul saith "he heard say"; he could not tell whether it were so or no. But he took occasion of hearing say to set out a good and wholesome doctrine: *His autem qui sunt ejusmodi praecipimus et obsecramus.* "We command and desire you, for the reverence of God, if there be any such, that they will do the works of their vocation and go quietly to their occupation and so eat their own bread" (*ibid.,* 3:12). Else it is not their own; it is other men's meat.

Our Saviour Christ, before He began His preaching, lived of His occupation; He was a carpenter and gat His living with great labor. Therefore let no man disdain or think scorn to follow Him in a mean living, a mean vocation, or a common calling and occupation. For as He blessed our nature with taking upon Him the shape of man, so in His doing He blessed all occupations and arts. This is a notable example to signify that He abhors all idleness. When He was a carpenter, then He went and did the work of His calling; and when He was a preacher, He did the works of that calling. He was no unpreaching prelate. The Bishop of Rome should have learned that of Him. And these gainers with false arts, what be they? They are never content with that they have, though it be never so much. And they that are true dealers are satisfied with that God sends, though it be never so little. *Quaestus magnus pietas cum animo sua sorte contento,* "Godliness is great gain; it is lucre enough, it is vantage enough, to be content with that that God sends" (I Tim. 6:6). The faithful cannot lack; the unfaithful is ever lacking, though he have never so much.

I will now make an end. *Labores manuum tuarum;* let us all labor. Christ teacheth us to labor; yea, the Bishop of Rome himself He teacheth him to labor, rather than to be head of the church. Let us put our trust in God; *Labores manuum tuarum.* "Cast thy care upon the Lord, and He will nourish thee and feed thee" (Psalm 55:22). Again, the prophet saith, *Nunquam vidi justum derelictum, nec semen ejus quaerens panem,* "I never saw the righteous man forsaken nor his seed to seek his bread" (Psalm 37:25). It is infidelity, infidelity, that mars all together.

Well, to my text: *Labores manuum tuarum quia manducabis, beatus es, et bene tibi erit, etc.,* "Because thou eatest the labors of thy hands, that that God sends thee of thy labor" (Psalm 128:2). Every man must labor; yea, though he be a king yet he must labor. For I know no man hath a greater labor than a king. What is his labor? To study God's book, to see that there be no unpreaching prelates in his realm nor bribing judges, to see to all estates, to provide for the poor, to see victuals good cheap. Is not this a labor, trow ye? Thus if thou dost labor, exercising the works of thy vocation, thou eatest the meat that God sends thee. And then it followeth, *Beatus es,* "Thou art a blessed man in God's favor," *et bene tibi erit,* "and it shall go well with thee in this world," both in body and soul, for God provides for both. How shalt thou provide for thy soul? Go hear sermons. How for the body? Labor in thy vocation. And then shall it be well with thee, both here and in the world to come, through the faith and merits of our Saviour Jesus Christ, to Whom with the Father and the Holy Ghost be praise for ever and ever, world without end. Amen.

The End of the Sixth Sermon

SEVENTH SERMON BEFORE KING EDWARD VI APRIL 19, 1549

THE SEVENTH SERMON OF MASTER HUGH LATIMER, WHICH HE PREACHED BEFORE THE KING'S MAJESTY WITHIN HIS GRACE'S PALACE AT WESTMINSTER THE NINETEENTH DAY OF APRIL

Quaecumque scripta sunt ad nostram doctrinam scripta sunt (Romans 15:4)
"All things that be written, they be written to be our doctrine."

BY OCCASION of this text, most honorable audience, I have walked this Lent in the broad field of scripture and used my liberty and entreated of such matters as I thought meet for this auditory. I have had ado with many estates, even with the highest of all. I have entreated of the duty of kings, of the duty of magistrates and judges, of the duty of prelates, allowing that that is good and disallowing the contrary. I have taught that we are all sinners. I think there is none of us all, neither preacher nor hearer, but we may be amended and redress our lives. We may all say, yea, all the pack of us, *Peccavimus cum patribus nostris,* "We have offended and sinned with our forefathers" (Psalm 106:6). *In multis offendimus omnes;*

there is none of us all but we have in sundry things grievously offended Almighty God. I here entreated of many faults and rebuked many kinds of sins. I intend today, by God's grace, to show you the remedy of sin. We be in the place of repentance. Now is the time to call for mercy, whiles we be in this world. We be all sinners, even the best of us all; therefore it is good to hear the remedy of sin.

This day is commonly called Good Friday. Although every day ought to be with us Good Friday, yet this day we are accustomed specially to have a commemoration and remembrance of the Passion of our Saviour Jesus Christ. This day we have in memory His bitter Passion and death, which is the remedy of our sin. Therefore I intend to entreat of a piece of the story of His Passion; I am not able to entreat of all. That I may do that the better, and that it may be to the honor of God and edification of your souls and mine both, I shall desire you to pray, etc. In this prayer I will desire you to remember the souls departed, with lauds and praise to Almighty God that He would vouchsafe to assist them at the hour of their death. In so doing you shall be put in remembrance to pray for yourselves that it may please God to assist and comfort you in the agonies and pains of death.

The place that I will entreat of is in the twenty-sixth chapter of St. Matthew. Howbeit, as I entreat of it, I will borrow part of St. Mark and St. Luke, for they have somewhat that St. Matthew hath not, and especially Luke. The text is, *Tunc cum venisset Jesus in villam, quae dicitur Gethsemani* (Matt. 26:36), "Then when Jesus came"; some have *in villam,* some *in agrum,* some *in praedium.* But it is all one; when Christ came into a grange, into a piece of land, into a field, it makes no matter; call it what ye will. At what time He had come into an honest man's house and there eaten His paschal lamb and instituted and celebrated the Lord's Supper and set forth the blessed Communion; then when this was done He took His way to the place where He knew Judas would come. It was a solitary place, and thither He went with His eleven apostles. For Judas, the twelfth, was about his business; he was occupied about his merchandise and was providing among the bishops and priests to come with an imbushment of Jews to take our Saviour Jesus Christ. And when He was come into this field or grange, this village or farmplace which was called Gethsemane, there was a garden, saith Luke, into the which He goeth, and leaves eight of His disciples without. Howbeit He appointed them what they should do. He saith, *Sedete hic donec vadam illuc et orem,* "Sit you here, whiles I go yonder and pray" (*ibid.*). He told them that He went to pray to monish them what they should do, to fall to prayer as He did. He left them there and took no more with Him but three, Peter, James, and John, to teach us that a solitary place is meet for prayer. Then when He was come into this garden, *coepit expavescere,* "He began to tremble" (*ibid.,* 26:37). Insomuch He said, *Tristis est anima mea usque ad mortem,* "My soul is heavy and pensive even unto death" (*ibid.,* 26:38).

This is a notable place and one of the most especial and chiefest of all that be in the story of the Passion of Christ. Here is our remedy. Here we must have in consideration all His doings and sayings, for our learning, for our edification, for our comfort and consolation. First of all, He set His three disciples that He took with Him in an order and told them what they should do, saying, *Sedete hic, et vigilate mecum, et orate* (*ibid.,* 26:41), "Sit here, and pray that ye enter not into temptation." But of that I will entreat afterward. Now when He was in the garden *coepit expavescere,* He began to be heavy, pensive, heavy-hearted. I like not Origen's playing with this word *coepit.*[1] It was a perfect heaviness; it was such a one as was never seen the greater; it was not only the beginning of a sorrow. These doctors, we have great cause to thank God for them, but yet I would not have them always to be allowed. They have handled many points of our faith very godly and we may have a great stay in them in many things; we might not well lack them. But yet I would not

[1] Origen minimizes the human suffering of Jesus in the garden by making a distinction between *began to be sorrowful* and *was sorrowful* (Migne, *Patrologiae Graecae,* ser. 2, XIII, col. 1741).

have men to be sworn to them and so addict as to take hand over head whatsoever they say; it were a great inconvenience so to do.

Well, let us go forward. He took Peter, James, and John into this garden. And why did He take them with Him rather than other? Marry, those that He had taken before, to whom He had revealed in the hill the transfiguration and declaration of His deity, to see the revelation of the majesty of His Godhead, now in the garden He revealed to the same the infirmity of His manhood. Because they had tasted of the sweet, He would they should taste also of the sour. He took these with Him at both times, for two or three is enough to bear witness. And He began to be heavy in His mind; He was greatly vexed within Himself; He was sore afflicted; it was a great heaviness. He had been heavy many times before and He had suffered great afflictions in His soul, as for the blindness of the Jews; and He was like to suffer mo pangs of pain in His body. But this pang was greater than any He ever suffered. Yea, it was a greater torment unto Him, I think a greater pain, than when He was hanged on the cross; than when the stour [2] nails were knocked and driven through His hands and feet; than when the sharp crown of thorns was thrust on His head. This was the heaviness and pensiveness of His heart, the agony of the spirit. And as the soul is more precious than the body, even so is the pain of the soul more grievous than the pains of the body. Therefore there is another which writeth, *Horror mortis gravior ipsa morte,*[3] "The horror and ugsomeness [4] of death is sorer than death itself." This is the most grievous pain that ever Christ suffered, even this pang that He suffered in the garden. It is the most notable place, one of them in the whole story of the Passion, when He said, *Anima mea tristis est usque ad mortem,* "My soul is heavy to death"; and *cum coepisset expaves-*

[2] *Stour:* hard, rough.

[3] Latimer is quoting, with his usual freedom, from Erasmus' commentary on this passage: *Est autem mortis horror, si quando corripuit hominem, vel ipsa morte acerbior* (*Paraphraseon . . . in Novum Testamentum* [Basle, 1535], I, sig. O4v).

[4] *Ugsomeness:* loathsomeness.

cere, "When He began to quiver, to shake." The grievousness of it is declared by His prayer that He made: *Pater, si possibile est, etc.,* "Father, if it be possible, away with this cup; rid me of it" (*ibid.,* 26:39). He understood by this cup His pains of death, for He knew well enough that His Passion was at hand, that Judas was come upon Him with the Jews to take Him.

There was offered unto Him now the image of death, the image, the sense, the feeling of hell, for death and hell go both together. I will entreat of this image of hell which is death. Truly, no man can show it perfectly, yet I will do the best I can to make you understand the grievous pangs that our Saviour Christ was in when He was in the garden. As man's power is not able to bear it, so no man's tongue is able to express it. Painters paint death like a man without skin and a body having nothing but bones. And hell, they paint it horrible flames of burning fire. They bungle somewhat at it; they come nothing near it. But this is no true painting. No painter can paint hell unless he could paint the torment and condemnation both of body and soul, the possession and having of all infelicity. This is hell, this is the image of death, this is hell. Such an evil-favored face, such an ugsome countenance, such an horrible visage our Saviour Christ saw of death and hell in the garden. There is no pleasure in beholding of it, but more pain than any tongue can tell. Death and hell took unto them this evil-favored face of sin and thorough sin. This sin is so highly hated of God that He doth pronounce it worthy to be punished with lack of all felicity, with the feeling of infelicity. Death and hell be not only the wages, the reward, the stipend of sin; but they are brought into the world by sin. *Per peccatum mors,* saith St. Paul, "Through sin death entered into the world" (Romans 5:12). Moses showeth the first coming-in of it into the world. Whereas our first father Adam was set at liberty to live forever, yet God, inhibiting him from eating of the apple, told him, "If thou meddle with this fruit, thou and all thy posterity shall fall into necessity of death. From ever living, *morte morieris,* thou and all thy posterity shall be subject to death" (Gen. 2:17). Here came in death and hell. Sin was their mother; therefore they must have such an image as their mother, Sin, would give them.

An ugsome thing and an horrible image must it needs be that is brought in by such a thing so hated of God; yea, this face of death and hell is so terrible that such as hath been wicked men had rather be hanged than abide it. As Achitophel, that traitor to David, like an ambitious wretch thought to have come to higher promotion and therefore conspired with Absalom against his master David. He, when he saw his counsel took no place, goes and hangs himself in contemplation of this evil-favored face of death. Judas also, when he came with bushments [5] to take his master Christ, in beholding this horrible face, hanged himself. Yea, the elect people of God, the faithful, having the beholding of this face—though God hath always preserved them, such a good God He is to them that believe in Him, that "He will not suffer them to be tempted above that that they have been able to bear" (I Cor. 10:13)—yet for all that there is nothing that they complain more sore than of this horror of death.

Go to Job, what saith he? *Pereat dies in quo natus sum, suspendium elegit anima mea,* "Woe worth the day that I was born in (Job 3:3), my soul would be hanged" (*ibid.,* 7:15), saying in his pangs almost he wist not what. This was when with the eye of his conscience and the inward man he beheld the horror of death and hell. Not for any bodily pain that he suffered; for when he had boils, botches, blains,[6] and scabs, he suffered them patiently. He could say then, *Si bona suscepimus de manu Domini, etc.,* "If we have received good things of God, why should we not suffer likewise evil?" (*ibid.,* 2:10). It was not for any such thing that he was so vexed. But the sight of this face of death and hell was offered to him so lively that he would have been out of this world. It was this evil-favored face of death that so troubled him. King David also said in contemplation of this ugsome face, *Laboravi in gemitu meo,* "I have been sore vexed with sighing and mourning" (Psalm 6:7). *Turbatus est a*

[5] *Bushments:* a surprise party of soldiers. [6] *Botches, blains:* ulcerous sores.

furore oculus meus, "Mine eye hath been greatly troubled in my rage" (*ibid.,* 6:8). A strange thing! When he had to fight with Goliath, that monstrous giant, who was able to have eaten him, he could abide him and was nothing afraid. And now what a work! What exclamations makes he at the sight of death! Jonah likewise was bold enough to bid the shipmen cast him into the sea. He had not yet seen that face and visage. But when he was in the whale's belly and had there the beholding of it, what terror and distress abode he! Hezekiah, when he saw Sennacherib besieging his city on every side most violently, was nothing afraid of the great host and mighty army that was like to destroy him out of hand; yet he was afraid of death. When the prophet came unto him and said, *Dispone domui tuae, morte morieris et non vives* (II Kings 20:1), it struck him so to the heart that he fell aweeping. O Lord, what an horror was this! There be some writers that say that Peter, James, and John were in this feeling at the same time; and that Peter, when he said, *Exi a me Domine, quia homo peccator sum* (Luke 5:8), did taste some part of it. He was so astonished, he wist not what to say. It was not long that they were in this anguish; some say longer, some shorter. But Christ was ready to comfort them and said to Peter, *Ne timeas,* "Be not afraid" (Luke 5:10).

A friend of mine told me of a certain woman that was eighteen years together in it. I knew a man myself, Bilney,[7] little Bilney, that blessed martyr of God, what time he had borne his fagot and was come again to Cambridge, had such conflicts within himself, beholding this image of death, that his friends were afraid to let him be alone. They were fain to be with him day and night and comforted

[7] Thomas Bilney, who was the agent of Latimer's "conversion" twenty-five years earlier (see Latimer's account in the "First Sermon on the Lord's Prayer," p. 167 below). Latimer here refers to the fact that in 1527 Bilney was convicted of heresy, recanted, and as penance was required to stand bareheaded, with a fagot on his shoulder, during the whole of a sermon at Paul's Cross. Bilney never recovered from the feeling that he had betrayed his own conscience and subsequently resumed his dangerous preaching. In 1531 he was condemned as a relapsed heretic and burned in the Lollards' Pit at Norwich.

him as they could, but no comforts would serve. As for the comfortable places of scripture, to bring them unto him it was as though a man would run him through the heart with a sword. Yet afterward, for all this, he was revived and took his death patiently and died well against the tyrannical see of Rome. Woe will be to that bishop [8] that had the examination of him if he repented not! Here is a good lesson for you, my friends. If ever ye come in danger, in durance, in prison for God's quarrel and His sake, as he did for purgatory matters, and put to bear a fagot for preaching the true Word of God against pilgrimage and suchlike matters, I will advise you first and above all things to abjure all your friends, all your friendship. Leave not one unabjured. It is they that shall undo you, and not your enemies. It was his very friends that brought Bilney to it.

By this it may somewhat appear what our Saviour Christ suffered; He doth not dissemble it Himself when He saith, "My soul is heavy to death." He was in so sore an agony that there issued out of Him, as I shall entreat anon, drops of blood. An ugsome thing surely, which His fact and deed showeth us what horrible pains He was in for our sakes! But you will say, "How can this be? It were possible that I and such other as be great sinners should suffer such affliction. The Son of God—what, our Saviour Christ—never sinned. How can this stand that He should be thus handled? He never deserved it."

Marry, I will tell you how. We must consider our Saviour Christ two ways, one way in His manhood, another in His Godhead. Some places of scripture must be referred to His deity and some to His humanity. In His Godhead He suffered nothing. But now He made Himself void of His deity, as scripture saith, *Cum esset in forma Dei, exinanivit seipsum,* "Whereas He was in the form of God (Phil. 2:6), He emptied himself of it" (*ibid.,* 2:7). He did hide it

[8] The allusion is probably to Richard Nix, Bishop of Norwich, who, it was charged, ordered the burning of Bilney without waiting for the royal warrant. But it was one Dr. Pellis, the chancellor of the diocese, who presided over Bilney's last examination, ordered his degradation, and delivered him to the secular arm for execution.

and used Himself as though He had not had it. He would not help Himself with His Godhead. "He humbled Himself with all obedience unto death, even to the death of the cross" (*ibid.,* 2:8). This was in that He was man. He took upon Him our sins, our sins. Not the work of sins; I mean not so; not to do it, not to commit it; but to purge it, to cleanse it, to bear the stipend of it. And that way He was the great sinner of the world. He bare all the sin of the world on His back; He would become debtor for it.

Now to sustain and suffer the dolors of death is not to sin. But He came into this world with His Passion to purge our sins. Now this that He suffered in the garden is one of the bitterest pieces of all His Passion. This fear of death was the bitterest pain that ever He abode, due to sin which He never did, but became debtor for us. All this He suffered for us; this He did to satisfy for our sins. It is much like as if I owed another man twenty thousand pounds and should pay it out of hand or else go to the dungeon of Ludgate.[9] And when I am going to prison, one of my friends should come and ask, "Whither goeth this man?" And, after he had heard the matter, should say, "Let me answer for him, I will become surety for him; yea, I will pay all for him." Such a part played our Saviour Christ with us. If He had not suffered this, I for my part should have suffered, according to the gravity and quantity of my sins, damnation. For the greater the sin is, the greater is the punishment in hell. He suffered for you and me in such a degree as is due to all the sins of the whole world. It was as if you would imagine that one man had committed all the sins since Adam. You may be sure he should be punished with the same horror of death in such a sort as all men in the world should have suffered. Feign and put case, our Saviour Christ had committed all the sins of the world; all that I for my part have done, all that you for your part have done, and that any man else hath done. If He had done all this Himself, His agony that He suffered

[9] The prison where freemen of the City of London were confined for debt, trespass, and the like. Those guilty of a felony were confined in Newgate, which was much less commodious.

should have been no greater nor grievouser than it was. This that [He] suffered in the garden was a portion, I say, of His Passion, and one of the bitterest parts of it.

And this He suffered for our sins and not for any sins that He had committed Himself—for all we should have suffered, every man according to his own deserts. This He did of goodness, partly to purge and cleanse our sins, partly because He would taste and feel our miseries, *quo possit succurrere nobis,* "that He should the rather help and relieve us"; and partly He suffered to give us example to behave ourselves as He did. He did not suffer to discharge us clean from death, to keep us clean from it, not to taste of it. Nay, nay, you must not take it so. We shall have the beholding of this ugsome face, every one of us; we shall feel it ourselves. Yet our Saviour Christ did suffer to the intent to signify to us that death is overcomeable. We shall indeed overcome it if we repent and acknowledge that our Saviour Jesus Christ pacified with His pangs and pains the wrath of the Father, having a love to walk in the ways of God. If we believe in Jesus Christ, we shall overcome death. I say it shall not prevail against us.

Wherefore, whensoever it chanceth thee, my friend, to have the tasting of this death, that thou shalt be tempted with this horror of death, what is to be done then? Whensoever thou feelest thy soul heavy to death, make haste and resort to this garden; and with this faith thou shalt overcome this terror when it cometh. Oh, it was a grievous thing that Christ suffered here! Oh, the greatness of His dolor that He suffered in the garden, partly to make amends for our sins and partly to deliver us from death; not so that we should not die bodily, but that this death should be a way to a better life and to destroy and overcome hell! Our Saviour Christ had a garden, but little pleasure in it. You have many goodly gardens; I would you would in the midst of them consider what agony our Saviour Christ suffered in His garden. A goodly meditation to have in your gardens! It shall occasion you to delight no farther in vanities but to remember what He suffered for you. It may draw you from sin. It is a good monument, a good sign, a good monition, to consider how He behaved Himself in this garden.

Well, He saith to His disciples, "Sit here and pray with me." He went a little way off, as it were a stone's cast from them, and falls to His prayer, and saith: *Pater, si possibile est, transeat a me calix iste,* "Father, if it be possible, away with this bitter cup, this outrageous pain." Yet after He corrects Himself, and says, *Veruntamen non sicut ego volo, sed sicut tu vis,* "Not My will, but Thy will be done, O Father" (Matt. 26:39). Here is a good meditation for Christian men at all times, and not only upon Good Friday. Let Good Friday be every day to a Christian man, to know to use His Passion to that end and purpose, not to read the story but to take the fruit of it. Some men, if they had been in this agony, would have run themselves through with their swords, as Saul did: some would have hanged themselves, as Achitophel did. Let us not follow these men; they be no examples for us. But let us follow Christ, which in His agony resorted to His Father with His prayer. This must be our pattern to work by.

Here I might dilate the matter as touching praying to saints. Here we may learn not to pray to saints. Christ bids us, *Ora Patrem qui est in coelis,* "Pray to thy Father that is in heaven"; [10] to the Creator and not to any creature. And therefore away with these avowries; [11] let God alone be our avowry. What have we to do to run hither or thither, but only to the Father of heaven? I will not tarry to speak of this matter.

Our Saviour Christ set His disciples in an order and commanded them to watch and pray, saying, *Vigilate et orate,* "Watch and pray." Whereto should they watch and pray? He saith by and by, *ne intretis in tentationem,* "that ye enter not into temptation" (*ibid.,* 26:41). He bids them not pray that they be not tempted; for that is as much to say, as to pray that we should be out of this world. There

[10] Here, for his immediate purpose, the preacher conflates "Pray to thy father which is in secret" (Matt. 6:6) and "Our Father which art in heaven" (Matt. 6:9).

[11] *Avowries:* patron saints.

is no man in this world without temptation. In the time of prosperity we are tempted to wantonness, pleasures, and all lightness; in time of adversity, to despair in God's goodness. Temptation never ceases. There is a difference between being tempted and entering into temptation. He bids therefore not to pray that they be not tempted, but that they enter not into temptation. To be tempted is no evil thing. For what is it? No more than when the flesh, the devil, and the world doth solicit and move us against God. To give place to these suggestions and to yield ourselves and suffer us to be overcome of them, this is to enter into temptation. Our Saviour Christ knew that they should be grievously tempted, and therefore He gave them warning that they should not give place to temptation, nor despair at His death; and if they chanced to forsake Him or to run away, in case they tripped or swerved, yet to come again.

But our Saviour Christ did not only command His disciples to pray, but fell down upon His knees flat upon the ground and prayed Himself, saying, *Pater, si fieri potest, transeat a me calix iste,* "Father, deliver me of this pang and pain that I am in, this outrageous pain." This word "Father" came even from the bowels of His heart when He made His moan; as who should say, "Father, rid me; I am in such pain that I can be in no greater! Thou art my Father, I am thy Son. Can the Father forsake His Son in such anguish?" Thus He made His moan. "Father, take away this horror of death from Me; rid Me of this pain; suffer Me not to be taken when Judas comes; suffer Me not to be hanged on the cross; suffer not My hands to be pierced with nails nor my heart with the sharp spear." A wonderful thing that He should so oft tell His disciples of it before and now, when He cometh to the point, to desire to be rid of it, as though He would have been disobedient to the will of His Father. Afore He said He came to suffer; and now He says "Away with this cup." Who would have thought that ever this gear should have come out of Christ's mouth? What a case is this! What should a man say? You must understand that Christ took upon Him all our infirmities, of the which this was one, to be sorry at death. Among the stipends of sin this was one, to tremble at the cross. This is a punishment for our sin.

It goeth otherways with us than with Christ. If we were in like case and in like agony, almost we would curse God, or rather wish that there were no God. This that He said was not of that sort; it was referring the matter to the will of His Father. But we seek by all means, be it right, be it wrong, of our own nature to be rid out of pain. He desired it conditionally, as it might stand with His Father's will, adding a *veruntamen* to it. So His request was to show the infirmity of man. Here is now an example what we shall do when we are in like case. He never deserved it. We have. He had a *veruntamen,* a "notwithstanding"; let us have so too. We must have a "nevertheless, Thy will be done, and not mine; give me grace to be content, to submit my will unto Thine." His fact teacheth us what to do. This is our surgery, our physic, when we be in agony. And reckon upon it, friends, we shall come to it; we shall feel it at one time or another.

What does He now? What came to pass now when He had heard no voice, His Father was dumb? He resorts to His friends, seeking some comfort at their hands. Seeing He had none at His Father's hand, He comes to His disciples and finds them asleep. He spake unto Peter, and said, "Ah, Peter, art thou asleep?" Peter before had bragged stoutly, as though he would have killed—God have mercy upon his soul—and now when he should have comforted Christ he was asleep. Not once buff nor baff[12] to Him; not a word. He was fain to say to His disciples, *Vigilate et orate,* "Watch and pray; the spirit is ready, but the flesh is weak." He had never a word of them again. They might at the least have said, "Oh, sir, remember Yourself; are not You Christ? Came not You into this world to redeem sin? Be a good cheer, be a good comfort; this sorrow will not help You; comfort Yourself by Your own preaching. You have said *Oportet Filium hominis pati* (Mark 8:31). You have not deserved anything, it is not Your fault." Indeed, if they had done this with Him,

[12] *Not . . . baff:* nothing at all. Both *buff* and *baff* seem to refer originally to the barking of a dog.

they had played a friendly part with Him; but they gave Him not so much as one comfortable word. We run to our friends in our distresses and agonies, as though we had all our trust and confidence in them. He did not so; He resorted to them but trusted not in them. We will run to our friends, and come no more to God; He returned again. What! Shall we not resort to our friends in time of need? And trow ye we shall not find them asleep? Yes, I warrant you, and when we need their help most we shall not have it. But what shall we do when we shall find lack in them? We will cry out upon them, upbraid them, chide, brawl, fume, chafe, and backbite them. But Christ did not so; He excused His friends, saying, *Vigilate et orate; spiritus quidem promptus est, caro autem infirma.* "Oh," quoth He, "watch and pray. I see well the spirit is ready, but the flesh is weak" (Matt. 26:41).

What meaneth this? Surely it is a comfortable place. For as long as we live in this world, when we be at the best we have no more but *promptitudinem spiritus cum infirmitate carnis,* the readiness of the spirit with the infirmity of the flesh. The very saints of God said, *Velle adest mihi,* "My will is good, but I am not able to perform it" (Romans 7:18). I have been with some, and fain they would, fain they would. There was readiness of spirit, but it would not be; it grieved them that they could not take things as they should do. The flesh resisteth the work of the Holy Ghost in our hearts and lets it, lets it. We have to pray ever to God. Oh, prayer, prayer, that it might be used in this realm, as it ought to be of all men, and specially of magistrates, of counselors, of great rulers; to pray, to pray that it would please God to put godly policies in their hearts. Call for assistance.

I have heard say when that good queen[13] that is gone had ordained in her house daily prayer both before noon and after noon, the Admiral[14] gets him out of the way, like a mole digging in the

[13] Catherine Parr, Henry VIII's sixth and last queen.

[14] In 1547, shortly after Henry's death, Catherine secretly married Thomas Seymour, Lord High Admiral and brother of the Protector Somerset. He conspired against his brother and was attainted of treason and executed on March 22, 1549. In

earth. He shall be Lot's wife to me as long as I live. He was a covetous man, an horrible covetous man. I would there were no more in England! He was an ambitious man. I would there were no mo in England! He was a seditious man, a contemner of common prayer. I would there were no mo in England! He is gone. I would he had left none behind him! Remember you, my lords, that you pray in your houses to the better mortification of your flesh. Remember, God must be honored. I will you to pray that God will continue His Spirit in you. I do not put you in comfort that if ye have once the Spirit ye cannot leese it. There be new spirits start up now of late that say after we have received the Spirit we cannot sin. I will make but one argument. St. Paul had brought the Galatians to the possession of the faith and left them in that state; they had received the Spirit once, but they sinned again, as he testified of them himself. He saith, *Currebatis bene* (Gal. 5:7); ye were once in a right state; and again, *Recepistis Spiritum ex operibus legis an ex justitia fidei?* [15] (*ibid.,* 3:2). Once they had the Spirit by faith; but false prophets came, when he was gone from them, and they plucked them clean away from all that Paul had planted them in. And then said Paul unto them, *O stulti Galati, quis vos fascinavit?* (*ibid.,* 3:1). If this be true, we may leese the Spirit that we have once possessed. It is a fond thing; I will not tarry in it. But now to the Passion again.

Christ had been with His Father and felt no help; He had been

---

his "Fourth Sermon before Edward VI," Latimer charged that Seymour, in the Tower awaiting execution, sent letters to the Princesses Mary and Elizabeth urging them to conspire against the Protector. In the "Fifth Sermon" the preacher reported that his allusions to the Lord Admiral had led to charges that he had been suborned and that he was like "Dr. Shaw that preached at Paul's Cross that King Edward [IV]'s sons were bastards." In the "Last Sermon" (see below, p. 143) Latimer denied charges that he had been paid by the Protector's wife to denounce the Lord Admiral. In the period between the death of Catherine Parr in September, 1548, and his attainder in March, 1549, the Lord Admiral seems to have schemed to marry the Princess Elizabeth. It is therefore not surprising that all the passages dealing with the Lord Admiral were deleted from editions of the sermons published during the reign of Elizabeth.

[15] But the Vulgate reads *ex auditu fidei.*

with His friends and had no comfort; He had prayed twice and was not heard. What did He now? Did He give prayer over? No, He goeth again to His Father and saith the same again: "Father, if it be possible, away with this cup." Here is an example for us. Although we be not heard at the first time, shall we give over our prayer? No, we must to it again; we must be importune upon God; we must be instant in prayer. He prayed thrice and was not heard; let us sinners pray threescore times. Folks are very dull nowadays in prayer, to come to sermons, to resort to common prayer. You housekeepers, and especially great men, give example of prayer in your houses.

Well, did His Father look upon Him this second time? No, He went to His friends again, thinking to find some comfort there, but He finds them asleep again, more deeper asleep than ever they were. Their eyes were heavy with sleep; there was no comfort at all; they wist not what to say to Him. A wonderful thing, how He was tossed from post to pillar, one while to His Father and was destitute at His hand, another while to His friends and found no comfort at them! His Father gave Him looking on and suffered Him to bite the bridle awhile. Almighty God beheld this battle that He might enjoy that honor and glory, "that in His name all knees should bow, *coelestium, terrestrium et infernorum,* in heaven, earth, and hell" (Phil. 2:10). This, that the Father would not hear His own Son, was another punishment due to our sin. When we cry unto Him He will not hear us. The prophet Jeremiah saith, *Clamabunt ad me et ego non exaudiam eos* (Jer. 11:11). These be Jeremiah's words; here he threateneth to punish sin with not hearing their prayers. The prophet saith, "They have not had the fear of God before their eyes, nor have not regarded discipline and correction."

I never saw, surely, so little discipline as is nowadays. Men will be masters; they will be masters and no disciples. Alas, where is this discipline now in England? The people regard no discipline; they be without all order. Where they should give place, they will not stir one inch. Yea, where magistrates should determine matters, they will break into the place before they come and at their coming not move a whit for them. Is this discipline? Is this good order? If a man say anything unto them, they regard it not. They that be called to answer will not answer directly but scoff the matter out. Men, the more they know, the worse they be; it is truly said, *Scientia inflat,* "Knowledge maketh us proud and causeth us to forget all and set away discipline." Surely in popery they had a reverence; but now we have none at all. I never saw the like. This same lack of the fear of God and discipline in us was one of the causes that the Father would not hear His Son. This pain suffered our Saviour Christ for us, who never deserved it. Oh, what it was that He suffered in this garden till Judas came! The dolors, the terrors, the sorrows that He suffered be unspeakable! He suffered it partly to make amends for our sins, and partly to give us example what we should do in like case. What comes of this gear in the end?

Well, now He prayeth again; He resorteth to His Father again. *Angore correptus prolixius orabat* (Luke 22:44). He was in sorer pains, in more anguish than ever He was; and therefore He prayeth longer, more ardently, more fervently, more vehemently than ever He did before. Oh, Lord, what a wonderful thing is this! This horror of death is worse than death itself, more ugsome, more bitter than any bodily death. He prayeth now the third time. He did it so instantly, so fervently, that it brought out a bloody sweat and such plenty that it dropped down even to the ground. There issued out of His precious body drops of blood. What a pain was He in when these bloody drops fell so abundantly from Him! Yet for all that, how unthankful do we show ourselves toward Him that did it only for our sakes and for the remedy of our sins! Oh, what blasphemy do we commit day by day! What little regard have we to His blessed Passion thus to swear by God's blood, by Christ's Passion! We have nothing in no pastime but "God's blood," "God's wounds." We continually blaspheme His Passion in hawking, hunting, dicing, and carding. Who would think He should have such enemies among those that profess His name?

What became of His blood that fell down, trow ye? Was the

blood of Hales[16] of it? Woe worth it! What ado was it to bring this out of the King's head! This great abomination of the blood of Hales could not be taken a great while out of his mind. You that be of the Court, and especially ye sworn chaplains, beware of a lesson that a great man taught me at my first coming to the Court. He told me for good will; he thought it well. He says unto me, "You must beware, howsoever ye do, that ye contrary not the King; let him have his sayings; follow him; go with him." Marry, out upon this counsel! Shall I say as he says? Say your conscience, or else what a worm shall ye feel gnawing, what a remorse of conscience shall ye have when ye remember how ye have slacked your duty! It is a good wise verse, *Gutta cavat lapidem non vi sed saepe cadendo,* "The drop of rain maketh a hole in the stone not by violence but by oft falling."[17] Likewise a prince must be turned, not violently, but he must be won by a little and a little. He must have his duty told him; but it must be done with humbleness, with request of pardon, or else it were a dangerous thing. Unpreaching prelates have been the cause that the blood of Hales did so long blind the King. Woe worth that such an abominable thing should be in a Christian realm! But thanks be to God, it was partly redressed in the King's days that dead is, and much more now. God grant good will and power to go forward, if there be any such abomination behind, that it may utterly be rooted up!

Oh, how happy are we that it hath pleased Almighty God to vouchsafe that His Son should sweat blood for the redeeming of our sins. And again, how unhappy are we if we will not take it thankfully but that was redeemed so painfully! Alas, what hard hearts have we! Our Saviour Christ never sinned, and yet sweat He blood for our sins. We will not once water our eyes with a few tears.

[16] A famous relic preserved in the Abbey of Hales, which lay in Latimer's old diocese of Worcester. One of the more ardent reformers declared that it was the blood of duck, regularly renewed, but Latimer, in a formal report made in 1538, described it as an "unctuous gum."

[17] There are many variations of this proverb. In Lucretius it is *stilicidi casus lapidem cavat* (*De rerum natura,* I, 314).

What an horrible thing is sin that no other thing would remedy and pay the ransom for it but only the blood of our Saviour Christ! There was nothing to pacify the Father's wrath against man but such an agony as He suffered. All the passion of all the martyrs that ever were, all the sacrifices of patriarchs that ever were, all the good works that ever were done, were not able to remedy our sin, to make satisfaction for our sins, nor anything besides, but this extreme Passion and bloodshedding of our most merciful Saviour Christ.

But to draw toward an end. What became of this threefold prayer? At the length, it pleased God to hear His Son's prayer and sent Him an angel to corroborate, to strengthen, to comfort Him. Christ need no angel's help if He had listed to ease Himself with His deity. He was the Son of God. What then? Forsomuch as He was man, He received comfort at the angel's hand, as it accords to our infirmity. His obedience, His continuance and suffering, so pleased the Father of heaven that for His Son's sake, be he never so great a sinner, leaving his sin and repenting for the same, he will owe him such favor as though he had never committed any sin. The Father of heaven will not suffer him to be tempted with this great horror of death and hell to the uttermost and above that he is able to bear. Look for it, my friends, by Him and through Him ye shall be able to overcome it. Let us do as our Saviour Christ did and we shall have help from above. We shall have angels' help. If we trust in Him, heaven and earth shall give up rather than we shall lack help. He saith He is *adjutor in necessitatibus,* "an helper in time of need" (Psalm 46:1).

When the angel had comforted Him and when this horror of death was gone, He was so strong that He offered Himself to Judas and said, "I am He." To make an end. I pray you take pains. It is a day of penance, as we use to say; give me leave to make you weary this day. The Jews had Him to Caiaphas and Annas, and there they whipped Him and beat Him; they set a crown of sharp thorn upon His head and nailed Him to a tree. Yet all this was not so bitter as this horror of death and this agony that He suffered in the garden, in such a degree as is due to all the sins of the world and not to one man's sin. Well, this Passion is our remedy; it is the satisfaction for our sins.

His soul descended to hell for a time. Here is much ado! These new upstarting spirits say, "Christ never descended into hell, neither body nor soul." In scorn they will ask, "Was He there? What did He there?" What if we cannot tell what He did there? The creed goeth no further but saith He descended thither. What is that to us if we cannot tell, seeing we were taught no further? Paul was taken up into the third heaven; ask likewise what he saw when he was carried thither. You shall not find in scripture what he saw or what he did there. Shall we not, therefore, believe that he was there? These arrogant spirits, spirits of vainglory, because they know not by any express scripture the order of His doings in hell, they will not believe that ever He descended into hell. Indeed this article hath not so full scripture, so many places and testimonies of scriptures, as other have; yet it hath enough. It hath two or three texts; and if it had but one, one text of scripture is of as good and lawful authority as a thousand and of as certain truth. It is not to be weighed by the multitude of texts. I believe as certainly and verily that this realm of England hath as good authority to hear God's word as any nation in all the world. It may be gathered by two texts. One of them is this: *Ite in universum mundum, et praedicate evangelium omni creaturae,* "Go into the whole world, and preach the gospel to all creatures" (Mark 16:15). And again, *Deus vult omnes homines salvos fieri,* "God will have all men to be saved" (I Tim. 2:4). He excepts not the Englishmen here nor yet expressly nameth them. And yet I am as sure that this realm of England by this gathering is allowed to hear God's word as though Christ had said a thousand times, "Go preach to Englishmen; I will that Englishmen be saved." Because this article of His descending into hell cannot be gathered so directly, so necessarily, so formally, they do utterly deny it.

This article hath scriptures two or three, enough for quiet minds. As for curious brains, nothing can content them. This the devil's stirring up of such spirits of sedition is an evident argument that the light is come forth; for His word is abroad when the devil rusheth, when he roareth, when he stirreth up such busy spirits to slander it. My intent is not to entreat of this matter at this time. I trust the people will not be carried away with these new arrogant spirits. I doubt not but good preachers will labor against them.

But now I will say a word and herein, I protest first of all, not arrogantly to determine and define it. I will contend with no man for it. I will not have it be prejudice to anybody, but I offer it unto you to consider and weigh it. There be some great clerks that take my part, and I perceive not what evil can come of it, in saying that our Saviour Christ did not only in soul descend into hell, but also that He suffered in hell such pains as the damned spirits did suffer there. Surely, I believe verily, for my part, that He suffered the pains of hell proportionably as it corresponds and answers to the whole sin of the world. He would not suffer only bodily in the garden and upon the cross, but also in His soul when it was from the body, which was a pain due for our sin. Some write so, and I can believe it, that He suffered in the very place—and I cannot tell what it is, call it what ye will—even in the scalding house, in the ugsomeness of the place, in the presence of the place, such pain as our capacity cannot attain unto. It is somewhat declared unto us when we utter it by these effects, "by fire, by gnashing of teeth, by the worm that gnaweth on the conscience." Whatsoever the pain is, it is a great pain that He suffered for us.

I see no inconvenience to say that Christ suffered in soul in hell. I singularly commend the exceeding great charity of Christ that for our sakes would suffer in hell in His soul. It sets out the unspeakable hatred that God hath to sin. I perceive not that it doth derogate anything from the dignity of Christ's death; as in the garden, when He suffered, it derogates nothing from that He suffered on the cross. Scripture speaketh on this fashion: *Qui credit in me habet vitam aeternam,* "He that believeth in me, hath life everlasting" (John 6:47). Here He sets forth faith as the cause of our justification; in other places, as high commendation is given to works. And yet are the works any derogation from that dignity, faith? No. And again, scripture saith, *Traditus est propter peccata nostra, et exsuscitatus propter justificationem, etc.* (Romans 4:25). It attributeth here our justification to His resurrection. And doth this derogate anything from His death? Not a whit. It is whole Christ. What with His nativity; what with His circumcision; what with His incarnation and the whole process of His life; with His preaching; what with His ascending, descending; what with His death; it is all Christ that worketh our salvation. He sitteth on the right hand of the Father, and all for us. All this is the work of our salvation. I would be as loath to derogate anything from Christ's death as the best of you all. How unestimably are we bound to Him! What thanks ought we to give Him for it! We must have this continually in remembrance: *Propter te morti tradimur tota die,* "For Thee we are in dying continually." The life of a Christian man is nothing but a readiness to die and a remembrance of death.

If this that I have spoken of Christ's suffering in the garden and in hell derogate anything from Christ's death and Passion, away with it. Believe me not in this. If it do not, it commends and sets forth very well unto us the perfection of the satisfaction that Christ made for us and the work of a redemption, not only before witness in this world, but in hell, in that ugsome place, whereto, whether He suffered, or wrestled with the spirits, or comforted Abraham, Isaac, and Jacob, I will not desire. If ye like not that which I have spoken of His suffering, let it go. I will not strive in it; I will be prejudice to nobody; weigh it as ye list. I do but offer it you to consider. It is like His soul did somewhat the three days that His body lay in the grave. To say He suffered in hell for us derogates nothing from His death, for all things that Christ did before His suffering on the cross and after do work our salvation. If He had not been incarnate, He had not died. He was beneficial to us with all things He did. Christian people should have His suffering for them in remembrance. Let your gardens monish you, your pleasant gardens, what Christ suffered for you in the garden, and what commodity you have by His suffering. It is His will ye should so do; He would be had in remembrance. Mix your pleasures with the remembrance of His bitter Passion. The whole Passion is satisfaction for our sins and not the bare death, considering it so nakedly by itself. The manner of speaking of scripture is to be considered. It attributeth our salvation now to one thing, now to another that Christ did; where indeed it pertained to all.

Our Saviour Christ hath left behind Him a remembrance of His Passion, the blessed Communion, the celebration of the Lord's Supper. Alack! it hath been long abused, as the sacrifices were before in the old law. The patriarchs used sacrifice in the faith of the seed of the woman, which should break the serpent's head. The patriarchs sacrificed on hope, and afterward the work was esteemed. There comes other after, and they consider not the faith of Abraham and the patriarchs but do their sacrifice according to their own imagination. Even so came it to pass with our blessed Communion. In the primitive church, in plagues when their friends were dead, they used to come together to the Holy Communion. What? To remedy them that were dead? No, not a straw; it was not ordained for no such purpose. But then they would call to remembrance God's goodness and His Passion that He suffered for us, wherein they comforted much their faith.

Other came afterward and sets up all these kinds of massing, all these kinds of iniquity. What an abomination is it, the foulest that ever was, to attribute to man's work our salvation! God be thanked that we have this blessed Communion set forth so now that we may comfort, increase, and fortify our faith at that blessed celebration! If he be guilty of the body of Christ that takes it unworthily, he fetcheth great comfort at it that eats it worthily. He doth eat it worthily that doth it in faith. In faith? In what faith? Not long ago a great man said in an audience, "They babble much of faith; I will go lie with my whore all night and have as good a faith as the best of them all." I think he never knew other but the whoremonger's faith. It is no such faith that will serve. It is no bribing judge's or justice's faith, no rent raiser's faith, no whoremonger's faith, no leasemonger's faith, no seller of benefices' faith, but the faith in the Passion of our Saviour Christ. We must believe that our Saviour Christ hath taken us again to His favor, that He hath delivered us His own body and blood, to plead with the devil, and by merit of His own Passion, of His own mere liberality. This is the faith, I tell you, that we must come to the Communion with, and not the whoremonger's faith. Look where remission of sin is, there is acknowledging of sin also.

Faith is a noble duchess.[18] She hath ever her gentleman-usher going before her, the confessing of sins. She hath a train after her, the fruits of good works, the walking in the commandments of God. He that believeth will not be idle; he will walk; he will do his business. Have ever the gentleman-usher with you. So if ye will try faith, remember this rule; consider whether the train be waiting upon her. If you have another faith than this, a whoremonger's faith, you are like to go the scalding house, and there you shall have two dishes, weeping and gnashing of teeth. Much good do it you! You see your fare. If ye will believe and acknowledge your sins, you shall come to the blessed Communion of the bitter Passion of Christ worthily and so attain to everlasting life, to the which the Father of heaven bring you and me! Amen.

Finis

[18] Latimer's friend and patroness, Catherine Willoughby, Duchess of Suffolk, and her gentleman-usher, Richard Bertie, were certainly present at the sermon, and it cannot be doubted that Latimer is here paying them a not very subtle compliment. The Duchess and Bertie were married in 1553, with Latimer probably officiating.

LAST SERMON BEFORE KING EDWARD VI LENT, 1550[1]

A MOST FAITHFUL SERMON PREACHED BEFORE THE KING'S MOST EXCELLENT MAJESTY AND HIS MOST HONORABLE COUNCIL IN HIS COURT AT WESTMINSTER BY THE REVEREND FATHER MASTER HUGH LATIMER, ANNO DOMINI 1550

Videte et cavete ab avaritia (Luke 12:15)
"Take heed and beware of covetousness."

"TAKE heed and beware of covetousness." "Take heed and beware of covetousness." "Take heed and beware of covetousness." And what and if I should say nothing else these three or four hours—for I know it will be so long in case I be not commanded to the contrary

[1] The title page of STC 15289 reads:
"¶A Moste faithfull Sermon preached before the Kynges most excellent Maiestye, and hys most honorable Councell, in hys Courte at Westminster, by the reuerend Father Master Hughe Latimer. Anno Domi. M.D.L."

The colophon reads: "¶Imprynted at London by Ihon Day: dwelling ouer Aldersgate beneth S. Martins. These bookes are to be sold at his shop by the litle Cunduite in Chepeside. Cum priuilegio ad imprimendum solum. Per septenium."

This sermon, Latimer's longest, is in two parts. Only the first part is reprinted in the present volume.

—but these words, "Take heed and beware of covetousness"? It would be thought a strange sermon before a king, to say nothing else but *Cavete ab avaritia,* "Beware of covetousness." And yet, as strange as it is, it would be like the sermon of Jonah, that he preached to the Ninevites as touching the shortness and as touching the paucity or fewness of the words. For his sermon was, *Adhuc quadraginta dies, et Ninive subvertetur,* "There is yet forty days to come and Nineveh shall be destroyed" (Jonah 3:4). Thus he walked from street to street and from place to place round about the city and said nothing else but "There is yet forty days," quoth he, "and Nineveh shall be destroyed." There is no great odds nor difference at the leastwise in the number of words, no nor yet in the sense or meaning, between these two sermons—"There is yet forty days and Nineveh shall be destroyed" and these words that I have taken to speak of this day, "Take heed and beware of covetousness." For Nineveh should be destroyed for sin, and of their sins covetousness was one and one of the greatest, so that it is all one in effect.

And as they be like concerning the shortness, the paucity of words, the brevity of words, and also the meaning and purpose, so I would they might be like in fruit and profit. For what came of Jonah's sermon? What was the fruit of it? *Ad praedicationem Jonae crediderunt Deo,* "At the preaching of Jonah they believed God" (Jonah 3:5). Here was a great fruit, a great effect wrought. What is that same? "They believed God." They believed God's preacher, God's officer, God's minister, Jonah, and were converted from their sin. They believed that, as the preacher said, if they did not repent and amend their life, the city should be destroyed within forty days. This was a great fruit. For Jonah was but one man, and he preached but one sermon, and it was but a short sermon, neither, as touching the number of words, and yet he turned all the whole city, great and small, rich and poor, king and all.

We be many preachers here in England and we preach many long sermons, and yet the people will not repent nor convert. This was the fruit, the effect, and the good that his sermon did, that all the whole city at his preaching converted and amended their evil living and did penance in sackcloth. And yet here in this sermon of Jonah is no great curiousness, no great clerkliness, no great affectation of words nor of painted eloquence. It was none other but *Adhuc quadraginta dies, et Ninive subvertetur,* "Yet forty days," *et Ninive subvertetur,* "and Nineveh shall be destroyed." It was no more. This was no great curious sermon, but this was a nipping sermon, a pinching sermon, a biting sermon. It had a full bite. It was a nipping sermon, a rough sermon, and a sharp biting sermon. Do you not here marvel that these Ninevites cast not Jonah in prison, that they did not revile him and rebuke him? They did not revile him nor rebuke him, but God gave them grace to hear him and to convert and amend at his preaching. A strange matter, so noble a city to give place to one man's sermon!

Now England cannot abide this gear; they cannot be content to hear God's minister and his threatening for their sin, though the sermon be never so good, though it be never so true. It is a naughty fellow, a seditious fellow; he maketh trouble and rebellion in the realm; he lacketh discretion. But the Ninevites rebuked not Jonah that he lacketh discretion or that he spake out of time, that his sermon was out of season made. But in England, if God's preacher, God's minister, be anything quick or do speak sharply, then he is a foolish fellow, he is rash, he lacketh discretion. Nowadays if they cannot reprove the doctrine that is preached, then they will reprove the preacher that he lacketh due consideration of the times, and that he is of learning sufficient but he wanteth discretion. "What a time is this picked out to preach such things! He should have a respect and a regard to the time and to the state of things and of the commonweal." It rejoiceth me sometimes when my friend cometh and telleth me that they find fault with my discretion, for by likelihood, think I, the doctrine is true. For if they could find fault with the doctrine, they would not charge me with the lack of discretion; but they would charge me with my doctrine, and not with the lack of discretion or with the incontinency of the time.

I will now ask you a question. I pray you, when should Jonah have preached against the covetousness of Nineveh if the covetous men should have appointed him his time? I know that preachers ought to have a discretion in their preaching, and that they ought to have a consideration and respect to the place and to the time that he preacheth in, as I myself will say here that I would not say in the country for no good. But what then? Sin must be rebuked; sin must be plainly spoken against. And when should Jonah have preached against Nineveh if he should have forborne for the respects of the times or the place or the state of things there? For what was Nineveh? A noble, a rich, and a wealthy city. What is London to Nineveh? Like a village, as Islington or such another in comparison of London. Such a city was Nineveh, it was three days' journey to go through every street of it and to go but from street to street. There was noblemen, rich men, wealthy men; there was vicious men and covetous men and men that gave themselves to all voluptuous living and to worldliness of getting riches. Was this a time well chosen and discreetly taken of Jonah to come and reprove them of their sin, to declare unto them the threatenings of God, and to tell them of their covetousness, and to say plainly unto them that except they repented and amended their evil living they and their city should be destroyed of God's hand within forty days? And yet they heard Jonah and gave place to his preaching. They heard the threatenings of God and feared His stroke and vengeance and believed God. That is, they believed God's preacher and minister; they believed that God would be true of His word that He spake by the mouth of His prophet, and thereupon did penance to turn away the wrath of God from them.

Well, what shall we say? I will say this and not spare. Christ saith Nineveh shall arise against the Jews at the last day and bear witness against them [2] because that they, hearing God's threatenings for sin, *Ad praedicationem Jonae in cinere et sacco egerunt poenitentiam,* "They did penance at the preaching of Jonah in ashes and

[2] The reference is to Matt. 12:41 and Luke 11:32.

sackcloth," as the text saith there (Jonah 3:6). And I say Nineveh shall arise against England, thou England. Nineveh shall arise against England because it will not believe God, nor hear His preachers that cry daily unto them, nor amend their lives, and especially their covetousness. Covetousness is as great a sin now as it was then, and it is the same sin now it was then. For God hateth sin and all covetousness as much now as He did then, and He will as sure strike for sin now as He did then.

But, ah, good God, that would give them a time of repentance after His threatening. First, to see whether they would amend or not, or He would destroy them. For even from the beginning of the world they fell to sin. The first age from Adam, which was about two thousand years, they fell ever to sin, and they had preachers, Noah and Enoch and other holy fathers. And in that time a great multiplication was that grew in two thousand years, for the scripture saith, "The sons of God saw the daughters of men that they were fair, and they took them wives from among all that they had chosen" (Gen. 6:2). This is a long matter to speak of all. But what meaneth this—"the sons of God saw the daughters of men"? Who were these sons of God? The sons of God were those that came of the good men, of the good preachers and of the holy fathers that were God's men, as they that came of Seth and Enoch that were good men and of others. For our grandmother Eve, when Cain had killed Abel and then she had another son by Adam, who was called Seth, what did she? She gave thanks to God for him and acknowledged that God it was which had given him unto her. For she said, *Dedit mihi Deus semen pro Abel quem occidit Cain*. "God," said she, "hath given me another seed instead of Abel whom Cain slew" (Gen. 4:25). Here is a long matter to talk on. Some will say, "Was this a natural mother, was this naturally done, to publish the sin of her own son? What needed she to speak of that matter or to make any rehearsal of that matter, to open the sin of her son? What needed she this to do?" Yes, she was now a good woman. When she believed the serpent, she was not good. But now she hath repented that deed and had taken hold of the promise of God that there should come of her a seed that should tread down and destroy the head of the serpent. She had taken hold of this promise and was now a good woman and a godly woman; she opened the fault of her son and hid it not.

Here could I say somewhat to them, if I would, that spake so much against me for my preaching here the last year. Oh, what a great matter is made of it and what ado, and what great fault is found with me for speaking that I did of the Lord Admiral.[3] A great matter is made of it. But I will tell you and I will speak now with a clear conscience. If it were to do again, and having the occasion that I then had, I would speak it again, every word of it, yea, and a great deal more too. I spake it for none hatred. I spake it but for an example of others to beware thereby. And if it were in the like occasion to be spoken again, I would speak it again. There be some that think and say that I was hired to it and that my Lady of Somerset's Grace hired me to it and that I was her feed man and had money of her to speak it. Well, so God help me, and as I shall answer in my conscience, in my remembrance I never talked with Her Grace touching that man in my life, nor never gave she me anything in her life for any such purpose. And therefore they are to blame that speak so of me. But, iwis,[4] I could say somewhat to them again if I would. I know the botts [5] that nip them by the guts.

But to return to Eve and declare that the sons of God are to be understanded those that came of good men, as of Seth and Enoch and the same good part of generation. And the daughters of men are to be understanded of them that came of Cain and of his seed. And therefore our grandmother Eve bade beware of marrying with Cain's seed for fear of falling from God to wickedness thereby.

And here I would say a thing to Your Majesty. I shall speak it of good will to Your Highness. I would I were able to do Your Grace

[3] See note 14 to the preceding sermon, pp. 127–128.

[4] *Iwis:* assuredly.

[5] *Botts:* maggots.

good service in anything; ye should be sure to have it. But I will say this. For God's love beware where you marry; choose your wife in a faithful stock. Beware of this worldly policy. Marry in God. Marry not for the great respect of alliance, for thereof cometh all these evils of breaking of wedlock which is among princes and noblemen. And here I would be a suitor unto Your Majesty, for I come now rather to be a suitor and a petitioner than a preacher. For I come now to take my leave and to take my *ultimum vale,* at leastwise in this place; for I have not long to live, so that I think I shall never come here into this place again. And therefore I will ask a petition of Your Highness. For the love of God, take an order for marriages here in England. For here is marriage for pleasure and voluptuousness and for goods, and so that they may join land to land and possessions to possessions. They care for no more here in England. And that is the cause of so much adultery and so much breach of wedlock in the noblemen and gentlemen and so much divorcing. And it is not now in the noblemen only, but it is come now to the inferior sort. Every man, if he have cause, will cast off his old wife and take a new and will marry again at his pleasure. And there be many that have so done.

I would therefore wish that there were a law provided in this behalf for adulterers and that adultery should be punished with death, and that might be a remedy for all this matter. There would not then be so much adultery, whoredom, and lechery in England as there is. For the love of God, take heed to it and see a remedy provided for it. I would wish that adultery should be punished with death, and that, the woman being an offender, if her husband would be a suitor for her, she should be pardoned for the first time, but not for the second time, and the man being an offender should be pardoned if his wife be a suitor for him for the first time but not for the second time, not if he offended twice. If this law were made there would not be so much adultery nor lechery used in the realm as there is. Well, I trust once yet, as old as I am, to see the day that lechery shall be punished. It was never more need, for there was never more lechery used in England as there is at this day and maintained. It is made but a laughing matter and a trifle, and it is a sad matter and an earnest matter. For lechery is a great sin; Sodom and Gomorrah was destroyed for it. And it was one of the sins reigning in Nineveh for which it should have been destroyed.

But think ye that lechery was alone? No, no, covetousness was joined with it. Covetousness followeth lechery and commonly they go together. For why? They that be given to voluptuousness and to the vice of lechery must have wherewith to maintain it, and that must be gotten by covetousness. For at the first when men fell to sin, and chiefly to lechery, wherefore the world should be destroyed, the book saith, "There were giants in the earth in those days: and after that the sons of God had come to the daughters of men, and there had engendered with them, the same became mighty men of the world and men of renown," etc. (Gen. 6:4). This is covetousness; for the book saith, *Terra erat repleta iniquitate,* "The earth was replete with iniquity" (Gen. 6:5). For they oppressed the poor. They made them slaves, peasants, villeins, and bondmen unto them. These were giants, so called of the property of giants, for they oppress the weaker and take from them what they list by force, violence, and oppression. They were giants of the property of giants, not that they were greater men of stature and strength of body than other men were. For certain writers, speaking of this matter, say that they were giants for their cruelty and covetous oppression and not in stature or procerity[6] of body. For there is no reason why Seth's children could beget on Cain's daughters greater men than others were in stature of body. But they were giants in the property of giants, for oppressing of others by force and violence. And this was covetousness, where-with God was so displeased that He repented that He had made man and resolved utterly to destroy the world, and so called to Noah and told him of it. "And I will not dispute the matter with them," saith God, "from day to day, and never the near; but if they will not amend within an hundredth and twenty years (Gen. 6:3), I shall

[6] *Procerity:* height.

bring in an universal flood over their ears and destroy them all." This was preached by Noah to them; and so that God of His goodness, patience, and long-sufferance gave them a time to repent and amend after His threatenings, because they should see their evil doings and return to God. So they had an hundredth and twenty years to repent. This Noah was laughed to scorn; they, like dodipoles,[7] laughed this godly father to scorn.

Well, ye think little of the history. If ye will know the meaning of it, it is a great show what anger God hath to sin. But how long hast thou, England, thou England? I cannot tell, for God hath not revealed it unto me; if He had, so God help me, I would tell you of it. I would not be afraid nor spare to tell it you for the good will I bear you. But I cannot tell how long time ye have, for God hath not opened it unto me. But I can tell you that this lenity, this long forbearing and holding of His hand, provoketh us to repent and amend. And I can tell that whosoever contemneth this riches and treasure of God's goodness, of His mercy, His patience and long-suffering, shall have the more grievous condemnation. This I can tell well enough; Paul telleth me this. And I can tell that ye have time to repent as long as you live here in this world; but after this life I can make no warrant of any further time to repent. Therefore repent and amend while ye be here, for when ye are gone hence ye are past that. But how long that shall be, whether tomorrow or the next day or twenty year or how long, I cannot tell. But in the meantime ye have many Jonahs to tell you of your faults and to declare unto you God's threatenings except ye repent and amend.

Therefore, to return to my matter, I say as I said at the beginning, *Videte et cavete ab avaritia. Videte,* "See it." First see it and then amend it. For I promise you, great complaints there is of it, and much crying out and much preaching, but none amendment that I see. But *Cavete ab avaritia,* "Beware of covetousness." And why of covetousness? *Quia radix omnium malorum avaritia et cupiditas,*

[7] *Dodipoles:* blockheads.

"For covetousness is the root of all evil and of all mischief" (I Tim. 6:10). This saying of Paul took me away from the gospel that is read in the church this day; it took me from the epistle, that I would preach upon neither of them both at this time. I cannot tell what ailed me; but—to tell you my imperfection—when I was appointed to preach here, I was new come out of a sickness whereof I looked to have died, and weak I was. Yet, nevertheless, when I was appointed unto it I took it upon me, howbeit I repented afterward that I had done. I was displeased with myself; I was testy, as Jonah was when he should go preach to the Ninevites.

Well, I looked on the gospel that is read this day; tut, it liked me not. I looked on the epistle; tush, I could not away with that neither. And yet I remember I had preached upon this epistle once afore King Henry the Eighth; but now I could not frame with it, nor it liked me not in no sauce. Well, this saying of Paul came to my mind, and at last I considered and weighed the matter deeply, and then thought I thus with myself. Is covetousness the root of all mischief and of all evil? Then have at the root and down with all covetousness. So this place of Paul brought me to this text of Luke, "See and beware of covetousness."

Therefore, you preachers, out with your swords and strike at the root. Speak against covetousness and cry out upon it. Stand not ticking [8] and toying at the branches nor at the boughs, for then there will new boughs and branches spring again of them. But strike at the root, and fear not these giants of England, these great men and men of power, these men that are oppressors of the poor. Fear them not, but strike at the root of all evil, which is mischievous covetousness. For covetousness is the cause of rebellion. I have forgotten my logic, but yet I can jumble at a syllogism and make an argument of it to prove it by. Covetousness is the root of all evil; rebellion is an evil; *ergo,* covetousness is the root of rebellion.

And so it was indeed. Covetousness was the cause of rebellion this

[8] *Ticking:* striking lightly.

last summer;[9] and both parties had covetousness, as well the gentlemen as the commons. Both parties had covetousness, for both parties had an inordinate desire to have that they had not, and that is covetousness, an inordinate desire to have that one hath not. The commons would have had from the gentlemen such things as they desired; the gentlemen would none of it; and so was there covetousness on both sides. The commons thought they had a right to the things that they inordinately sought to have. But what then? They must not come to it that way. Now on the other side the gentlemen had a desire to keep that they had, and so they rebelled too against the King's commandment and against such good order as he and his Council would have set in the realm. And thus both parties had covetousness, and both parties did rebel. I heard say that there was godly ordinances devised for the redress of it. But the giants would none of it in no sauce. I remember mine own self a certain giant, a great man, who sat in commission about such matters; and when the townsmen should bring in what had been enclosed, he frowned and chafed and so near looked and threatened the poor men that they durst not ask their right.

I read of late in an act of Parliament; and this act made mention of an act that was made in King Henry's days, the Third I trow it was; yea, and such another business there was in King Edward's time, the Second also.[10] In this Parliament that I speak of the gentlemen and the commons were at variance, as they were now of late. And there the gentlemen that were landlords would needs have away much lands from their tenants; and would needs have an act of Parliament, that it might be lawful for them to enclose and make several[11] from their tenants and from the commons such portions of

[9] The rebellions in Yorkshire, Northampton, Norfolk, and Suffolk in 1549 were provoked chiefly by social and economic grievances. The most formidable of these was the rising in Norfolk, commonly called "Kett's Rebellion."

[10] The acts referred to are 3 and 4 Edward VI, c. 3; 20 Henry III, c. 4; and Statutes of Westminster, 2 and 13 Edward I, statute 1, c. 46. Latimer's attribution of the latter to the reign of Edward II was an error.

[11] *Several:* private.

their lands as they thought good. Much ado there was about this act. At last it was concluded and granted that they might so do, provided alway that they should leave sufficient to the tenant. Well, it was well that they were bound to leave sufficient for them. But who should be the judge to limit what was sufficient for them? Or who shall now judge what is sufficient? Well, I for my part cannot tell what is sufficient. But methought it was well that the tenants and poor commons should have sufficient. For if they had sufficient, thought I, they had cause to be quiet. And then fell I to make this argument within myself. If at that time it were put in their will and power that they might enclose, leaving to the tenant that were sufficient for him, if they had it then in their power, thought I, that they might this do, they would leave no more than sufficient. If they left to the tenants and poor commons no more in those days but sufficient, then if they had any more taken from them since that time, then had they now not sufficient.

They in Christ are equal with you. Peers of the realm must needs be. The poorest plowman is in Christ equal with the greatest prince that is. Let them therefore have sufficient to maintain them and to find them their necessaries. A plowland must have sheep. Yea, they must have sheep to dung their ground for bearing of corn, for if they have no sheep to help to fat the ground, they shall have but bare corn and thin. They must have swine for their food, to make their veneries [12] or bacon of. Their bacon is their venison, for they shall now have *hangum tuum* [13] if they get any other venison; so that bacon is their necessary meat to feed on, which they may not lack. They must have other cattles, as horses to draw their plow and for carriage of things to the markets, and kine for their milk and

[12] *Veneries:* meat (but it usually refers only to game).

[13] *Hangum tuum:* the *OED* comments as follows: "Humorous. Perhaps a parody on *judicium tuum* or *et ideo habeat judicium suum,* 'and therefore let him have his judgment,' a phrase found in court rolls, referring to hanging." This explanation seems highly unlikely. In any case, the sense of the passage is that the shooting of deer was restricted to royalty and nobility; the penalty for poaching was hanging, and thus common folk had to be content with bacon instead of venison.

cheese, which they must live upon and pay their rents. These cattle must have pasture, which pasture if they lack the rest must needs fail them. And pasture they cannot have if the land be taken in and enclosed from them. So, as I said, there was in both parts rebellion. Therefore, for God's love, restore their sufficient unto them, and search no more what is the cause of rebellion.

But "see and beware of covetousness," for covetousness is the cause of rebellion. Well now, if covetousness be the cause of rebellion, then preaching against covetousness is not the cause of rebellion. Some say that the preaching nowadays is the cause of all sedition and rebellion. For, since this new preaching hath come in, there hath been much sedition; and therefore it must needs be that the preaching is the cause of rebellion here in England. Forsooth, our preaching is the cause of rebellion much like as Christ was cause of the destruction of Jerusalem. For, saith Christ, *Si non venissem et locutus fuissem eis, peccatum non haberent, etc.* "If I had not come," saith Christ, "and spoken to them, they should have no sin" (John 15:22). So we preachers have come and spoken to you. We have drawn our swords of God's word and stricken at the roots of all evil to have them cut down. And if ye will not amend, what can we do more?

And preaching is cause of sedition here in England much like as Elijah was the cause of trouble in Israel. For he was a preacher there and told the people of all degrees their faults, and so they winched[14] and kicked at him and accused him to Ahab the king that he was a seditious fellow and a troublous preacher and made much uproar in the realm. So the King sent for him and he was brought to Ahab the king, who said unto him, "Art thou he that troubleth all Israel?" And Elijah answered and said, "Nay, thou and thy father's house are they that trouble all Israel" (I Kings 18:17–18). Elijah had preached God's word; he had plainly told the people of their evil doings; he had showed them God's threatenings. In God's behalf I speak. There is neither king nor emperor, be they never in so great

[14] *Winched:* kicked impatiently.

estate, but they are subject to God's word. And therefore he was not afraid to say to Ahab, "It is thou and thy father's house that causeth all the trouble in Israel." Was not this presumptuously spoken to a king? Was not this a seditious fellow? Was not this fellow's preaching a cause of all the trouble in Israel? Was he not worthy to be cast in Bocardo [15] or Little-Ease? [16] No, but he had used God's sword, which is His word, and done nothing else that was evil; but they could not abide it. He never disobeyed Ahab's sword, which was the regal power; but Ahab disobeyed his sword, which was the word of God. And therefore by the punishment of God much trouble arose in the realm for the sins of Ahab and the people. But God's preacher, God's prophet, was not the cause of the trouble. Then is it not we preachers that trouble England.

But here is now an argument to prove the matter against the preachers. Here was preaching against covetousness all the last year in Lent, and the next summer followed rebellion; *ergo,* preaching against covetousness was the cause of the rebellion. A goodly argument! Here now I remember an argument of Master More's which he bringeth in in a book [17] that he made against Bilney. And here by the way I will tell you a merry toy. Master More was once sent in commission into Kent to help try out, if it might be, what was the cause of Goodwin Sands and the shelf that stopped up Sandwich haven. Thither cometh Master More and calleth the country afore him, such as were thought to be men of experience and men that could of likelihood best certify him of that matter concerning the stopping-up of Sandwich haven. Among others came in before him

[15] The notorious Oxford prison, which Miles Coverdale described as "a stinking and filthy prison for drunkards, whores, and harlots." It was here that Cranmer, Latimer, and Ridley were incarcerated from March 25, 1554, until the disputations the following month. Ridley wittily remarked that the place had become a "very college of quondams."

[16] A dungeon in the Tower of London and also a place of punishment in the Guildhall. Also, the pillory.

[17] *A dialogue concerning heresies,* which was directed against Tyndale, not Bilney. More tells the story which follows but does not say that he himself was present.

an old man with a white head and one that was thought to be little less than an hundredth years old. When Master More saw this aged man, he thought it expedient to hear him say his mind in this matter; for, being so old a man, it was likely that he knew most of any man in that presence and company.

So Master More called this old aged man unto him and said, "Father," said he, "tell me, if ye can, what is the cause of this great arising of the sands and shelves here about this haven, the which stop it up that no ships can arrive here. Ye are the eldest man that I can espy in all this company, so that if any man can tell any cause of it, ye of likelihood can say most in it, or at leastwise more than any other man here assembled." "Yea, forsooth, good master," quoth this old man, "for I am wellnigh an hundredth years old and no man here in this company anything near unto mine age." "Well then," quoth Master More, "how say you in this matter? What think ye to be the cause of these shelves and flats that stop up Sandwich haven?" "Forsooth, sir," quoth he, "I am an old man; I think that Tenterton steeple is the cause of Goodwin Sands. For I am an old man, sir," quoth he, "and I may remember the building of Tenterton steeple, and I may remember when there was no steeple at all there. And before that Tenterton steeple was in building there was no manner of speaking of any flats or sands that stopped the haven. And therefore I think that Tenterton steeple is the cause of the destroying and the decaying of Sandwich haven." And even so, to my purpose, is preaching of God's word the cause of rebellion as Tenterton steeple was cause that Sandwich haven is decayed. And is not this a gay matter, that such should be taken for great wise men that will thus reason against the preacher of God's word?

But here I would take an occasion by the way of a digression to speak somewhat to my sisters, the women, to do them some good too, because I would do all folks good if I could before I take my *ultimum vale,* at leastwise here of this place. For I think I shall no more come here, for I think I have not long to live, so that I judge I take my leave now of the Court forever and shall no more come in this place. Ahab was a king, but Jezebel, Jezebel, she was the perilous woman. She would rule her husband the king; she would bear a stroke in all things and she would order matters as pleased her. And so will many women do; they will rule their husbands and do all things after their own minds. They do therein against the order by God appointed them; they break their injunction that God gave unto them. Yea, it is now come to the lower sort, to mean men's wives. They will rule and apparel themselves gorgeously, and some of them far above their degrees, whether their husbands will or no. But they break their injunction and do therein contrary to God's ordinance.

God saith, *Subdita eris sub potestate viri,* "Thou shalt be subject under the power of thy husband" (I Cor. 7:4). Thou shalt be subject. Women are subjects; ye be subjects to your husbands. At the first the man and the woman were equal. But after that she had given credit to the serpent, then she had an injunction set upon her. *Subdita eris sub potestate viri,* "Thou shalt be subject under the power of thy husband." And as for one part of her injunction, she taketh; and she taketh one part of her penance because she cannot avoid it, and that is, *In dolore paries,* "Thou shalt bring forth children with pain and travail" (Gen. 3:16). This part of their injunction they take. And yet is the same so grievous that Chrysostom saith if it were not for the ordinance of God, which cannot be made frustrate by man, they would never come to it again for no worldly good.[18] But God hath provided herein. And as Christ saith in the gospel, *Mulier cum parit tristitiam habet, etc.,* "The woman when she beareth child hath sorrow, but afterward she remembereth not the pain because there is a soul brought forth into the world" (John 16:21). But as it is a part of your penance, ye women, to travail in bearing your children, so it is a part of your penance to be subjects unto your husbands. Ye are underlings, underlings, and must be obedient. But this is now made a trifle and a small matter;

[18] Chrysostom, *In cap. III Genesim, Homilia XVII* (Migne, *Patrologiae Graecae,* ser. 2, LIII, col. 144).

and yet it is a sad matter, a godly matter, a ghostly matter, a matter of damnation and salvation.

And Paul saith that a woman ought to have a power on her head. What is this, "to have a power on her head"? It is a manner of speaking of the scripture; and to have her power on her head is to have a sign and a token of power, which is by covering of her head declaring that she hath a superior above her by whom she ought to be ruled and ordered. For she is not immediately under God, but mediately. For by their injunction the husband is their head under God, and they subjects unto their husbands. But this "power" that some of them have is disguised gear and of strange fashions. They must wear French hoods,[19] and I cannot tell you, I, what to call it. And when they make them ready and come to the covering of their head, they will call and say, "Give me my French hood, and give me my bonnet, or my cap," and so forth. I would wish that the women would call the covering of their heads by the terms of the scripture, as when she would have her cap I would she would say, "Give me my power." I would they would learn to speak as the Holy Ghost speaketh and call it by such name as St. Paul doth. I would they would—as they have much pricking[20] when they put on their cap—I would they would have this meditation, "I am now putting on my power upon my head." If they had this thought in their minds, they would not make so much pricking up of themselves as they do nowadays. But now here is a vengeance devil. We must have our power from Turkey, of velvet and gay it must be, farfet, dear bought. And when it cometh, it is a false sign. I had rather have a true English sign than a false sign from Turkey. It is a false sign when it covereth not their heads as it should do. For if they would keep it under the power as they ought to do, there should not any such tussocks nor tufts be seen as there be, nor such laying-out of the hair nor braiding to have it open.

[19] *French hood:* a small hood made on a stiff frame and worn far back on the head. The back of the crown was raised into a horseshoe-shaped curve.

[20] *Pricking:* primping.

I would marvel of it, how it should come to be so abused and so far out of order, saving that I know by experience that many will not be ruled by their husbands as they ought to be. I have been desired to exhort some, and with some I could do little in that matter. But there be now many Adams that will not displease their wives, but will in this behalf let them have all their own minds and do as them listeth. And some others again there be nowadays that will defend it and say it may be suffered well enough because it is not express in scripture nor spoken of by name. Though we have not expressed mention in scripture against such laying-out of the hair in tussocks and tufts, yet we have in scripture express mention *de tortis crinibus* (I Tim. 2:9), of writhen[21] hair, that is, for the nonce forced to curl. But of these tussocks that are laid out nowadays there is no mention made in scriptures because they were not used in scripture-time. They were not yet come to be so far out of order as to lay out such tussocks and tufts. But I will tell thee, if thou wilt needs lay it out, or if thou wilt needs show thy hair and have it seen, go and poll thy head or round it, as men do. For to what purpose is it to pull it out so and to lay it out? Some do it, say they, of a simplicity; some do it of a pride and some of other causes. But they do it because they will be quartermasters[22] with their husbands. Quartermasters? Nay, half-masters; yea, some of them will be whole masters, and rule the roast[23] as they list themselves.

But these defenders of it will not have it evil because it is not spoken of in scripture. But there be other things as evil as this which are not spoken of in scripture expressly; but they are implied in scripture as well as though they were expressly spoken of. For the prophet Isaiah saith: *Vae qui consurgitis mane ad comessandum, ad ebrietatem sectandam et potando usque ad vesperam, ut vino aestuetis,* "Woe unto you that arise early in the morning, and go to

[21] *Writhen:* curled by plaiting.

[22] Latimer was probably unaware that "quarter" in *quartermaster* is etymologically related to the fraction one-fourth. He is simply punning.

[23] *Rule the roast:* be master of the feast. "Rule the roost" arises from a later misunderstanding of the expression.

drinking until night, that ye may swim in wine" (Isa. 5:11). This is the scripture against banqueting and drunkenness. But now they banquet all night and lie abed in the daytime till noon, and the scripture speaketh nothing of that. But what then? The devil hath his purpose this way as well as the other. He hath his purpose as well by reveling and keeping ill rule all night as by rising early in the morning and banqueting all day. So the devil hath his purpose both ways.

Ye noblemen, ye great men, I wot not what rule ye keep. For God's sake, hear the complaints and suits of the poor. Many complain against you that ye lie abed till eight or nine or ten of the clock. I cannot tell what revel ye have overnight, whether in banqueting or dicing or carding or how it is; but in the morning when poor suitors come to your houses ye cannot be spoken withal. They are kept sometimes without your gates, or if they be let into the hall, or some utter [24] chamber, out cometh one or other, "Sir, ye cannot speak with my lord yet; my lord is asleep; or he hath had business of the King's all night," etc. And thus poor suitors are driven off from day to day, that they cannot speak with you in three or four days, yea, a whole month. What, shall I say more? Yea, a whole year sometimes ere they can come to your speech to be heard of you. For God's love, look better to it. Speak with poor men when they come to your houses and dispatch poor suitors, as indeed some noblemen do.

And would Christ that all noblemen would so do! But some do. I went one day myself betime in the morning to a great man's house to speak with him in business that I had of mine own. And methought I was up betimes, but when I came thither the great man was gone forth about such affairs as behooved him ere I came. Well, yet, thought I, this is well, I like this well. This man doth somewhat regard and consider his office and duty. I came too late for mine own matter and lost my journey and my early rising too, and yet I was glad that I had been so beguiled. For God's love, follow this exam-

[24] *Utter:* outer.

ple, ye great men, and arise in the mornings and be ready for men to speak with them and to dispatch suitors that resort unto you. But all these I bring to disprove them that defend evil things because they be not expressly spoken against in the scripture. But what forceth that, when the devil hath his purpose and is served as well one way as another way? Though it be not expressly spoken against in scripture, yet I reckon plainly enough implied in the scripture.

But now to come to my matter again: *Videte et cavete ab avaritia,* "See and beware of covetousness." And I shall desire you to consider four things: *Quis dicat; quid dicat; cui dicat; et quare dicat.* Who speaketh it, what he speaketh, to whom he speaketh, and wherefore he speaketh it. As here, Christ speaketh to a rich man against avarice. And why against avarice? What shall be the end of all covetous persons? Eternal damnation. "For the covetous persons," saith Paul, "shall not possess nor enter into the kingdom of God." Here therefore I shall desire you to pray, etc.

FIRST SERMON ON THE LORD'S PRAYER 1552[1]

"Our Father which art in heaven" (Matt. 6:9)

I HAVE entered of late in the way of preaching and spoken many things of prayer, and rather of prayer than of any other thing. For I think there is nothing more necessary to be spoken of nor more abused than prayer was by the craft and subtlety of the devil, for many things were taken for prayer when they were nothing less. Therefore at this same time also I have thought it good to entreat of prayer, to the intent that it might be known what a precious thing right prayer is. I told you, first, what prayer is. Secondarily, to whom we ought to pray. Thirdly, where and in what place we ought to pray. And fourthly, I told you the diversity of prayer, namely, of the common prayer and the private. These and suchlike things I have dilated and expounded unto you of late in the open pulpit.

Now at this present time I intend as by the way of a lecture, at the

[1] The volume (STC 15276) in which this sermon was first printed is in two parts. The title page reads, in part: "27 Sermons Preached by the ryght Reuerende father in God and constant Matir of Iesus Christe, Maister Hugh Latimer. . . . Imprinted at London by Iohn Day, dwelling ouer Aldersgate. . . . Anno. 1562."

Part II, in which the present sermon occurs, is headed: "Certaine sermons made by the right reuerende father in God, maister doctor Latymer, before the right vertuous and honorable lady, Katherine duchesse of Suffolke, in the yere of our Lord. 1552."

request of my most gracious Lady, to expound unto you, her household servants, and other that be willing to hear, the right understanding and meaning of this most perfect prayer which our Saviour Himself taught us at the request of His disciples, which prayer we call the *Pater Noster*. This prayer of our Lord may be called a prayer above all prayers, the principal and most perfect prayer, which prayer ought to be regarded above all others, considering that our Saviour Himself is the author of it. He was the maker of the prayer, being very God and very man. He taught us this prayer, Which is a most perfect schoolmaster, and commanded us to say it. Which prayer containeth great and wonderful things, if a learned man had the handling of it. But as for me, such things as I have conceived by the reading of learned men's books, so far forth as God will give me His grace and Spirit, I will show unto you touching the very meaning of it and what is to be understand by every word contained in that prayer. For there is no word idle or spoken in vain. For it must needs be perfect, good, and of great importance, being our Saviour's teaching, which is the wisdom of God itself.

There be many other psalms and prayers in scripture very good and godly, and it is good to know them; but it is with this prayer, the Lord's Prayer, I say, like as with the law of love. All the laws of Moses as concerning what is to be done to please God, how to walk before Him uprightly and godly, all such laws are contained in this law of love. *Diliges Dominum Deum tuum ex toto corde tuo, et in tota anima tua, et in tota mente tua, et proximum sicut teipsum,* "Thou shalt love the Lord thy God with all thy heart, with all thy soul, and with all thy mind, and thy neighbor as thyself" (Matt. 22:37, 39). Even so is it with this prayer. For like as the law of love is the sum and abridgment of the other laws, so this prayer is the sum and abridgment of all other prayers. All the other prayers are contained in this prayer; yea, whatsoever mankind hath need of to soul and body, that same is contained in this prayer.

This prayer hath two parts: it hath a preface, which some call a salutation or a loving entrance; secondarily, the prayer itself. The entrance is this: *Cum oratis, dicite, Pater Noster, qui es in coelis,* "Our Father, which art in heaven" (Matt. 6:9). As who [should] say, "You Christian people, you that bear the name of Christians, you must pray so." Before I go any further, I must put you in remembrance to consider how much we be bound to our Saviour Christ that He would vouchsafe to teach us to pray and in this prayer to signify unto us the good will which our Heavenly Father beareth towards us. Now to the matter.

"Our Father." These words pertain not to the petitions; they be but an entering, a seeking favor at God's hand. Yet if we well weigh and consider them, they admonish us of many things and strengthen our faith wondrous well. For this word "Father" signifieth that we be Christ's brothers and that God is our Father. He is the eldest Son. He is the Son of God by nature; we be His sons by adoption through His goodness. Therefore He biddeth us to call Him our Father, which is to be had in fresh memory and great reputation. For here we are admonished how that we be reconciled unto God; we which beforetimes were His enemies are made now the children of God and inheritors of everlasting life. Thus we be admonished by this word "Father." So that it is a word of much importance and great reputation, for it confirmeth our faith when we call Him "Father." Therefore our Saviour, when He teacheth us to call God "Father," teacheth us to understand the fatherly affection which God beareth towards us; which thing maketh us bold and hearty to call upon Him, knowing that He beareth a good will towards us and that He will surely hear our prayers. When we be in trouble, we doubt of a stranger whether he will help us or not; but our Saviour, commanding us to call God "Father," teacheth us to be assured of the love and good will of God toward us. So by this word "Father" we learn to stablish and to comfort our faith, knowing most assuredly that He will be good unto us. For Christ was a perfect schoolmaster; He lacked no wisdom. He knew His Father's will and pleasure; He teacheth us, yea, and most certainly assureth us, that God will be no cruel judge but a loving Father. Here we see what commodities we have in this word "Father."

Seeing now that we find such commodities by this one word, we ought to consider the whole prayer with great diligence and earnest mind. For there is no word nor letter contained in this prayer but it is of great importance and weight; therefore it is necessary for us to know and to understand it thoroughly, and then to speak it considerately with great devotion. Else it is to no purpose to speak the words without understanding; it is but lip-labor and vain babbling and so unworthy to be called prayer, as it was in times past used in England. Therefore, when you say this prayer, you must well consider what you say, for it is better once said deliberately with understanding than a thousand times without understanding, which is in very deed but vain babbling and so more a displeasure than pleasure unto God. For the matter lieth not in much saying but in well saying. So if it be said to the honor of God, then it hath his effect and we shall have our petitions. For God is true in His promises, and our Saviour, knowing Him to be well affected towards us, commandeth us therefore to call Him "Father."

Here you must understand that like as our Saviour was most earnest and fervent in teaching us how to pray and call upon God for aid and help and for things necessary both to our souls and bodies, so the devil, that old serpent, with no less diligence endeavoreth himself to let and stop our prayers, so that we shall not call upon God. And amongst other his lets he hath one especially wherewith he thinketh to keep us from prayer, which is the remembrance of our sins. When he perceiveth us to be disposed to pray, he cometh with his craft and subtle conveyances, saying, "What, wilt thou pray unto God for aid and help? Knowest thou not that thou art a wicked sinner and a transgressor of the law of God? Look rather to be damned and judged for thy ill doings than to receive any benefit at His hands. Wilt thou call Him 'Father' which is so holy a God, and thou art so wicked and miserable a sinner?" This the devil will say and trouble our minds, to stop and let us from our prayer, and so to give us occasion not to pray unto God.

In this temptation we must seek for some remedy and comfort, for the devil doth put us in remembrance of our sins to that end, to keep us from prayer and invocation of God. The remedy for this temptation is to call our Saviour to remembrance, Who hath taught us to say this prayer. He knew His Father's pleasure; He knew what He did. When He commanded us to call God our Father, He knew we should find fatherly affections in God towards us. Call this, I say, to remembrance, and then again remember that our Saviour hath cleansed through His Passion all our sins and taken away all our wickedness, so that as many as believe in Him shall be the children of God. In such wise let us strive and fight against the temptations of the devil, which would not have us to call upon God because we be sinners. Catch thou hold of our Saviour, believe in Him, be assured in thy heart that He with His suffering took away all thy sins. Consider again, that our Saviour calleth us to prayer and commandeth us to pray. Our sins let us and withdraw us from prayer, but our Saviour maketh them nothing. When we believe in Him, it is like as if we had no sins. For He changeth with us. He taketh our sins and wickedness from us and giveth unto us His holiness, righteousness, justice, fulfilling of the law, and so, consequently, everlasting life. So that we be like as if we had done no sin at all, for His righteousness standeth us in so good stead as though we of our own selves had fulfilled the law to the uttermost.

Therefore our sins cannot let us nor withdraw us from prayer, for they be gone. They are no sins; they cannot be hurtful unto us, Christ dying for us, as all the scripture both of the New and Old Testament witnesseth. *Dolores nostros ipse portavit,* "He hath taken away our sorrows" (Isa. 53:4). Like as when I owe unto a man an hundreth pound. The day is expired, he will have his money; I have it not, and for lack of it I am laid in prison. In such distress cometh a good friend and saith, "Sir, be of good cheer, I will pay thy debts," and forthwith payeth the whole sum and setteth me at liberty.

Such a friend is our Saviour. He hath paid our debts and set us at liberty, else we should have been damned world without end in everlasting prison and darkness. Therefore, though our sins condemn us, yet when we allege Christ and believe in Him our sins shall not hurt us. For St. John saith, *Si quis peccaverit, advocatum habemus apud Patrem, Jesum Christum justum,* "We have an advocate with God the Father, Jesus Christ the righteous" (I John 2:1). Mark that he saith *advocatum, non advocatos.* He speaketh singularly, not plurally. We have one advocate, not many, neither saints nor anybody else but only Him and none other, neither by the way of mediation nor by the way of redemption. He only is sufficient, for He only is all the doer. Let Him have all the whole praise. Let us not withdraw from Him His majesty and give it to creatures. For He only satisfieth for the sins of the whole world, so that all that believe in Christ be clean from all the filthiness of their sins. For St. John Baptist saith, *Ecce Agnus Dei qui tollit peccata mundi,* "Behold the Lamb of God, which taketh away the sins of the world" (John 1:29). Doth the devil call thee from prayer? Christ calleth thee unto it again. For so it is written, *In hoc apparuit Filius Dei, ut destruat opera diaboli,* "To that end the Son of God appeared, to destroy the works of the devil" (I John 3:9).

But mark here. Scripture speaketh not of impenitent sinners. Christ suffered not for them; His death remedieth not their sins. For they be the bondmen of the devil and his slaves, and therefore Christ's benefits pertain not unto them. It is a wonderful saying that St. John hath, "Behold the Lamb of God that taketh away the sins of the world." The devil saith unto me, "Thou art a sinner." "No," saith St. John, "the Lamb of God hath taken away thy sins." *Item, Habentes igitur pontificem magnum qui penetravit coelos, Jesum Filium Dei, accedamus cum fiducia ad thronum gratiae, ut consequamur misericordiam,* "We therefore having a great high Priest, Which hath passed through the heavens, even Jesus the Son of God, let us with boldness go unto the seat of His grace that we may obtain mercy" (Hebrews 4:14, 16). Oh, it is a comfortable thing that we have an access unto God! Isaiah saith, *In livore ejus sanati sumus,* "The pain of our punishment was laid upon Him and with His stripes are we healed" (Isa. 53:5). Further, in the New Testament we read, *Huic omnes prophetae testimonium perhibent, remissionem peccatorum accipere per nomen ejus omnes qui credunt in eum,* "Unto the same bear all prophets witness, that all they do receive forgiveness of sins by His name which believe on Him" (Acts 10:43).

Now you see how ye be remedied from your sins; you hear how you shall withstand the devil, when he will withdraw you from prayer. Let us therefore not give over prayer but stick unto it. Let us rather believe Christ our Saviour than the devil, which was a liar at the beginning. You know now how you may prevent him, how you may put him off and avoid his temptations.

There is one other addition, afore we come to the petitions, which doth much confirm our faith and increase the same: *Qui es in coelis,* "Which art in heaven." These words put a diversity between the Heavenly Father and our temporal fathers. There be some temporal fathers which would fain help their children, but they cannot; they be not able to help them. Again, there be some fathers which are rich and might help their children, but they be so unnatural they will not help them. But our Heavenly Father, in that we call Him "Father" we learn that He will help, that He beareth a fatherly love towards us.

"In heaven." Here we learn that He is able to help us, to give us all good things necessary to soul and body, and is mighty to defend us from all ill and peril. So it appeareth that He is a Father Which will help and that He, being celestial, Which is able to help us. Therefore we may have a boldness and confidence that He may help us and that He will help us where and whensoever we call. He saith, *Coelum et terram impleo,* "I fill heaven and earth" (Jer. 23:24). And again, *Coelum mihi sedes est, et terra scabellum pedum meorum,* "Heaven is My seat and the earth is My footstool" (Isa. 66:1), where we see that He is a mighty God, that He is in heaven and earth with His power and might. In heaven He is apparently, where face to face He showeth Himself unto His angels and saints. In earth He is not so apparently, but darkly and obscurely He exhibiteth Himself unto us, for our corrupt and feeble flesh could not bear His majesty. Yet He filleth the earth; that is to say, He ruleth and governeth the same, ordering all things according unto His will and pleasure. Therefore we must learn to persuade ourselves and undoubtedly believe that He is able to help, and that He beareth a good and fatherly will towards us, that He will not forget us. Therefore the King and prophet David saith, *Dominus de coelo prospexit,* "The Lord hath seen down from heaven" (Psalm 53:2). As far as the earth is from heaven, yet God looketh down; He seeth all things, He is in every corner.

He saith the Lord hath looked down, not the saints. No, he saith not so, for the saints have not so sharp eyes to see down from heaven. They be spur-blind,[2] and sand-blind; [3] they cannot see so far nor have not so long ears to hear. And therefore our petition and prayer should be unto Him Which will hear and can hear. For it is the Lord that looketh down. He is here in earth, as I told you, very darkly, but He is in heaven most manifestly, where He showeth Himself unto His angels and saints face to face. We read in scripture that Abel's blood did cry unto God.[4] Where it appeareth that He can hear, yea, not only hear but also see and feel. For He seeth over all things, so that the least thought of our hearts is not hid from Him. Therefore ponder and consider these words well, for they fortify our faith. We call Him "Father" to put ourselves in remembrance of His good will towards us. "Heavenly" we call Him, signifying His might and power that He may help and do all things according to His will and pleasure. So it appeareth most manifestly that there lacketh neither good will nor power in Him. There was

[2] *Spur-blind* (= *purblind*): totally blind. [3] *Sand-blind:* half-blind.

[4] Gen. 4:1–16.

once a prophet which, when he was ill entreated of King Joash, said, *Dominus videat et requirat,* "The Lord look upon it and require it" (II Chron. 24:22). There be many men in England, and otherwhere else, which care not for God—yea, they be clean without God—which say in their hearts, *Nubes latibulum ejus, nec nostra considerat, et circa cardines coeli ambulat,* "Tush, the clouds cover Him that He may not see, and He dwelleth above in heaven" (Job 22:14). But, as I told you before, Abel's blood may certify us of His present knowledge. Let us therefore take heed that we do nothing that might displease His majesty, neither openly nor secretly, for He is everywhere and nothing can be hid from Him. *Videt et requiret,* "He seeth it and will punish it."

Further, this word "Father" is not only apt and convenient for us to strengthen our faith withal, as I told you, but also it moveth God the sooner to hear us when we call Him by that name, "Father." For He, perceiving our confidence in Him, cannot choose but show Him like a Father. So that this word "Father" is most meet to move God to pity and to grant our requests. Certain it is, and proved by Holy Scripture, that God hath a fatherly and loving affection towards us far passing the love of bodily parents to their children. Yea, as far as heaven and earth is asunder, so far His love towards mankind exceedeth the love of natural parents to their children. Which love is set out by the mouth of His holy prophet Isaiah, where he saith, *Num oblivioni tradet mulier infantem suum, quo minus misereatur filii uteri sui? Si esto obliviscatur illae, ego tamen tui non obliviscar,* "Will a wife forget the child of her womb and the son whom she hath borne? And though she do forget him, yet will I not forget thee" (Isa. 49:15). Here are showed the affections and unspeakable love which God beareth towards us. He saith, *nunquid potest mulier,* "may a woman?" He speaketh of the woman, meaning the man too; but because women most commonly are more affected towards their children than men be, therefore He nameth the woman. And it is a very unnatural woman that hateth her child or neglecteth the same.

But, oh, Lord, what crafts and conveyances useth the devil abroad that he can bring his matters so to pass that some women set aside not alonely all motherly affections but also all natural humanity, insomuch that they kill their own children, their own blood and flesh! I was alate credibly informed of a priest which had taken in hand to be a midwife. Oh, what an abominable thing is this! But what followed? He ordered the matter so that the poor innocent was lost in the mean season. Such things the devil can bring to pass, but what then? God saith, "Though a woman do forget her children, though they kill them, yet will I not forget thee, saith the Lord God Almighty." Truth it is there be some women very unnatural and unkind, which shall receive their punishments of God for it; but for all that we ought to beware and not believe every tale told unto us and so rashly judge. I know what I mean. There hath been alate such tales spread abroad and most untruly. Such false tale tellers shall have a grievous punishment of the Lord when He shall come to reward everyone according unto his deserts.

Here I have occasion to tell you a story which happened at Cambridge. Master Bilney—or rather St. Bilney, that suffered death for God's word sake [5]—the same Bilney was the instrument whereby God called me to knowledge.[6] For I may thank him, next to God, for that knowledge that I have in the Word of God. For I was as obstinate a papist as any was in England, insomuch that when I should be made Bachelor of Divinity, my whole oration went against Philip Melanchthon and against his opinions. Bilney heard me at that time and perceived that I was zealous without knowledge; and he came to me afterward in my study and desired me, for God's sake, to hear his confession. I did so; and, to say the truth, by his confession I learned more than afore in many years. So from that time forward I began to smell the Word of God and forsook the school doctors and such fooleries.

Now, after I had been acquainted with him, I went with him to

[5] See the "Seventh Sermon before Edward VI," pp. 120–121.

[6] I.e., knowledge of the true faith.

visit the prisoners in the Tower at Cambridge,[7] for he was ever visiting prisoners and sick folk. So we went together and exhorted them as well as we were able to do, moving them to patience and to acknowledge their faults. Among other prisoners there was a woman which was accused that she had killed her own child, which act she plainly and steadfastly denied and could not be brought to confess the act. Which denying gave us occasion to search for the matter, and so we did. And at the length we found that her husband loved her not, and therefore he sought means to make her out of the way. The matter was thus: a child of hers had been sick by the space of a year and so decayed as it were in a consumption. At the length it died in harvest time. She went to her neighbors and other friends to desire their help to prepare the child to the burial. But there was nobody at home; every man was in the field. The woman, in a heaviness and trouble of spirit, went and, being herself alone, prepared the child to the burial. Her husband, coming home, not having great love towards her, accused her of the murder; and so she was taken and brought to Cambridge. But as far forth as I could learn through earnest inquisition, I thought in my conscience the woman was not guilty, all the circumstances well considered.

Immediately after this I was called to preach before the King, which was my first sermon that I made before His Majesty, and it was done at Windsor,[8] where His Majesty, after the sermon was done, did most familiarly talk with me in a gallery. Now, when I saw my time, I kneeled down before His Majesty, opening the whole matter, and afterwards most humbly desired His Majesty to pardon that woman. For I thought in my conscience she was not guilty, else I would not for all the world sue for a murderer. The King most graciously heard my humble request, insomuch that I had a pardon ready for her at my return homeward. In the mean

[7] The tower of the castle built by William the Conqueror on Castle Hill on the north side of the town. Although by Latimer's time much of the castle had been demolished and the materials used by the builders of the colleges, the tower itself continued to be used as a prison.

[8] On March 13 (the second Sunday in Lent), 1530.

season that same woman was delivered of a child in the Tower at Cambridge, whose godfather I was, and Mistress Cheke[9] was godmother. But all that time I hid my pardon and told her nothing of it, only exhorting her to confess the truth. At the length the time came when she looked to suffer. I came, as I was wont to do, to instruct her. She made great moan to me and most earnestly required me that I would find the means that she might be purified before her suffering, for she thought she should have been damned if she should suffer without purification. Where Master Bilney and I told her that that law was made unto the Jews and not unto us, and that women lying in childbed be not unclean afore God. Neither is purification used to that end that it should cleanse from sin, but rather a civil and politic law, made for natural honesty sake, signifying that a woman before the time of her purification, that is to say as long as she is a green woman,[10] is not meet to do such acts as other women nor to have company with her husband. For it is against natural honesty and against the commonwealth. To that end purification is kept and used, not to make a superstition or holiness of it, as some do which think that they may not fetch neither fire nor anything in that house where there is a green woman, which opinion is erroneous and wicked. For women, as I said afore, be as well in the favor of God before they be purified as after. So we travailed with this woman till we brought her to a good trade[11] and at the length showed her the King's pardon and let her go.

This tale I told you by this occasion, that though some women be very unnatural and forget their children, yet when we hear anybody so report, we should not be too hasty in believing the tale but rather suspend our judgments till we know the truth.[12] And again, we shall

[9] The mother of Sir John Cheke, the distinguished humanist.

[10] *Green woman:* a woman recently delivered of a child.

[11] *Trade:* frame of mind.

[12] Twice in this sermon (see above, p. 167) Latimer alludes to false reports that a woman has neglected her children. One wonders whether such reports could have circulated concerning the Duchess of Suffolk, whose two sons by her first husband, Charles Brandon, had died of the sweating sickness a year earlier.

mark hereby the great love and loving-kindness of God our loving Father, who showeth Himself so loving unto us that, notwithstanding women forget sometimes their own natural children, yet He will not forget us. He will hear us when we call upon Him, as He saith by the evangelist Matthew: "Ask and it shall be given unto you; seek and ye shall find; knock and it shall be opened unto you," etc. (Matt. 7:7). Then He cometh and bringeth in a pretty similitude, saying: "Is there any man amongst you which, if his son ask bread, will offer him a stone? If ye then," *cum sitis mali,* "being evil, can give your children good gifts," etc. (Matt. 7:11). In these words, where He saith *cum sitis mali,* "which be evil," He giveth us our own proper name. He painteth us out; He pincheth us; He cutteth off our combs; He plucketh down our stomachs. And here we learn to acknowledge ourselves to be wicked and to know Him to be the wellspring and fountain of all goodness and that all good things come of Him.

Therefore let every man think lowly of himself, humble himself, and call upon God, Which is ready to give us not only bread and drink or other necessaries but the Holy Ghost. To whom will He give the Holy Ghost? To lords and ladies, to gentlemen or gentlewomen? No, not so. He is not ruled by affections; He hath not respect unto personages. *Poscentibus,* saith He, "unto those which call upon Him," being rich or poor, lords or knights, beggars or rich; He is ready to give unto them when they come to Him. And this is a great comfort unto those which be poor and miserable in this world, for they may be assured of the help of God, yea, and as boldly go unto Him and desire His help as the greatest king in earth. But we must ask, we must inquire for it; He would have us to be importune, to be earnest and diligent in desiring. Then we shall receive when we come with a good faith and confidence. To whom shall we call? Not unto the saints. *Poscentibus illum,* saith He. Those that call upon Him shall be heard. Therefore we ought to come to Him only and not unto His saints.

But one word is left which we must needs consider—*noster,* "our." He saith not "my," but "our." Wherefore saith He "our?" This word "our" teacheth us to consider that the Father of heaven is a common Father, as well my neighbor's Father as mine, as well the poor man's Father as the rich. So that He is not a peculiar Father but a Father to the whole church and congregation, to all the faithful. Be they never so poor, so vile, so foul and despised, yet He is their Father as well as mine. And therefore I should not despise them but consider that God is their Father as well as mine. Here may we perceive what communion is between us, so that when I pray, I pray not for myself alone but for all the rest. Again, when they pray, they pray not for themselves only but for me. For Christ hath so framed this prayer that I must needs include my neighbor in it. Therefore all those which pray this prayer, they pray as well for me as for themselves, which is a great comfort to every faithful heart when he considereth that all the church prayeth for him. For amongst such a great number there be some which be good and whose prayer God will hear. As it appeared by Abraham's prayer, which prayer was so effectuous that God would have pardoned Sodom and Gomorrah if He might have found but ten good persons therein.[13] Likewise St. Paul in shipwreck preserved his company by his prayer.[14] So that it is a great comfort unto us to know that all good and faithful persons pray for us.

There be some learned men which gather out of scripture that the prayer of St. Stephen was the occasion of the conversion of St. Paul. St. Chrysostom saith that that prayer that I make for myself is the best and is of more efficacy than that which is made in common.[15] Which saying I like not very well. For our Saviour was better learned than St. Chrysostom. He taught us to pray in common for all. Therefore we ought to follow Him and to be glad to pray one

[13] Gen. 18:23–33. [14] Acts 27.

[15] I have not discovered this statement, or anything resembling it, in the writings of Chrysostom.

for another, for we have a common saying amongst us, "Whosoever loveth me, loveth my hound." [16] So whosoever loveth God will love his neighbor, which is made after the image of God.

And here is to be noted that prayer hath one property before all other good works. For with my alms I help but one or two at once, but with my faithful prayer I help all. I desire God to comfort all men living, but specially *domesticos fidei,* "those which be of the household of God" (Gal. 6:10). Yet we ought to pray with all our hearts for the other which believe not, that God will turn their hearts and renew them with His Spirit. Yea, our prayer reacheth so far that our very capital enemy ought not to be omitted. Here you see what an excellent thing prayer is. When it proceedeth from a faithful heart, it doth far pass all the good works that men can do.

Now to make an end. We are monished here of charity and taught that God is not only a private Father but a common Father unto the whole world, unto all faithful. Be they never so poor and miserable in this world, yet He is their Father. Where we may learn humility and lowliness; specially great and rich men shall learn here not to be lofty or to despise the poor. For when ye despise the poor miserable man, whom despise ye? Ye despise him which called God his Father as well as you, and peradventure more acceptable and more regarded in His sight than you be. Those proud persons may learn here to leave their stubbornness and loftiness. But there be a great many which little regard this. They think themselves better than other men be and so despise and contemn the poor, insomuch that they will not hear poor men's causes nor defend them from wrong and oppression of the rich and mighty.[17] Such proud men despise the Lord's Prayer. They should be as careful for their brethren as for themselves. And such humility, such love and carefulness towards our neighbors, we learn by this word "our." Therefore I desire you, on God's behalf, let us cast away all disdainfulness,

[16] This saying goes back at least to St. Bernard's *qui me amat, amet et canem meum* in *Sermo in Festo Sancti Michaelis* (ca. 1150).

[17] See the "Second Sermon before Edward VI," pp. 86–89.

all proudness, yea, and all bibble-babble.[18] Let us pray this prayer with understanding and great deliberation, not following the trade of monkery, which was without all devotion and understanding.

There be but few which can say from the bottom of their hearts, "Our Father," a little number. Neither the Turks, neither the Jews, nor yet the impenitent sinners, can call God their Father. Therefore it is but vain babbling, whatsoever they pray. God heareth them not; He will not receive their prayers. The promise of hearing is made unto them only which be faithful and believe in God, which endeavor themselves to live according unto His commandments. For scripture saith, *Oculi Domini super justos,* "The eyes of the Lord are over the righteous and His ears open unto their prayers" (Psalm 33:18). But who are those righteous? Every penitent sinner that is sorry from the bottom of his heart for his wickedness and believeth that God will forgive him his sins for His Son our Saviour Jesus Christ's sake. This is called in scripture "a just man," that endeavoreth himself to leave all wickedness. In such sort Peter and Paul were just, because they did repent and believed in Christ and so endeavored themselves to live according unto God's laws. Therefore, like as they were made just before God, so may we too, for we have even the selfsame promise. Let us therefore follow their ensample. Let us forsake all sins and wickedness; then God will hear our prayers. For scripture saith, *Dominus facit quicquid volunt timentes eum, et clamorem eorum exaudit ac servat eos,* "The Lord fulfilleth the desire of them that fear Him; He also will hear their cry and help them" (Psalm 145:19). In another place He saith, *Si manseritis in sermone meo, et verba mea custodiveritis, quicquid volueritis petentes accipietis,* "If ye abide in Me, and My words abide in you, ask what you will, and it shall be done for you" (John 15:7). So we see that the promises pertain only to the faithful, to those which endeavor themselves to live according to God's will and pleasure, which can be content to leave their wickedness and follow

[18] *Bibble-babble:* idle talk.

godliness. Those God will hear at all times, whensoever they shall call upon Him.

Remember now what I have said. Remember what is meant by this word "our," namely, that it admonisheth us of love and charity; it teacheth us to beware of stubbornness and proudness, considering that God loved as well the beggar as the rich man, for He regardeth no persons. Again, what is to be understood by this word "Father," namely, that He beareth a good will towards us, that He is ready and willing to help us. "Heavenly," that admonisheth us of His potency and ability, that He is ruler over all things. This, I say, remember and follow it. Then we shall receive all things necessary for this life and finally everlasting joy and felicity. Amen. Let us pray, "Our Father."

SERMON FOR CHRISTMAS DAY 1552[1]

A SERMON MADE ON CHRISTMAS DAY BY MASTER HUGH LATIMER AT BAXTERLEY, THE TWENTY-FIFTH OF DECEMBER, 1552

Factum est autem in diebus illis, exiit decretum a Caesare Augusto, etc. (Luke 2:1)

THIS Gospel maketh specially mention of the nativity of our Saviour Jesus Christ, declaring how Mary with her husband Joseph came, after the commandment of the Emperor, from Nazareth unto Bethlehem, the city of David, of whose lineage and tribe she was; what miseries and calamities she suffered by the way; and how poor and miserable she was, having nothing that pertained to a woman being in her case, you may right well consider. And as touching His

[1] The title page of the volume (STC 15277) in which this and the following sermon were first printed reads in part as follows: "Frutefull Sermons Preached by the right reuerend father, and constant Martyr of Iesus Christ M. Hugh Latymer newly Imprinted: with others, not heretofore set forth in print, to the edifying of all which will dispose them selues to the readyng of the same. . . . 1571. ¶At London, Printed by Iohn Daye, dwelling ouer Aldersgate. Cum priuilegio Regiae Maiestatis per Decennium."

nativity, His poverty, how He was born in a stable among beasts, lacking all manner of necessary things which appertained to young children, insomuch that He had neither cradle nor clouts. Wherefore Mary, His mother, wrapped Him, as it is most like, in her own apparel and laid Him in a manger, where He was showed, not to the rulers of this world, neither to kings, potentates, or bishops, but rather to simple shepherds and poor servants keeping their sheep in the field. To these poor wretches the angel of God was sent, which proclaimed these great things unto them, saying: "Be not afraid, for behold, I bring you tidings of great gladness, that shall come to all people: for unto you is born this day in the city of David a Saviour, which is Christ the Lord," etc. (Luke 2:10–11).

This is the greatest comfort in the world, to know that our Saviour is born, that He is abroad and at hand unto everyone that calleth upon Him. What greater gladness can be unto a man that feeleth his sin and seeth his damnation before his eyes? Unto such a man nothing is more acceptable than to hear that there is a Saviour which will help him and heal his sores. Therefore this message of the angel was a very joyful tidings.

The angel bade them go unto Bethlehem and to search for the child. And forthwith a great many of angels came together rejoicing, singing, and praising God for our sakes, that the Redeemer of mankind was born into the world. For without Him nothing availeth in the sight of God the Father. Without Him no man can praise God, because it hath pleased God for His Son's sake only to show Himself favorable and loving unto mankind, and to receive only that prayer which is made unto Him in the name of Christ our Saviour. Therefore all those which come without Him before God shall be rejected as persons rebellious against God and His constitutions. For the will, pleasure, and counsel of God is to receive only those which come to Him in the name of His Son our Saviour, which know themselves, lament their own sins, and confess their own naughtiness and wickedness, and put their whole trust and confidence only in the Son of God, the Redeemer of mankind, as the angels themselves testify.

Here in this gospel note that here was singing and rejoicing for the great and unspeakable goodness and mercy of Almighty God the Father, Whom it pleased to redeem mankind through the death of His only, natural, and most dearly beloved Son, our Saviour and Redeemer Jesus Christ; very God and very man; the Son of God after His Godhead; the Son of Mary after His manhood, which He hath taken upon Him for man's sake, to redeem and deliver the same from all misery and to set him at unity with God the Father and finally to bring him to everlasting life.

Now it followeth in the text, "As soon as the angels were gone from them," etc. (Luke 2:15). Mark here that the angels, as soon as they had done their business, they returned unto their master which had sent them. By the which all good and godly servants may learn that whensoever their masters send them on their business, they ought to do the same diligently and quickly to return again to their masters, not spending the time in loitering and lewdness,[2] as the common sort of servants do in these days, clean contrary to the ensample of these angels of God, which returned to God immediately after their message[3] was done. And I would to God that all servants would consider this and keep in remembrance these angels of God! For if this were well considered, there would not be so great complaint of the lewd[4] service of servants, as there is everywhere. God amend it!

We read here that the angels appeared visibly and in sight. By the which we shall consider that whensoever or wheresoever the word of God is preached, there are the angels present, which keep in safe custody all those which receive the word of God and study to live after it, for St. Paul calleth them *administratores Spiritus,* that is to say, "the administrators and servants of the Spirit" (Heb. 1:14). Therefore, seeing the angels are present, it is meet for us to come

[2] *Lewdness:* foolishness. [3] *Message:* errand, task. [4] *Lewd:* worthless.

with great reverence to the word of God, where Himself with His angels are present.

"The angels return to heaven," etc. (Luke 2:15). Here I will not dispute before you where heaven is nor how many heavens there be. Such obscure questions appertain not to you that are ignorant and unlearned. For this is sufficient for you to know, that wheresoever God doth exhibit and show Himself, there is heaven. God is everywhere, as He saith, *Coelum et terram impleo* (Jer. 23:24). But wheresoever most apparently He exhibiteth Himself to His saints and angels, the same properly is called "heaven"; and thither went these angels after they had done their message, to wait upon the Lord, ready to go and do all that which He would command them. Wherein you may learn the great love and kindness of God, the Heavenly Father, which hath made and created them for our sakes, to this end, that they should defend and keep us from our strong and mighty enemy and prince of this world, the devil, whose power passeth all man's power; insomuch that except God did preserve us from him by the ministration of His obedient angels we should all perish both soul and body. But thanks be unto God, Which never ceaseth to provide for us, to preserve both our souls and bodies! But mark here that we are not bound to call upon the angels when we hear that they serve us, but rather to give God thanks in them, that He hath vouchsafed to set such watchmen about us. Therefore learn only to hope and trust in the Lord and give laud and thanks unto Him, like as the angels themselves do, singing with great pleasant voice, as Luke saith. This is enough of the angels. Now let us come to the shepherds.

"The shepherds said one to another, 'Let us go unto Bethlehem and see these things which we hear say is happened, that the Lord hath showed unto us'" (Luke 2:15). Here note the faith of these poor shepherds, which believed the saying of the angels so steadfastly that they were ready to go and do after the commandment of the said angels. They did not as many of us do, which are so slothful that we will not scant abide one hour to hear the word of God, and, when we have heard the same, we believe it not, we regard it not; it goeth in at one ear and out at the other. Wherefore it is not to be marveled that God is angry with us, seeing we are so forgetful and unthankful for His great and exceeding benefits showed unto us in these later days of the world.

This is a comfortable place for servants, which should be more diligent in their business than they be, considering that God regardeth them so much that He is content to open His great and high mysteries unto servants first, setting aside all kings and rulers in this world, which are only esteemed in the sight of men. Here, therefore, learn, O ye servants, and consider that God no less regardeth you than the greatest lords in the world if you live after His commandments, which is that you shall serve your masters truly and uprightly and not with a feigned heart.

"Let us go to Bethlehem," saith the shepherds. Here is to be noted in these shepherds a great charity among themselves, in that one exhorteth another to go to follow the word of God. Many folks nowadays agree and exhort themselves to do wickedly, to steal, to pick,[5] and to do all lewdness, but to exhort their neighbors to any goodness, as those shepherds did, they will not agree. Therefore let us not be ashamed to learn of these poor shepherds to follow their ensamples. When we hear the word of God, let one exhort another to follow the same, and let us agree in goodness to seek Christ and to follow Him according to His word, and then we shall find Him. Let the curate exhort his parishioners to follow the commandments of God. Let the householder exhort his wife, children, servants, and family to the seeking of Christ. Let every neighbor exhort another to goodness. Yea, let everyone consider that no one person is born into the world for his own sake but for the commonwealth sake. Let us therefore walk charitably, not seeking our own commodities[6] but the honor and glory of God and the wealth of our even Christian,[7] with exhortations, admonitions, and prayers one for another, that

[5] *Pick:* rob. [6] *Commodities:* interests, benefits.
[7] *Even Christian:* fellow Christian.

the name of God may be magnified among us and His will known and fulfilled. Of these poor shepherds we may learn much goodness; yea, the best doctor of divinity need not be ashamed to learn of them and to follow their ensamples, which are now saints in heaven and the inheritors of everlasting life.

But yet we must beware that we go not too far. For we may not make gods of them nor call upon them, as we have been taught in times past, because God will be called upon, honored, and worshiped alone. He may not suffer any to be fellow with Him; as He Himself saith, "I give Mine honor to none" (Isa. 42:8). Therefore we must call upon Him only and seek all manner of comfort at His hand, which is the fountain of all goodness, and not at the saints'. But if you will needs worship them, will you hear how you shall worship them? Live godly and uprightly after their example; follow their charitable life and steadfast faith; then you worship them as they ought to be worshiped. But to call upon them is not a worship but a detestable idolatry, because, as I said before, we must call upon God only and not saints. For when we call upon them, we make them gods; and then we put God out of His seat and place them in it. Which manner of doing God cannot suffer unpunished, and therefore beware.

Farther, we learn in this gospel the nature of very true and unfeigned faith. These shepherds, as soon as the angels were gone from them, they laid their heads together and consulted what was best to do, and at the length with one consent concluded to forsake and set aside all their flocks of sheep and cattle and to go unto Bethlehem to seek the Saviour. Here appeareth their excellent, marvelous, and great faith, for they were in peril of body and goods. To leave a flock of sheep a whole night without a shepherd could not be done without great danger; for that the same country, as is said before, brought forth many wild and harmful beasts, ready to devour the whole flock of sheep in one night: as we read of a lion that killed a prophet, but not without the sufferance of God; [8] also

[8] I Kings 13:23–26.

of the lion which Samson killed when he went to see his new married wife;[9] also we read in the scripture of two bears that killed at one instant forty-four young children that mocked the prophet Elisha.[10]

So that it appeareth, partly by the Holy Scripture and partly by other writers (as Josephus), that the same country is full of such manner of devouring beasts. Therefore, to leave a flock of sheep without a shepherd was a great matter for them to do, which were but servants and were bound to make amends for all that should happen to be lost, as we read of Jacob, which ever made good out of his own flock unto Laban, his father-in-law, when anything had been lost.[11] So it appeareth that these shepherds were in peril of body and goods, for if they had not been able to make amends, then they themselves should have been sold to perpetual slavery and bondage, like horses or brute beasts. But faith, when it is not feigned, feareth no peril nor danger; a faithful man knoweth that God is able to defend him and to help him in all tribulation. And herein is verified the saying of our Saviour Christ that "Whosoever shall lose his life, shall find it" (Matt. 16:25). These shepherds put their lives in adventure,[12] yea, they put themselves in the greatest peril that might be, but at the length they found the Saviour, Which restored to them their souls and bodies and everlasting life.

Here we may learn to be hearty[13] and to do manfully for the gospel's sake, believing undoubtedly that God is able and will preserve us in the midst of all our tribulations, so that we do that which our duty is to do, that is, to live and die in God's quarrel, and so to forsake ourselves that we may find Him Which will give us life everlasting. Further, here may all those be ashamed which set so much by this world that they cannot find in their hearts to forego one farthing for God's sake. Such shall receive their judgment of

[9] Judges 14.

[10] Here Latimer's memory played him false. The number given in II Kings 2:24 is forty-two.

[11] Gen. 30:25–43.

[12] *Adventure:* jeopardy.

[13] *Hearty:* courageous.

these shepherds that were so hearty in God's cause, and not without peril of their lives. Therefore return, O thou covetous heart, return to God, amend thy life. Consider the momentany and short time that thou hast here to live, and that when thou shalt depart hence thou must be judged after thine own wickedness. And, the more careful that thou art to keep thy money and substance, the sooner shalt thou lose both that and thy soul also, which is the greatest treasure above all other.

"They came with haste unto Bethlehem," etc. (Luke 2:16). Here let every man learn quickly to go about his business to the which God hath appointed him. And specially servants may learn here to do their business truly and speedily, not spending the time in vain going up and down when their masters are absent, but rather to be diligent, knowing that they serve not only their bodily master but Christ Himself, as St. Paul saith. Therefore consider this, O ye servants, and know that God will reward you for your well doings and, again, punish you for your slothfulness and deceitful doings.

"They found Mary and Joseph, and the babe laid in a manger, according to the saying of the angel," etc. (Luke 2:16). Here let every man follow the ensample of the angel, which told the shepherds no lies; so let every man be upright in his talk and talk nothing abroad except he be sure that it be so. For when you do otherwise, you follow not this angel. Make no manner of promise, neither great nor small, except you be able to keep it. Above all things, beware of perjury and lies, which are abominable in the face of God; as the prophet saith, *Odisti qui loquuntur mendacium linguis suis:* that is to say, "Thou hatest those, O God, that speak lies with their tongues."[14] But God knoweth that many things are now promised and nothing performed. Every man is more liberal in speech than in deed, whereas it should be contrary. Likewise, servants are not angels when they deal deceitfully with their masters and when they are slothful in their doings, not regarding their promise

[14] The reference is apparently to Prov. 6:16–17. But there is little verbal correspondence to any other Latin or English version.

made unto their masters. For they promise to serve diligently in all manner of business, which God knoweth is not kept by a great many of servants. Yea, there is none that serve as they ought for to do; therefore all such are not angels.

"The same Mary, Joseph, and the babe," etc. Here we may not take heed of the order of this speech or writing; as, Mary is set before her child, *ergo,* she hath more authority than her child hath. As the Bishop of Rome maketh an argument, saying Peter is ever first named before the apostles; *ergo,* he is the principal and chief apostle and all the other are subjects unto him. Which manner of reasoning is false. For after that reasoning, Mary should be more esteemed than our Saviour, which were abominable and clean against the verity of the scripture. And therefore the setting and placing of names in scripture is not to be observed, nor no argument may be made after that manner, which be set first or last.

"They find Mary and Joseph, and the child lying in a manger." Here is the faith of the shepherds proved. They had heard a voice from heaven which promised unto them a Saviour; and now when they come they find nothing but a poor infant lying in a manger. This was a great matter to them. For they thought they should have found Him keeping a state after His name, that is, like a Saviour, but they found a poor child which, after man's reason, was not able to help himself. Notwithstanding, they had conceived such a strong and hearty faith, which faith preserved them from all such outward storms and offenses. By the which we may learn of these shepherds not to be offended with the poor kingdom that our Saviour kept in this world, for we see, most commonly, that the rich and wealthy of this world despise and contemn the word of God. Let us therefore be despised in this world with Christ our King, that we may have afterward with Him everlasting life, when the proud and sturdy [15] fellows shall be thrust into everlasting fire.

For these shepherds were not offended with the poverty of our Saviour and did therefore stay and meddle no farther; but they went

[15] *Sturdy:* obstinate.

forth and preached and talked of it to other folks, which thing they could not do without peril of their lives. For the Pharisees and spiritualty were so stubborn that they would suffer none other doctrine to be taught than their own fantasies, as it appeared afterward when they killed Christ Himself and after Him a great number of the apostles. Yet, for all that, these poor shepherds were content to lose their lives in God's quarrel. Therefore they go and teach their neighbors and others how the Messiah and Saviour of the world was born of a virgin, and how the angel of God had opened it unto them. But what followed of their teaching, or what became of it? It begat a wondering and a gazing. Everybody marveled at it and was desirous to talk of it, because it was a new matter; as we see in this our time a great number of people pretend the gospel and bear the name of gospelers, because it is a new thing and therefore it is the more pleasant unto them. So was it at that same time. Everybody would talk of it in all places, but there were few or none that believed. For we read not that any of them went forth to seek the child and so to confirm his or their faith. No, there was none. It was but a talk, and so they used it.

Wherein you may note the unfaithfulness and unthankfulness of this world, which will not receive the great benefits of God offered unto us. The shepherds told them how the angel of God had opened the matter to them, but the foolish people would not believe it. And even so at this time. The preachers go abroad and show unto the people what God hath done for them, how He hath delivered them from sin, death, and hell; but the people are so blinded with unthankfulness that they will not believe the benefits of God, nor receive them, but make a gazing and wondering at the matter.

But what did Mary the mother of Christ? What did she? The evangelist saith, "She pondered it in her heart" (Luke 2:19); she weighed the matter with herself. She did not as our well-spoken dames do; she took not in hand to preach. She knew that silence in a woman is a great virtue; therefore she made nothing of the matter. She boasted not of her stock to be of the lineage of noble King

David; neither did she praise her own child, but would rather hear Him to be praised of another. She tarried until the Lord Himself had opened the matter; neither would she be too hasty in promoting herself to honor. Here may all women learn to follow the example of Mary, to leave their talk and vain speaking and to keep silence. For what was the cause of the fall of mankind but the unmeasurable talk of Eve, which took in hand to reason the matter with the serpent? She thought herself very learned and able to convince him. So are there too many now which take too much upon them. Such women may learn here of Mary to keep their tongues in better order. All women commonly make much of the mother of Christ; yea, some call upon her. But for all that, they will not follow her example and goodness.

Farther, here is to be noted the temptation and trial wherewith Mary was tempted and tried. She heard of the angel that she should bring forth a Saviour Whose kingdom should last forever. And now that He is born there cometh nobody to visit Him but poor shepherds, which seemed strange unto her and such as might make her much to marvel at the matter and to overthrow her faith. But Mary comforted herself with word and promise of God, which was that her Son should reign forever. This she believed, and therefore took no harm of the said temptation or trial but rather much good; for this visitation of the shepherds was an establishment of her faith and a great increase of the same. And here is verified the saying of St. Paul: *Bonis omnia cooperantur in bonum:* that is, "All things work for the best to them that love God" (Romans 8:28).

Farther, by these shepherds we learn that God is not partial. He hath not respect to any person, neither to the rich, wise, nor mighty; but He delighteth in those which are meek and lowly in spirit. Unto such God openeth Himself, as Christ saith, *Ago tibi gratias, Pater,* "I thank thee, Heavenly Father, that Thou hast hidden these things from the wise men of this world and hast opened them unto the simplest" (Matt. 11:25). Which saying of Christ is verified now upon us, for God hath hidden the divine mysteries of His word from the

Pope, cardinals, bishops, and the great learned of this world and hath opened it unto us. Therefore let us be thankful for His innumerable benefits poured upon us so richly and abundantly. Let us follow therefore the example of these shepherds. Let us come to Bethlehem, that is, to Christ, with an earnest mind and hearty zeal to hear the word of God and then to follow it indeed. For not the hearer shall be saved but the doer and follower thereof, as He saith: "Not those that call me, Lord, Lord, shall enter into the kingdom of God, but those which do the will of My Father which is in heaven" (Matt. 7:21). Wherefore let us follow the word of God; let us glorify and magnify His holy name in all our works and conversations, wherein consisteth the very thankfulness and true service which we owe unto Him.

"And the shepherds returned, lauding and praising God for all the things that they had heard and seen," etc. (Luke 2:20). They were not made religious men nor monks but returned again to their business and to their occupation. Where we learn every man to follow his occupation and vocation, and not to leave the same except God call him from it to another. For God will have every man to live in that order that He hath ordained for him. And no doubt the man that plieth his occupation truly, without any fraud or deceit, the same is acceptable to God and he shall have everlasting life.

We read a pretty story of St. Anthony,[16] which, being in the wilderness, led there a very hard and strait life, insomuch as none at that time did the like, to whom came a voice from heaven, saying, "Anthony, thou art not so perfect as is a cobbler that dwelleth at Alexandria." Anthony, hearing this, rose up forthwith and took his staff and went till he came to Alexandria, where he found the cobbler. The cobbler was astonied to see so reverend a father come to his house. Then Anthony said unto him, "Come and tell me thy whole conversation and how thou spendest thy time." "Sir," said the cobbler, "as for me, good works have I none, for my life is but simple and slender; I am but a poor cobbler. In the morning when I

[16] Latimer had used this story also in his fifth sermon on the Lord's Prayer.

rise I pray for the whole city wherein I dwell, specially for all such neighbors and poor friends as I have. After, I set me at my labor, where I spend the whole day in getting my living. And I keep me from all falsehood, for I hate nothing so much as I do deceitfulness; wherefore, when I make to any man a promise I keep it and do it truly. And so I spend my time poorly with my wife and children, whom I teach and instruct, as far as my wit will serve me, to fear and dread God. And this is the sum of my simple life." In this story you see how God loveth those that follow their vocation and live uprightly without any falsehood in their dealing. This Anthony was a great holy man, yet this cobbler was as much esteemed before God as he.

Here I might take occasion to speak of all estates and what pertaineth to every one of them, but the time is past. I will make an end without any rehearsal or recital of that which is already said. The Lord of heaven and earth make us diligent and ready to do His will and live after His commandments, and so to come finally to everlasting life, through Christ our Lord; to Whom, with God the Father and the Holy Ghost, be all honor and glory, for ever and ever, world without end! Amen, Amen.

SERMON FOR ST. STEPHEN'S DAY DECEMBER 26, 1552

A SERMON PREACHED BY MASTER HUGH LATIMER ON ST. STEPHEN'S DAY AT GRIMSTHORPE, ANNO 1552

"And it fortuned that while they were there her time was come that she should be delivered, and she brought forth her first begotten son and wrapped him in swaddling clothes and laid him in a manger, because there was no room in the inn." (Luke 2:6–7).

I SHOWED you yesterday, right worshipful audience, what was the occasion that Mary, the mother of Christ our Saviour and Redeemer, came to Bethlehem whereas it was prophesied that He should be born. The occasion was this. Octavius being Emperor over that great empire of Rome at that time when Christ should be born—as it was prophesied that He should be born whilst the second temple stood—now this Octavius sent out a general proclamation that all countries underneath his dominion should be taxed and to give him a certain money. Now God intended another thing. Octavius with this proclamation sought nothing but to fill his purse and to make money, but God sought occasion that way to fulfill His prophecy. For it was prophesied a long time that Christ should be born before at Bethlehem. Now she could not come thither except by some occasion, and therefore this was the occasion, namely, that she should come and be taxed and pay a certain money unto the officers.

And here we shall consider and weigh the obedience that Mary, the mother of Christ, and her husband showed towards the magistrate, that she was content to take such a great journey in hand with her husband Joseph to show herself obedient unto the magistrates. And here I took occasion the last time to speak somewhat of obedience, how we ought to show ourselves obedient in all things which be not against God. I think of this matter we cannot speak too much, for it is a thing most necessary to be known. For if the parents of our Saviour were content to be obedient unto a heathen king, how much more shall we show ourself obedient unto our natural king, which feedeth us with the holy word of God, and seeketh not alone our bodily health and wealth but also the health of the soul! How much more ought we reverence him and honor him which not tyrannously ruleth over us, as Octavius did over the Jews, but most lovingly governeth and ruleth us, seeking not his own commodities [1] but our good estate!

Now by this occasion, as I told you, namely, to show themselves obedient, came Joseph and Mary unto Bethlehem—a long journey, and poor folks, and peradventure on foot, for we read of no great horses that she had as our great ladies have nowadays, for truly she had no such jolly [2] gear. Now he that would show the good behavior that was between them two, he must have much time. We read of no falling-out between them or ill behaviors that was between them. And therefore all the husbands may learn by Joseph to do their duties towards their wives, and again all the wives may learn by her.

Well, she was great with child and was now come to Bethlehem. A wonderful thing to consider the works of God! The Emperor Octavius served God's purpose and yet knew nothing of Him, for he knew not what manner of man was born at that time when his

[1] *Commodities:* advantages. [2] *Jolly:* showy.

proclamation was sent out. But John Baptist, that went before our Saviour Christ, he showed what manner of man Christ was when he saith, *Ecce Agnus Dei, qui tollit peccata mundi,* "Lo! the Lamb of God, that taketh away the sins of the world" (John 1:29). By these words is showed to what end Christ was sent into this world, namely, to take away sins. And before this, Zacharias, the father of John Baptist, fell out in praising of God, saying, *Benedictus Deus Israel,* "Blessed be the Lord God of Israel, for He hath visited and redeemed His people, and hath set up a horn of salvation" (Luke 1:68–69).

Now if Zacharias because of the birth of John rejoiced in God, how much more shall we laud and praise God that Christ our Saviour Himself is born! For John Baptist was the precursor. He was but a servant of God, yet Zacharias his father so much rejoiced in him. How much, I say, shall we praise God that the Lord above all lords hath taken upon Him our humanity and is made man; for this great benefit, that He would vouchsafe to humble Himself so much as to take our nature upon Him; for this cause, to deliver us out of the hands of this old serpent the devil, in whose kingdom and dominion all mankind should have been if this Saviour had not come into the world! And thus His first coming is but very poorly, without any jollity or pomp; but His second coming (as I have told you many a time before) shall be a glorious coming, a beautiful coming. For He shall come accompanied with all His angels; He shall come with such clearness that the sun and the moon shall be darkened at His coming. Not that the sun itself of her substance shall be darkened, no, not so, for she shall give her light. But it shall not be seen for this great light and clearness wherein our Saviour shall appear. Now at the first He is come, not with glory or majesty, but with great poverty and misery which He hath sustained for our sakes.

We have here to consider the great benefits of God, the almighty Father, that it hath pleased Him, through His great goodness and love which He bare towards us which were His enemies, that it hath pleased Him, I say, to give unto us for our sakes His only Son into these miseries and calamities, and to suffer Him to take our nature upon Him, and to deliver us with His most painful and grievous Passion. We cannot express the worthiness of it; but though we are not able to express it, yet we shall do as much as we can.

Now for to come to the knowledge of this benefit, you must consider first what He was before He was incarnate and made man; for when we know what He was before He was made man, then we shall know what He hath done for us. Now, therefore, you must know that He was the natural Son of God, yea, God Himself, the Lord and King over heaven and earth, through Whom all things were made and created, and by Whom all things are kept and sustained, ruled and governed. That same God, that same Son of God, refused not to humble Himself far beyond all measure, to take upon Him such a vile nature, for He was made very man. You must not think as the Arians [3] did, which said that He was not a very man nor suffered very pains upon the cross but had a fantastical body. And I know where there was one of such an erroneous opinion, not many years ago; he belonged to a great man at the same time. Therefore I say we must beware of this opinion and believe steadfastly that He was a very natural man, sin excepted.

Again, we must believe that He was God's Son, not by adoption, as we be, for we all be adopted and taken up for the children of God. But He was before the world began with God, the very natural Son of God, and God Himself, very God's Son without a mother, like as He was very man without a father. I will prove Him to be very God, because we are commanded to call upon Him. Now ye know that to call upon God is to honor God. And God saith in His word that He will give His honor unto nobody. But Christ hath the honor of God, therefore He must needs be very God. And here we have occasion to be sorry that we have called upon the saints and so deprived God of His honor and dignity, and made them *Deos*

[3] The heresy here alluded to more closely resembles the Marcionite heresy than it does the Arian.

tutelares, we made gods of them. But Christ it is He in Whom we must call and put our confidence, for so it is written, *Adorabunt eum omnes reges terrae,* "All the kings of the world shall honor Him and call upon His name" (Psalm 72:11). And therefore here it appeareth most manifestly that He is very God, coequal unto the Father after His divinity.

You have heard this day, in the service of St. Stephen, how he called upon Christ, to Whom he saith, *Domine Jesu, suscipe spiritum meum,* "Lord Jesu, take Thou my spirit" (Acts 7:58). The Jews stoned him, but he made his prayer, saying, *Domine Jesu, suscipe spiritum meum,* "Lord Jesu, take Thou my spirit," lifting up his eyes unto heaven, signifying that Christ is very God, which thing no doubt St. Stephen would not have done if Christ had not been very God.

Now this day is St. Stephen's Day, which was put to death because he rebuked the stubbornness of the wicked priests and bishops, which bishops stirred up false witnesses against him and so stoned him. But well is he that ever he was born. Now, therefore, if you will worship St. Stephen I will tell you how you shall worship him. Consider his faith and heartiness[4] which he had in God's cause, and pray unto God that thou mayest have such a strong faith too, that thou mayest be ready to forsake the world and suffer for the word of God, like as he hath. And, further, pray unto God that thou mayest have such a strong faith to pray unto Him, like as St. Stephen had. This is the right worshiping of St. Stephen, to follow his example, and not to call upon him. But I marvel much how it chanced that upon this day we are wont to let the horses' blood. It is like as though St. Stephen had some government over the horses, which thing no doubt is a vain invention of man.[5] We ought to commit ourselves and all that we have under the governance of God, and not be so foolish as to commit them unto saints. God grant us that we may say with a good faith, from the bottom of our hearts,

[4] *Heartiness:* courage.

[5] St. Stephen was regarded as the protector of horses.

Domine Jesu, suscipe spiritum nostrum, "Lord Jesu, receive our spirits!"

Further, Christ Himself showed most manifestly what He was, for He hath witnesses enough—the Father, the Holy Ghost, John Baptist, and the works which He did. And finally He Himself witnesseth what He is, for He saith, *Qui credit in me habet vitam aeternam,* "He that believeth in Me hath everlasting life" (John 6:47). Here is evidently showed by His own words what He was, namely, the Redeemer of mankind and very God, for nobody can give everlasting life save only God. But Christ giveth everlasting life; *ergo,* He is very natural God. Item, in another place He saith, *Quemadmodum Pater mortuos suscitat, sic et Filius,* "Like as the Father raised up the dead, so doth the Son too" (John 5:21). Where it most manifestly appeareth that He is equal unto the Father; they work their works together unseparably. This I say unto you to that intent that you should consider with yourselves what Christ hath been before He took upon Him our nature, and again, to consider what He hath done for us and how exceedingly He hath humbled Himself.

Now I will show you what man is of his own nature, left unto himself. But I will not speak of that singular Son of Man which was Christ, for He had two natures in unity of persons; He was very God and very man. He was a privileged man from all other men; that man never sinned. Therefore I speak not of Him. I speak of that nature which mankind hath inherited of Adam after he had sinned, for as he was, that is, a sinful, wicked man, disobedient unto the word of God, such he brought into the world. Now what is man, what is the nature of the son of Adam? I speak not of Christ, for He was not born of the seed of Adam. When we know what man is, then we shall perceive what great benefit we have received of God, the Father Almighty, in that He hath sent His only Son to be a sacrifice for us, and to help us out of the estate of damnation, and to remedy this impureness of our nature.

Now this our nature David, the holy king and prophet, describeth with few words, saying, *Ecce iniquitatibus natus sum et in peccatis concepit,* "Lo, in iniquity am I born, and in sin hath my mother conceived me" (Psalm 51:5). Which words are not so to be understand as though the act of generation and the lawful use of matrimony be defiled and unclean before God. He speaketh here not of the lawful bed company that is between married folks, for this hath his warrant in scripture, in God's book. Therefore he speaketh not here of the company that is between man and wife; but he will signify by his words what he had inherited of his parents, of Adam, namely, sin and wickedness; and he speaketh not of himself only but of all mankind. He painteth us out in our own color; showing that all we be contaminate from our birth with sin, and so should justly be firebrands in hell, world without end. This the holy prophet showed us in these words, to put us in remembrance of our own wretchedness, to teach us to despair of our own holiness and righteousness, and to seek our help and comfort by that Messiah whom God had promised our forefathers and now hath fulfilled the same promise.

Another scripture signifieth unto us further what we be of ourselves, of our own nature. For it is written, *Omnis homo mendax,* "All men are liars" (Psalm 116:11); therefore man is not clean [6] but full of falsehood and deceit and all manner of sin and wickedness. Yet we may learn what we be of our own nature, namely, poisoned and corrupt with all manner of uncleanness. Another scripture we have which showeth us in the same thing: *Dominus de coelo despexit, et omnes declinaverunt, simul inutiles facti sunt,* "The Lord looked down from heaven, to see whether any man be that did well; but they are all declined, they were all naught together" (Psalm 14:2–3). God looked down to consider whether there were some that had understanding of Him or not. What brought He to pass? What found He when He made inquisition? Marry this, *Omnes declinaverunt,* "All have declined from God; there was not one that did good, no, not one."

[6] *Clean:* pure.

Here we may perceive what we be of our own selves, of our own nature. And again, here we may see what Christ, the Son of God, hath done for us, what inestimable benefits we have received at His hands: namely, to suffer for us and to cleanse us from all our sins and wickedness; to make us just before the face of God; to purge us from all iniquity, as well from original sin as actual. For, if He had not done so, we should never have been able to escape the wrath of God. For, *Quicquid natus ex carne caro est,* "Whatsoever is born of flesh is flesh" (John 3:6), that is to say, is sinful, wicked, and so destitute of the glory of God, and the child of the devil. If Christ had not been come and cleansed our filthiness, if He had not suffered death for us, we had perished. Now afore He suffered, He was born and lived a great while in the miserable world; or else He could not have suffered if He had not been born, for no man can suffer before he be alive. Further, it is written in God's book, *Conclusit Deus omnes sub peccato, ut omnium misereatur,* "God hath concluded[7] all mankind under sin" (Gal. 3:22), so that all mankind was sinful and destitute of the favor of God, save only Christ.

Wherefore, I pray you, have I rehearsed all these scriptures? Marry, to this intent I have rehearsed them, to bring you to knowledge how great need we have had of Christ. For no doubt if we had not had Him, all mankind should have been damned, yea, the best of us, world without end. But that we have deliverance, that the kingdom of heaven is opened unto us, that same brought He to pass with His Passion; for He took upon Him our nature, and so deserved for us everlasting life. For by Him we have it, and therefore we must thank Him for it, we must to Him give all honor and praise.

It is a great unity between the two natures in Christ, between the manhood and Godhead. For the body and soul make a man, but the manhood and the Godhead are joined so together they make but one Christ. And yet they are not confounded, so that the Godhead is not

[7] *Concluded:* included.

turned into the manhood, neither the manhood into the Godhead. And thus Christ, which was very God and very man, died not for Himself nor of necessity, for death had no right unto Him, because He was without sin. But He died for our sake, willingly, without any compulsion, moved by the great love that he bare unto man. And therefore He saith, *Nemo tollit animam meam a me, sed ego repono illam,* "No man taketh away my life, but I myself put it away (John 10:18). But I will receive it again. I am willing to die, for with my dying I will destroy the kingdom of the devil; and by my death all mankind shall be saved." And here He showed himself what He was, namely, very God; for He had power over death, and not death over Him; and so He died not by compulsion or necessarily, but willingly. For it was His will and pleasure to help us and deliver us from our wretchedness, for nothing could help us else but the death of the eternal Son of God.

And here you may note, by the way, what a heinous thing sin is before the face of God, how He abhorreth sin, that He would be with nothing reconciled save only with the death of His Son our Saviour Jesus Christ. And this shall make us to hate sin and to avoid all the occasions of sin, and not to fall willingly and wittingly to all kinds of sin again; but rather to live uprightly and godly, according unto His will and commandment, seeing that He beareth such a loving and fatherly heart towards us that He spared not His only Son, but gave Him even to the most vile and painfullest death for our sakes, for our sins and wickedness' sake.

David, that holy man, when he considered this great benefit, what saith he? He fell out into such words, *Quid retribuam Domino pro omnibus quae tribuit mihi?* "What shall I give unto the Lord for all those things which He hath given unto me?" (Psalm 116:12). Then he made himself answer and saith, *Nomen Domini invocabo,* "I will call upon the name of the Lord"; *Calicem salutaris accipiam,* "I will take the cup of health" (*ibid.,* 13); that is to say, I will bear His cross that He shall lay upon me, willingly, without any grudge or murmuring. Now, therefore, let us say so too: "O Lord, what shall we give unto Thee again? What amends shall we make Thee, seeing Thou hast given us Thine only natural Son, which took upon Him a vile nature and suffered most painful death?" For that we have a brother in heaven, what shall we now do? How shall we show ourselves thankful? Marry, *Nomen Domini invocabimus,* "We will call upon the name of the Lord." We will praise Him for all His goodness; we will show ourselves thankful with a godly, upright conversation. *Calicem salutaris accipiemus,* "We will take the cup of health; we will bear all calamities and crosses that Thou shalt lay upon us willingly, without any grudging."

This is all that we can do; and when the devil cometh and tempteth us, as no doubt he will not sleep, we shall defy him, knowing that we have a brother in heaven which hath overcome him and all his power. Therefore we shall not need to fear him or care for him, though he be busy with us and tempt us in all manner of things to bring us to destruction. Let us defy him and give God thanks which so mercifully hath dealt with us and delivered us from all our sins. Let us take the cross meekly, whatsoever it be, though we be in misery or poverty or other calamities. Let us be content withal; for they be but examinations and proofs, to provoke us to call upon God when we feel the burden. And no doubt we shall be heard when we call as we ought to do, that is to say, with a faithful heart. Then, no doubt, He will take them away, so that we shall be no more troubled with them. Or else He will mitigate and assuage them in such sort that we shall [be] able to bear the burden of them.

"And she brought forth her first-begotten Son." These words, after the outward appearance, sound as though Mary the mother of Christ had had more sons than Christ. And there was an heretic [8] which steadfastly said that Mary had more sons after she had brought forth Christ. And here he took his arguments, saying, "We

[8] Helvidius, ca. 380. His views were declared heretical by St. Augustine and provoked St. Jerome to write the treatise *De perpetua virginitate Beatae Mariae adversus Helvidium* (Migne, *Patrologiae Latinae,* XXIII, cols. 183–206).

read in scripture that Christ had brethren, which argueth that Mary had more sons besides Christ." Which indeed is a foolish argument against all learning, for we must consider the phrases of the Hebrew tongue.[9] The Jews in their tongue call all those which are kinsmen "brethren"; and so the kinsmen of our Saviour were called His brethren, after the manner of their language, not that they had one mother, or that Mary had more sons but Christ. Therefore these heretics go far wide to prove that Mary had more sons beside Christ because we read that He had brethren. Let them consider the propriety of the Hebrew tongue; then they shall soon perceive how fond and foolish their arguments be.

The second argument which [these] fond fellows make is this: the Evangelist saith, "And she brought forth her first-begotten son." By these words they will prove, *ergo,* she had more than one son; Christ was the first begotten, but she had more beside Him. Here I would have them to consider this word *primogenitum,* which signifieth Him *qui primo aperuit vulvam,* "Him that first opened the womb." But she had no more, neither before nor after, but was a clear[10] virgin before she brought forth, and after she brought forth Him she remained a virgin. And therefore these heretics do wrongfully violate, toss, and turmoil the scriptures of God, according to their own fantasies and foolish minds.

Another argument they make, taken out of the first chapter of Matthew, where the Evangelist saith, *Et non cognovit illam donec peperisset filium suum primogenitum,* "And Joseph took his wife and knew her not till she had brought forth her first-begotten son" (Matt. 1:24–25). Hereupon they make this argument: "Joseph knew her not till she had brought forth her first son; *ergo,*" say they, "he knew her after": which no doubt is a foolish argument. For the mind of the Evangelist, when he declared Christ to be the first son of Mary, was to prove that He was the son of a virgin, according to the prophecy that was of Him, and not to declare that Mary had more

[9] It is unlikely that Latimer had more than a smattering of Hebrew.

[10] *Clear:* pure.

children after Him, as some do fantasy. For we in our English tongue have such a manner of speaking when we say, "I will never forgive him so long as I live"; or when we be ill entreated in a city we say, "I will no more come thither so long as I live." By which manner of speaking we do not signify that we will come thither after our death, or forgive after our death. No. And so likewise it is here. When he saith, "He knew her not till she had brought forth her first-begotten son," it followeth not, *ergo,* he knew her after. Like as it followeth not when I say, "I will do this thing no more so long as I live," *ergo,* I will do it after I am dead. And here you may perceive how foolishly and fondly these heretics have handled the scripture.

Now let us go forward and consider His great extreme poverty. They came to Bethlehem, where they could get never a lodging in no inn, and so were compelled to lie in a stable. And there Mary the mother of Christ brought forth that blessed child through Whom and in Whom all the nations of the earth are and shall be blessed. And there "she wrapped Him in swaddling clothes and laid Him in a manger, because there was no room for them in the inn." Here began the misery of the Lord above all lords, even at His first coming into this world, when He was laid in a manger, as soon as He was born, to taste poverty and miseries, to make amends for our sins and wickedness, and so to take away from us the wrath of God, the Heavenly Father, which lay upon all mankind so heavy that they should all be condemned world without end if this child had not been born into this world.

And here we may learn by His poverty to comfort ourselves when God sendeth poverty unto us; and not to think, because we are poor, *ergo* God hateth us, or will condemn us; but rather consider with ourselves and call to remembrance the poverty of Christ our Saviour. He was the beloved Son of God, and God Himself; and yet He was content to be born in misery and to sustain most vile poverty and penury of all manner of those things which are required necessarily to the sustentation of this life. There be some which when they be in trouble say, "Oh, if God loved me, He would not punish me so; He would not suffer me to be vexed so grievously with poverty and lack of necessaries!" Which indeed is not so, for those whom God loveth He punisheth. Ensamples we have in David, what troubles, calamities, and miseries he had; and yet God loved him, insomuch that He called him a man after His heart's desire. But though he was well-beloved of God, yet he must taste of miseries and calamities, of which he had not a little: but he ever sticked unto God, who delivered him out of all his trouble.

Now some will say, when they hear what poverty our Saviour suffered and how Mary His mother was compelled to take a stable for lack of a better lodging, some will say now, "Oh, what a wicked city was this! What a cruel people was this!" But when we consider all things well, we shall find that we be even as wicked as they be. For are not we given nowadays to covetousness, so that we regard not the poor and miserable people? Seek we not our own commodities and despise and neglect the poor? Therefore if thou wilt cry out upon the Bethlehemites, then cry out on thyself; for thou art as wicked, yea, more wicked than they were. For the most part of all Bethlehem knew nothing of our Saviour Christ that He was born. But we know it; therefore we are inexcusable. God hath sent unto us His preachers, which teach us the way to heaven; they show us wherein standeth our redemption; they exhort us to godliness, to do good works, to be pitiful and liberal unto the poor, to help them and comfort them. But what do we? Marry, we despise the preachers, we abhor their doctrine, and so consequently refuse Christ Himself. For He saith, *Qui vos suscipit, me suscipit,* "He that receiveth you, receiveth Me" (Matt. 10:40). "He that refuseth you, refuseth Me." This Christ speaketh by His preachers. Therefore, as I said before, we need not to cry out against Bethlehem, but let us cry out on ourselves, for we are as ill in all points as they are.

But I warrant you, there was many a jolly damsel at that time at Bethlehem, yet amongst them all there was not one found that would humble herself so much as to go see poor Mary in the stable and to comfort her. No, no; they were too fine to take so much pain. I warrant you, they had bracelets and farthingales and such fine gear. They were trimmed with all manner of fine raiment, like as there be many nowadays amongst us which study nothing else but how they shall devise fine raiments. And in the mean season they suffer poor Mary to lie in the stable; that is to say, the poor people of God they suffer to perish for lack of necessaries. But what was her swaddling cloth wherein she laid the King of heaven and earth? No doubt it was poor gear; peradventure it was her kerchief which she took from her head or suchlike gear. For I think Mary had not much fine gear; she was not trimmed up as our women are nowadays. I think indeed Mary had never a farthingale, for she used no such superfluities as our fine damsels do nowadays. For in the old time women were content with honest and single garments. Now they have found out these roundabouts; they were not invented then. The devil was not so cunning to make such gear; he found it out afterward. Therefore Mary had it not. I will say this, and yet not judge other bodies' hearts, but only speak after daily appearance and experience. No doubt it is nothing but a token of fair pride to wear such farthingales, and I therefore think that every godly woman should set them aside.

It was not for nought that St. Paul advertised all women to give a good example of sadness, soberness, and godliness in setting aside all wantonness and pride. And he speaketh of such instruments of pride which were used at his time: *non tortis crinibus,* "not with laying out the hairs artificially" (I Tim. 2:9); *non plicatura capillorum,* "not with laying out the tussocks."[11] I doubt not but if farthingales had been used at that time, St. Paul would have spoken against them too, like as he spake against other things which women used at that time to show their wantonness and foolishness. Therefore, as I said before, seeing that God abhorreth all pride, and farthingales are nothing else but an instrument of pride, I would wish that women would follow the counsel of St. Paul and set aside such gorgeous

[11] *Tussocks:* tufts or locks of hair.

apparel, and rather study to please God than to set their mind upon pride. Or else, when they will not follow the counsel of St. Paul, let them scrape out these words wherewith he forbiddeth them their proudness, else the words of St. Paul shall condemn them at the last day. I say no more; wise folks will do wisely; the words of St. Paul are not written for nothing. If they will do after St. Paul's mind, they must set aside these foolish farthingales. But when they will go forward in their abominable pride, the reward which they shall have at the end shall not be taken from them.

Here is a question to be moved. Who fetched water to wash the child after it was born into the world, and who made a fire? It is like that Joseph himself did such things; for, as I told you before, those fine damsels thought it scorn to do any such thing unto Mary, notwithstanding that she had brought into the world the Lord over heaven and earth.

Alack! shall we murmur and grudge against God when we be in distress or poverty? Shall we cry out against Him, seeing that Christ the Saviour of the world Himself was handled so extremely? Therefore let us learn to be patient in all our troubles; let us be content with all that God shall send us. If we do so, He will plenteously reward us in everlasting life.

This day on which our Saviour was come into the world we were made one flesh with the Son of God. Oh, what a great honor is this unto us! Which honor exceedeth the dignity of the angels. For though the angels are better in substance, yet we are better in the benefit. For "Christ took not upon Him the nature of the angels, but He took our nature upon Him" (Heb. 2:16), man's nature, I say. Oh, what an exceeding thing is this! Oh, how much are we bound to give Him thanks for these His profound and inestimable benefits! We read a story, take it as you will, though it be not a true story.[12] The devil came once into the church whilst the priest was saying mass; and when he was at these words, *et homo factus est,* the devil looked about him, and, seeing no man kneel down or bow his knees,

[12] The story occurs in many places.

he strake one of them in the face, saying, "What! will ye not reverence Him for this great benefit which He hath done unto you? I tell you, if He had taken upon Him our nature, as He hath taken upon Him yours, we would more reverence Him than ye do." This story is prettily devised, for we should reverence Him; we should honor Him, and show ourselves thankful for His inestimable benefits that He hath showed upon us miserable wretched sinners in taking upon Him our nature.

Now the same Christ was born as this day of the virgin Mary, very man except sin, for sin hath not defiled His flesh. For He was not begotten of the seed of man, after the manner of other men, but by the power of the Holy Ghost. Mary was His very natural mother, and He was born to that end that He might deliver us from our sins and wickedness. To Whom, with God the Father, and the Holy Ghost, be praise and honor everlastingly, world without end! Amen.

INDEX

"Act Abolishing Diversity of Opinions" ("Six Articles"), x, xxii, xxiii
Aldersgate, 28 n., 50 n., 70 n., 138 n., 158 n., 175 n.
Alexander I, Pope, 46
Alexander III, Pope, 109 n.
Alexandria, 186
Alexandrines (canon law), 109
Algar, St., shrine of, 25
Ambrose, St., 98
Anthony, St., 186-187
Arches, Court of, 21
Arians, 191
Articles . . . to Stablish Christian Quietness and Unity ("Ten Articles"), x, xx
Augustine, St., 98-99, 197 n.
Augustus (Octavius), 175, 188, 189

Bale, John, 19 n., 46 n.
Balliol College, Oxford, xxxiv
Bankside, Southwark, 93
Barnes, Robert, xiv
Basel, Council of, 106 n.
Baxterley (Warwickshire), xxiii, 175
Baynton, Sir Edward, xix n.
Beaufort, Henry, Cardinal, 78-79
Becket, Gilbert, 98 n.
Becket, Thomas à, 98 n.
Becon, Thomas, 46 n.
Bello-Loco, Gaufridus de, 63 n.
Bernard, St., 20 n., 172 n.
Bernher, Augustine, xxvi-xxvii, xxviii
Berthelet, Thomas, 2
Bertie, Richard, 137 n.
Bible, English, xvi-xvii, 80-81
Bilney, Thomas, ix, xiv, xv, xxix-xxx, 120-121, 151, 167-169
"Bishops' Book" (*Institution of a Christian Man*), x, xx
Blackheath, battle of, 67
Blaise, St., shrine of, 25
Blanche of Castile, 63 n.
Blesis, *see* Blaise, St.
Bocardo prison, Oxford, xi, xxxiii, 151
Boleyn, Anne, Queen of England, xix, 9 n.
Boniface VIII, Pope, 110 n.
Bonner, Edmund, Bishop of London, 77
Book of Common Prayer, xxxii
Brandon, Charles, 169 n.
Bristol, x, xix
Buckenham, Robert, xvii
Bullinger, Heinrich, xxii n.

Cambridge, Tower of, 168, 169

Cambridge University, ix, xiii-xiv, xvi-xviii, xxx, 35, 167
Canon law, 109
Canterbury (episcopal mint), 38 n.
Canterbury, province of, xx
Capon, John, Bishop, 83 n.
Catherine of Aragon, Queen of England, ix, xviii
Chambers, John, Bishop, 83 n.
Chapel Royal, Westminster, xx, xxiv
Charterhouse, 107
Cheapside, 28 n., 71 n., 98 n., 138 n.
Cheke, Mistress, 169
Chrysostom, St. John, 65, 100-101, 153, 171
Clare Hall, Cambridge, ix, xiii
Clement V, Pope, 19 n., 109 n.
Clementines (canon law), 109
Convocation, x, xix, xx, xxi, 13-16, 21
Coverdale, Miles, 151 n.
Cranmer, Thomas, Archbishop of Canterbury, xi, xiii, xiv, xix, xx, xxi, xxii, xxvi, xxxii, xxxiii, xxxiv, 2, 31 n., 77, 102 n., 151 n.
Crome, Edward, x, xxviii
Cromwell, Thomas, xix, xxii
Curius (Roman consul), 13

Day, John, 29 n., 50 n., 70 n., 138 n., 158 n., 175 n.
Decretals (canon law), 109
Dionysius Carthusianus (Denis le Chartreux), 107, 109 n.
Dudley, John, Earl of Warwick and Duke of Northumberland, xxvi
"Dunstable way," 71
Durham (episcopal mint), 38 n.

Edward I, King of England, 140 n.
Edward II, King of England, 140 n.
Edward VI, King of England, x, xxiii, xxvii, xxxi, 18 n., 38, 39, 47, 53, 57-58, 60-66, 69, 70, 77-78, 81-82, 84, 88, 90, 101, 102 n., 114, 138, 143-144, 148 n.
Elizabeth I, Queen of England, 57, 128 n.
Enclosures, xxiv, xxv, 37, 66-68, 147-151
England, conditions in, 33-35, 38, 42, 48, 93, 100, 110, 133, 140, 142, 144, 146, 147-151
Episcopal mints, 38 n.
Erasmus, Desiderius, xiv, xv, 16, 72 n., 76 n., 117 n.
Eugenius IV, Pope, 106 n.
Extravagantines (canon law), 109, 110

Ficino, Marsilio, 94
Fleet prison, 88
Florence, Council of, 106
Fox, Edward, Bishop, xviii
Foxe, John, xvi, xvii, xviii, xxiii
Francis, St., 19 n.
Frith, John, xiv

Glover, Mary, xxiii
Glover, Robert, xxiii
Goodwin Sands, 151-152
Gorham, Nicholas, *see next entry*
Gorranus, Nicolaus, 96
Greek New Testament (*Novum testamentum*), xiv, xv
Grimsthorpe (Lincolnshire), x, xxvi-xxvii, 188
Guildhall, 151 n.

Hales, Blood of (shrine of), xxx, 131
Helvidius, 197 n.

Henry III, King of England, 148 n.
Henry VI, King of England, 78
Henry VII, King of England, 67
Henry VIII, King of England, ix, xviii, xix, xx, xxi, xxii, xxiii, xxx, 1, 9, 15, 59-60, 94, 127 n., 131, 147, 168-169
Hilles, Richard, xxii n.
Holy Communion, *see* Lord's Supper
"Homilies, Book of," 28 n., 31, 81
Humphrey, Duke of Gloucester, 78-79

Images, *see* Voluntary works
Injunctions of 1547, Royal, xxiv, 28-29 n., 81 n.
Institution of a Christian Man ("Bishops' Book"), x, xx
Islip, Simon, Archbishop, 25 n.

Jerome, St., 197 n.
John XXII, Pope, 110 n.
Josephus, 181

Kett's Rebellion, 148 n.

Lambeth Palace, xxvi, 87, 103
Lanfranc, Archbishop, 106 n.
Latimer, Hugh: chronological table, ix-xi; student at Cambridge, xiii-xiv; conversion to "New Learning," xv, 167; "Sermons on the Card," xvi-xviii; examined by Convocation on charges of heresy, xviii-xix; Bishop of Worcester, xx-xxii; deprived and silenced, xxi-xxiii; resumes preaching after accession of Edward VI, xxiii-xxvi; semiretirement in Lincolnshire, xxvi-xxvii; text and style of the sermons, xxvii-xxxi; imprisoned after accession of Mary Tudor, xxxi-xxxiii; the trial for heresy at Oxford, xxxiii-xxxiv; the martyrdom, xxxiv; biographical details and personal reminiscences in the sermons, 15, 30, 31, 59-60, 67, 80-81, 87, 91, 105, 120-121, 127-128, 130-131, 140, 143, 167-169
Leicestershire, 31
Lincoln, xiii
Lincolnshire, x, xxvii
"Little Ease" (prison), 151
Loci communes rerum theologicarum (Melanchthon), xv
Lollards' Pit (Norwich), xv, 120 n.
London, conditions in, 33-35, 93, 141
Lords, House of, xx
Lord's Supper, xxii, 43, 46, 77, 80-81, 111, 136-137
Louis IX, King of France ("St. Louis"), 62-63
Ludgate prison, 122
Luther, Martin, xiv, 109-110

Malvern, 25
Manes, 98 n.
Marcionite heresy, 191 n.
Margaret of Anjou, Queen of England, 79
Mariolatry, x, xix
Marshalsea prison, 77 n.
Martyrs' Memorial, Oxford, xiii
Mary Tudor, Queen of England, x, xxxi, xxxiii, 57, 128 n.
Melanchthon, Philip, xv, 167
Milan, 98
Mints, episcopal, 38 n.
More, Sir Thomas, 151-152
Morice, Ralph, xiv n.

"New Learning," ix, xiv, xviii
Newgate prison, 122 n.
Nicholas I, Pope, 106 n.
Nicholas V, Pope, 106 n.
Nix, Richard, Bishop, 121
Norfolk, rebellion in, 148 n.
Northampton, rebellion in, 148 n.
Norwich, xv, 120 n.
Novum testamentum (Greek New Testament), xiv, xv

Octavius, Emperor of Rome (Augustus), 175, 188, 189
Origen, 116
Oxford, xi, xxxii, xxxiii, xxxiv

Pardon bowls, 19, 46
Parr, Catherine, Queen of England, 127-128
Paul's Cross, x, xx, xxiv, xxvi, 18, 77 n., 120 n., 128
"Pilgrimage of Grace," xx
Pilgrimages, *see* Voluntary works
Pole, Reginald, xxxiv, 94
Prayer Book, *see* Book of Common Prayer
Preaching, importance of, xxiv, 7, 29-32, 49, 97-101, 103-105, 139
Privy Council, xxviii, xxxii, 38
Purgatory, xxiii, 15, 20-21, 41

Relics, *see* Voluntary works
Repps, William, *see* Rugg
Rich, Edmund, Archbishop, 24
Rich, Richard, Lord Chancellor, 86, 109
Ridley, Nicholas, Bishop, xi, xiii, xxxii-xxxiv, 151 n.
Robin Hood's Day, xxix, 105
Rogers, John, xxxiii
Rugg, William, Bishop, 83 n.

St. Edmundsbury, 79
St. Edward's, Cambridge, xvi
St. Martin-le-Grand, London, 93 n.
St. Mary Abchurch, London, ix, xix
St. Mary-le-Bow, London, 21 n.
St. Mary the Virgin, Oxford, xxxiii
St. Paul's, London, 28
St. Thomas of Acres, London, xxix, 98
Salcot, John, *see* Capon
Sampson, Richard, Bishop of Chichester, xxii
Sandwich Haven, 151-152
"Scala Coeli," 20 n., 82, 89
Seres, William, 28 n., 50 n., 70 n.
Seymour, Lady Anne, 143
Seymour, Edward, Duke of Somerset, Lord Protector, xxiv, xxv, xxvi, 32 n., 77, 86-87, 128 n.
Seymour, Jane, Queen of England, 9
Seymour, Thomas, Lord Admiral, 127 n., 128 n., 143
Shrines, *see* Voluntary works
Shrouds, the (St. Paul's churchyard), 28
"Six Articles," x, xxii, xxiii
Sixtus IV, Pope, 110 n.
Smith, Sir Thomas, 82 n.
Some, Thomas, xxviii
Stafford, George, xiv
Standish, Henry, 16 n.
Stokesley, John, Bishop, ix, x, xix
Stow, John, xxiii
Sudbury, Simon, Archbishop, 25 n.
Suffolk, rebellion in, 148 n.

"Ten Articles" (*Articles . . . to Stablish Christian Quietness and Unity*), x, xx
Tenterton (Tenterden, Kent), 152
Thurcaston (Leicestershire), ix, xii, xxxi
Tower of London, x, xi, xxiii, xxxii, 128 n., 151 n.
Tracy, William, 15 n.
Transubstantiation, xv, xxiii, xxxii-xxxiii
Tre Fontane, Abbey of, 20 n.
Tunstall, Cuthbert, Bishop, 38 n.
Tyndale, William, 97 n., 151 n.

Venutus, John, xvi
Vienne, Council of, 109 n.
Voluntary works, xv, xvi, xvii-xviii, 5-6, 18-20, 23-25, 47

Wakeman, John, Bishop, 83 n.
Waltham Abbey, 46
Wards, Court of, 39
Warwickshire, x
Watling Street, 71
West, Nicholas, Bishop of Ely, xvi
West Kington (Wiltshire), ix, xviii
Westminster Bridge, 108
Westminster Palace, xxiv, 50, 70, 90, 114, 138
"Whip with Six Strings," *see* "Act Abolishing Diversity of Opinions"
Will-works, *see* Voluntary works
William I, King of England, 168 n.
Willoughby, Catherine, Duchess of Suffolk, x, xxvi-xxvii, xxviii, 137 n., 158 n., 169 n.
Winchester, xx
Windsor, ix, xviii, 168
Wolsey, Thomas, Cardinal, ix, xvi
Worcester, diocese of, xxii

York (episcopal mint), 38 n.
Yorkshire, rebellion in, 148 n.